PRAISE FOR
BRAIN HABITS

At a time when there is urgency to isolate the signal from the noise, *Brain Habits* is a must read. This practical approach goes straight to the heart of the matter. It focuses on the science behind the most incredible machine on the planet: the human brain. I know, because I have reaped the benefits of this knowledge and approach in my personal and professional life. Read, change, succeed—it's all right here.

Joe Garbus | Executive Vice-President & Global Head of Talent Management, PVH

Success rarely happens in isolation. We see this most clearly among world-class athletes: it takes a team of coaches, doctors, and nutritionists combined with focused training to create sustained peak performance. In the professional world, we need to approach growth and performance similarly. Rather than upgrading what we know, *Brain Habits* offers tools to change how we learn. Like a training plan for your brain, investing time in the right activities can increase the brain's capacity to focus and perform at its best, much like an athlete in the right training program can reach peak performance. This reimagined perspective can change how we maximize individual potential with a novel approach to training and development.

Vickie Zalkin | Senior HR & Operations Executive, Top Global Management Consultancy

It is a remarkable idea to think that many of us travel well into adulthood, into successful careers, families, promotions, etc., without ever understanding how our own brain works. We continue to preach that the human brain is one of the most powerful forces on the planet, capable of enacting huge internal and external change, yet many of us have absolutely no idea how to think intentionally, much less how to leverage the subconscious parts of our brain. *Brain Habits* is a fascinating, and thought-provoking discussion on this subject.

Rick Orford | Co-Founder & Executive Producer at Travel Addicts Life, and Bestselling Author of *The Financially Independent Millennial*

"If your brain was an app, would you buy it?" What a simple and yet necessary question Phillip Campbell asks his readers in *Brain Habits*. It provokes a more profound question about what we invest in. We upgrade technology almost instinctively. So, why do we accept a lower standard when it comes to our brain? *Brain Habits* unpacks the mechanics behind cognitive development and the future of cognitive capital.

Jonathan Morgan | Chief Growth Officer, Symend

As we head into more complex and disruptive times, the need for a book like *Brain Habits* is increasingly necessary and yet extremely rare. Phillip Campbell captures the science of subconscious thinking habits and how they can dramatically impact professional and personal performance. In our current context of ongoing disruption, the need to look inward and approach development proactively has never been more essential.

Jon Davies | Managing Director, Head of Talent, Lightyear Capital

Phillip Campbell has done something remarkable with *Brain Habits*! In his scientific exploration into the both the conscious and 'inaccessible' subconscious areas of our brain, Campbell turns our preconceived notions about our own brain right on their heads. If you're looking for a way to become more adaptable, a better learner or to access more of your own potential, you'll definitely want to get your hands on a copy of this book!

Glenn Hopper | CFO, Sandline Global, and Bestselling Author of *Deep Finance*

A highly enjoyable read! *Brain Habits* is an explorative journey into the most relevant discoveries of neuroscience, neuroplasticity, and the utilization of the subconscious brain in developing more efficient learning patterns. Simply excellent.

Tamara Nall | CEO & Founder, The Leading Niche

The most impactful part of *Brain Habits* to me was the Four Pillars of Subconscious Success frameworks. Phillip's work flows seamlessly with the various concepts explored throughout the book. It will undoubtedly make a big impression in the publishing world offering a powerful and practical resource for those looking to really understand how our brains work. It is a considerable achievement in the field of optimizing cognitive performance. Impressively, it achieves this with a very approachable and light-hearted flare that keeps the pages turning with ease.

Socrates Jimenez | Market Growth & Operations Executive, Health Services

Facts are static, and knowledge is transient and quickly outdated. The knowledge economy is evolving, and the currencies holding their value are increasingly transferable skills. I highly recommend *Brain Habits*. It gives a wealth of insight to the reader, highlighting the connective tissue being the inner working of the brain and its practical impact on our day-to-day lives. The value of an efficient thinker and agile learner will only increase which makes it an imperative investment.

Garry Whatley | Managing Director, Business Services Sector

An intriguing journey into understanding how and why our brains operate the way they do—and more importantly, why our subconscious thinking habits impact our performance. *Brain Habits* will certainly leave you thinking long after you finish!

Shawn Johal | Business Growth Coach, Elevation Leaders, Bestselling Author of *The Happy Leader*

Do you wonder how you brain works? What are the key process that lead to optimal brain performance, innovation, and a better life. The potential is laid out in *Brain Habits*, which takes an amazing spin on how we thought learning works. Your brain is an amazing wonder; aren't you curious to know more about how to use it better and more effectively?

Mar Ricketts | Principal, GuildWorks

Brain Habits was like neuroscience for dummies! The sheer volume of information, concepts, and strategies was expertly balanced throughout by the author's clear and concise writing style. I felt like I was able to begin to understand the complexities of the brain, without being bogged down trying to decipher an endless barrage of technical terminology.

Rick Yvanovich | CEO, TRG

BRAIN HABITS

THE SCIENCE OF
SUBCONSCIOUS SUCCESS

PHILLIP JOHN CAMPBELL

DEDICATION

To my wife and business partner, Susan, who has robustly encouraged me to write this book for many years, and to our loving and supportive children, Alyssa and Matthew.

To my parents, Bruce and Morva Campbell, who encouraged me and gave me the opportunity to develop my adaptability and agility by continually exposing me to new environments during my school years.

TABLE OF CONTENTS

LIST OF FIGURES

LIST OF TABLES

FOREWORD

Most people I talk to are fascinated by the brain overall, and particularly about how their brain works; however, most of us have little idea about it. So I'd like to share my journey with the author of this book and how I came to a much better and pragmatic understanding of how our brains work, the associated thinking routines and habits, and the deep impact they have on our professional and personal lives.

Phillip John Campbell is a cognitive scientist with over 25 years' experience working with executives to enhance their cognitive capability. I met Phillip when he was initially launching his business in New York City in 2016. At the time, I was Managing Partner of Boston Consulting Group (BCG) New York, which was BCG's largest office worldwide. Having worked in the corporate sector for almost three decades, there wasn't much I hadn't seen before in the area of assessing and developing talent. However, Campbell's language around Fluid Thinking; Crystallized Knowledge; and how our brains think, learn, and adapt was very different and piqued my interest because I am always open to innovative concepts.

In my role as Managing Partner, I was always very conscious that our business was a 100 percent people business, all about who we could attract, retain, develop, and energize. And our business depended entirely on how well we could think—about new technologies, new markets, new ways for our clients to compete—and then help our clients think differently too. A mutual contact had invited me to attend a small breakfast launch of enigmaFIT's business in New York where I met the global head of talent of a major Fortune 500 company who was the guest speaker. She shared her experience of having her Fluid Thinking assessed and undertaking enigmaFIT's brain development program to enhance her cognitive capability, adaptability, agility, and flexibility.

Phillip kicked off by asking us how much we knew about how our brains worked and how we had been taught to think and learn. There were some brave attempts to answer the questions, but it quickly became apparent that none of us really knew. He pushed further, challenging us to identify any other critical asset in our business that we would indiscriminately accept despite not understanding how it worked and not having been taught how to use it effectively.

The guest speaker shared how the Fluid Thinking test had accurately identified her cognitive strengths and, more importantly, her cognitive derailers. In her view, gaining these insights was like finally having her own personalized brain manual. Even more significantly, she reported that the development program that followed enabled her to address many of her cognitive derailers rapidly and effectively, leading to more creative, more insightful, and more effective thinking—ultimately resulting in promotions to more senior and more impactful roles. The attendees were very familiar with professional development, and they all agreed that no other program addressed the underlying causes of their challenges the way enigmaFIT's does, as this is the only program that singularly focuses on understanding Fluid Thinking.

I knew it was time then to buckle up, and my HR Director and I decided to give it a go. We both found the test was unlike any assessment we had done before, and we were almost shocked by its accuracy and insight. We quickly expanded the opportunity to participate in the program, offering it to our top potential partners, both senior and up-and-coming. Over time, all experienced the rewards of this truly unique approach to professional development. I am told the program is still having a profound impact and receiving rave reviews almost five years later. Likewise, many of our client management teams with whom we shared the opportunity to participate continue to praise the program and enjoy tremendous success.

I think of this work—the assessment and then the training—as being akin to teaching old dogs new tricks. In one memorable moment, Phillip helped me understand that while I was okay at complex problem-solving, I tended to rely on go-to techniques that excluded potentially better alternatives. But it was the way I learned that lesson that was so powerful. We were talking about jigsaw puzzles (a bit of a passion of mine), and Campbell challenged me to reflect on alternative strategies for finding the edges and grouping the colors instead of doing it the same way that had served me well in the past. Only last month, I noted that a young woman had won a jigsaw competition by starting in the middle. Who knew!

Whether you are looking to improve your thinking skills and enhance your cognitive capability, adaptability, agility, and flexibility in order to deal proactively with this ever-changing world or you are responsible for talent development in your organization, I would recommend this book to you.

Enjoy getting to know your brain better and learning about how it works when you read this book.

Ross Love,
Managing Partner, BCG New York (2015-2018)
Non-Executive Director and Founder of Turton House Group (2019-present)

AUTHOR'S NOTE

This book is all about unpacking serious brain science in an approachable way. We will use several frameworks which I have created to guide your understanding of cognitive potential and the power of your brain on autopilot.

Brain Habits is written in six parts. The first part provides an overview of how our understanding of brain science has changed in recent decades and explains how these new insights are challenging traditional approaches to learning and education. In Part I, I provide a new framework for understanding the subconscious brain habits that underpin our thinking processes and introduce my own theory of how people think, learn, and adapt.

The next four parts describe each of the pillars in my framework, which I call the Four Pillars of Subconscious Success. Each pillar comprises up to three brain habits called Subconscious Thinking Habits.

Finally, Part VI explains my approach to unlocking your brain's potential and achieving a state of mental agility, competency, and adaptability that occurs when the brain's left and right hemispheres are optimally balanced to deliver peak performance.

Because my model is especially tailored to the needs of business leaders, I have replaced most of the technical jargon from brain science with business-oriented language, which is more intuitive and simpler to understand. Certain terms are specific to my framework, however, and I have included those in the glossary at the end of the book for easy reference.

Throughout this book, I use metaphors and analogies to illustrate various principles. I also use storytelling to help make the information more relatable and engaging to readers. While I have drawn heavily from my client case files for inspiration, the characters in these vignettes are not real people. Rather, they are composite characters based on several people who exhibited similar traits. Using composite characters allowed me to describe real-life situations while preserving the privacy and anonymity of the people involved. It is my hope that readers will see themselves or people they know in these stories.

I encourage you to explore a new way of thinking about thinking.

INTRODUCTION

What if your entire future depends on something you're not even aware of?

If you're like most people, your brain is your biggest asset. Your success depends on it. And yet, like most people, you probably don't know how your brain works or how to improve it. Unfortunately, no one is born with a user manual for their brain. But what if someone handed you a personalized manual that you could use to start upgrading your brain? Thanks to the latest research in brain science, we now have the capability to do just that. And it couldn't have happened at a more opportune time.

Today's world is moving at extraordinary velocity. Ongoing disruption is causing chaos across the global stage. Virtually everyone has been affected by COVID-19 in one way or another for the past couple of years, but that's just the beginning. Digital technologies such as Artificial Intelligence are transforming the way companies do business. And the entire world is facing massive challenges such as supply chain issues, soaring oil and energy prices, the war between Russia and Ukraine, skyrocketing inflation, and climate change. But the pain does not end here.

We are all dealing with disruption in our personal lives, too. In the post-COVID era, many of us are still finding ourselves struggling to adapt to working from home, and many also have reservations about returning to the office. Years of non-stop worry and physical isolation from friends, family, and co-workers have left millions of people mentally frazzled, their resilience ongoingly challenged by constant change and the stress it causes.

Companies no longer hire people based just on what they know but, rather, on how well they think and how quickly they can learn and adapt.

To make matters worse, the Fourth Industrial Revolution has arrived at the world's doorstep, threatening to make our job skills obsolete. The nature of work is evolving at warp speed. According to EAB, the half-life of professional skills has already been slashed to five years.[i] With the rapid advancement of technology, businesses are increasingly using computers and robots to perform routine tasks that were previously done by humans. These technologies have increased the value of non-conventional skill sets. Consequently, companies no longer hire people based just on what they know but, rather, on how well they think and how quickly they can learn and adapt.

Never before in history has there been a time when leaders needed to be more adaptable and agile. They need to become faster learners, better problem solvers, and more adept at thinking on their feet. Most importantly, leaders need to become better at dealing with novel situations that they have never encountered before.

Unfortunately, most people are ill-equipped to handle continuous upheaval in their careers and personal lives. It's impossible to thrive in a disruptive environment if you rely solely on your existing knowledge and past experiences. You need to think and learn differently, and you need to apply your knowledge more effectively.

In the near future, career success will depend on being proficient at fluid skills such as complex problem-solving, analytical thinking, and critical thinking. Now more than ever, businesses need people who are resilient and flexible. Creative people who can innovate, invent, and reinvent. Socially adept people who can collaborate with others. And leaders who can lead themselves and their organizations while inspiring their people to succeed. These are the qualities that will define top talent for the year 2025 and beyond.

While the demand for fluid skills is growing at an unprecedented rate, employers aren't investing enough in reskilling their workers. A 2018 survey by Accenture revealed that global executives estimate that only one-fourth of the workforce is adequately prepared to work with intelligent machines. Although organizations had increased spending on intelligent technology by over 60 percent between 2016 and 2017, only 3 percent of the organizations surveyed had planned for a significant increase in training for the following year.[ii] This is devastating news for workers who are struggling to acquire the skills they need, not just to keep their current jobs, but especially to progress to more senior leadership roles.

The message couldn't be more clear: individuals who want to advance in their careers will need to invest in their own education and development. But what kind of training program teaches people how to flourish in a world that's undergoing a revolution of disruption? A traditional college education is no longer enough, and it can take many years to earn a degree. Today, we no longer have the luxury of time to get up to speed. Learning through trial and error is another option, but that route is also time consuming and often costly. Besides, any knowledge and skills you acquire can become obsolete quickly, making it difficult to keep up in the never-ending race to acquire even more current knowledge and skills.

So, how do we stop this madness? Fortunately, you don't need to be the smartest person in the room to win this race, nor do you need to fill your brain with an immense library of information in order to gain a competitive advantage. The answer lies in becoming a more effective thinker and a more agile learner by leveraging the principles of neuroscience and your subconscious brain's innate capacity to rewire itself.

In the Introduction to his book, *A User's Guide to the Brain*, John Ratey states:

> Each of our one hundred billion neurons may have any-where from 1 to 10,000 synaptic connections to other neu-rons. This means that the theoretical number of different patterns of connections possible in a single brain is approx-imately 40,000,000,000,000,000—forty quadrillion… If changes in synaptic strengths (not merely the different arrangement of synapses) are the primary mechanism be-hind the brain's ability to represent the world, and each synapse has, say, ten different strengths, then the different electrochemical configurations in a single brain come to a staggering number: ten to the trillionth power. This is an unimaginably large number: most astrophysicists calculate the volume of the universe, in cubic meters, to be roughly ten to the eighty-seventh power.[iii]

Think of your brain as an iceberg. Your conscious mind is just the tip of the iceberg that sticks out of the water, whereas your subconscious is the huge mass that lies hidden and unknown underneath. This is why I focus on the subconscious brain—specifically, the brain habits that we perform automatically without even being aware of them. I call these hidden powerhouses *Subconscious Thinking Habits*. They underlie the processes that shape how we think, learn, and adapt and how we view and interact with the world.

There are a lot of books and programs on the market designed to help you develop new habits, but those resources focus on conscious mind habits. In other words, they take a traditional approach to delivering information that relies on the brain's language-based left hemisphere. However, this approach fails to tap into the brain's natural learning functions. But my approach is completely different. This book doesn't try to tell you how to change your habits. Rather, it explains that it is possible to *change your thinking* and achieve a state of cognitive mastery that will keep your brain operating in your high-performance zone with ease, even when you are under intense pressure.

Brain Habits is designed to help you learn what is possible for your brain and to empower you to understand that you can upgrade it by optimally balancing your brain's left and right hemispheres. It is not a do-it-yourself guide on how to gain subconscious success, as the process of cognitive development is highly personalized and deeply nuanced. (We tailor our brain coaching program to each client because no two brains are the same.) Rather, this book offers a fresh and candid take on some serious science and unpacks the reasons why developing your Subconscious Thinking Habits can create profound and sustainable behavioral changes that will bring success to virtually every area of your life and career.

As a cognitive scientist, I have always done things a little differently, and this book follows that pattern. It is my unequivocal opinion that everyone needs a brain upgrade in order to be optimally equipped to thrive in today's ever-changing world. If we, as the people of this planet, could collectively upgrade the learning engines of our brains, then our ability to learn new knowledge and skills quickly and effectively would radically increase.

In my 25 years as an executive brain coach, I have seen amazing transformations. Watching clients metamorphose—breaking through career ceilings, multiplying their yearly revenue, and finally achieving work/life balance—drives my passion and gives me tremendous joy. It is my hope that this book will help even more individuals begin the journey of unlocking their total potential and fully optimizing their performance.

Our brains love stories. They are one of the primary ways we learn and retain information. In fact, I learned a long time ago that all science and no story is like all work and no play. That's why nearly every chapter in this book includes stories. They set the scene to unpack the science in a more relatable way.

In life, we have a way of seeing things as good or bad—black or white—but I invite you to embrace the gray in this book. As you read these stories, keep an inquiring mind, and see how they might relate to you or remind you of people you know. Resist the temptation to label traits as positive or negative. Instead, simply observe and see what resonates.

PART I

THE BEST VERSION OF YOUR BRAIN

Chapter 1

YOUR BRAIN: A HAPPY ACCIDENT OR PURPOSELY DESIGNED?

If your brain was an app, would you buy it?

I have spoken to many leaders during my career as a CEO, brain coach, and cognitive scientist. Although I didn't know it at the time, a conversation with a business leader I'll call Amelia turned out to be a pivotal moment for my work.

I ran into Amelia at a networking event. Our paths had crossed before, and I was happy to see her familiar face. Amelia was a senior executive at a global financial organization, and I found her to be bright, curious, and quite insightful. After engaging in small talk for a few minutes, we shifted our conversation to her career goals. Amelia told me she was happy, and that she had successfully driven her business unit's growth. However, she now faced a pervasive business challenge: how to sustain the momentum?

I listened intently as Amelia explained that leveraging her thinking had been a significant factor in her success, but now she was finding it harder to come up with new ideas. She needed to upgrade her thinking to continue her trajectory, but how?

As Amelia spoke, I felt my mind being lulled by the fading sunlight on that brisk autumn afternoon. Suddenly, an idea struck me: a smartphone app is a great metaphor for the brain!

"What if your brain and its associated functions are like an app on a smartphone?"

Amelia looked at me quizzically. "Do you mean like a brain app?"

3

I nodded and asked, "If your brain was an app, would you buy it?"

After pondering my question for a moment, Amelia let out a soft "hmm" that told me her mind was open to this concept. Then, she smiled and said, "Probably not this version of my brain app, but maybe a new and improved version. Is that even possible?"

"Indeed it is," I assured her.

"How?" she asked, her curiosity piqued.

"Let me tell you a story…"

YOUR CURRENT BRAIN APP: A HAPPY ACCIDENT?

Several years ago, while facilitating a session at a multinational Chief Financial Officers (CFOs) conference, I asked the audience for a volunteer. I wanted someone who had a great sense of humor, a healthy ego, and a high level of resilience. A section of the attendees erupted with laughter, and before I knew it, Elliott was standing next to me. Although he had feigned reluctance, he seemed happy to have been offered up by his colleagues.

I asked Elliott to share his views on the role of a CFO with the group. He emphasized the intellectual rigor the job required and described the challenges CFOs faced, explaining that they had to switch rapidly between pre-emptively managing risk and thinking about growth and new opportunities. The audience murmured in agreement.

"Would you say your brain and your thinking capacity are two of your greatest professional assets?" I asked.

Elliott nodded emphatically.

"Would you agree they are two of the most critical assets required to perform your role as a CFO and that your future career growth depends on them?"

He replied, "Of course they are."

"I agree," I said. But here's where our conversation took a turn. I asked him a critical question: "So, Elliot, can you tell me…how does your brain work?"

Without hesitation, he replied that it worked poorly. His response evoked a mix of laughter and applause from the supportive attendees. When the laughter had simmered down, Elliott added, "Honestly, I don't really know how my brain works; it just does, for better or worse."

Probing further, I asked, "Can you recall how you were taught how to think and learn?"

Elliott replied, "I wasn't taught how. It just happened, just as it does for everyone else. A happy accident, I suppose."

Lighthearted chuckles echoed throughout the room. Because Elliott had been such a fantastic volunteer and was responding to my line of questioning with a good dose of humor, I pressed on with a final comment.

You believe your brain and thinking capacity are the most important personal assets in your career. But even though your brain is your biggest asset, you don't know how it works.

"Elliott, indulge me. Let me see if I have understood you correctly by summing up what I've heard. You believe your brain and thinking capacity are the most important personal assets in your career. But even though your brain is your biggest asset, you don't know how it works. Nobody ever taught you how to use your brain optimally to think and learn. The development of these core assets—your brain and your thinking—just happened as a 'happy accident.'"

There was a long pause. I had put Elliott's resilience and good nature to the test, and he grew visibly uncomfortable. The audience members whispered amongst themselves and a few people laughed nervously while we all waited for him to respond.

After he had composed himself, Elliot said, "When you put it like that, it is a bit confronting. I don't think I would've expressed it quite that way. But to be fair, it is hard to argue with your logic."

Elliott had made a salient point in acknowledging that he had never been taught how to think or learn. It had all happened by accident, but was it really a *happy* accident? Well, it would have been if Elliott's brain worked optimally, but our testing has shown that is rarely the case.

Although Elliott's teachers and professors had attempted to shape his learning capacity, they had not taught him how to think and learn in a clear and explicit way. Of course, for him to have become a CFO, there had obviously been some success in developing his thinking. Unfortunately, he had not taken an intentional approach to developing his thinking skills.

It is imperative to take a deliberate approach if we want to develop our ideal thinking capability. Career growth and long-term success depend on the ability to think optimally, and this need only increases with more senior roles.

IT IS INDEED POSSIBLE TO UPGRADE YOUR BRAIN APP

After sharing that story with Amelia, I said, "Like most executives and entrepreneurs, Elliott had developed his brain app accidentally and not by design. He needed to upgrade it."

Amelia shrugged wistfully and replied, "Even if my brain was an app that could be upgraded, I would have no idea how to do that. I wouldn't even know where to start."

"All of us are walking around with an accidental brain app," I explained. "Our brain doesn't come with a user manual—we just think how we think, and we are how we are. But like most things in life, our brains can change. We can redesign our brain app."

Intrigued, Amelia asked, "How?"

"By leveraging neuroscience and cognitive science research," I said. "You can generate your own brain user manual. I have developed a method to test people's subconscious thinking capabilities and identify their personal thinking and behavioral derailers. Once we know what's causing glitches in their brain, we can recode the underlying subconscious thinking capabilities and turn those derailers into strengths."

Amelia tilted her head thoughtfully and asked, "Are you saying that we think without even being aware of how we are thinking?"

"Yes," I explained. "Subconscious thinking operates below our conscious awareness. These subconscious processes develop in an unplanned way over time and become habits, which is why I call them Subconscious Thinking Habits. They underpin how we process information, think, learn, behave, and adapt."

Amelia's eyes had grown wide. "Wow, that's amazing!" she exclaimed. "But how do you know it works?"

"Because I have many clients who have successfully upgraded their brain app," I replied. "Not only do our clients' scores improve significantly when we retest them, but they also report that their entire lives change because their brain is functioning better. Most people gain an additional hour of productivity each day after brain coaching, and many have been promoted to more senior roles."

"Wow, I can see why you call it an upgrade!" Amelia quipped. "This is all very interesting. Can you tell me how it works?"

So, I launched into my explanation of cognitive development, which, like most things in life, starts at birth…

HOW YOUR BRAIN APP DEVELOPED

Many pioneers in early childhood development theory have laid a strong foundation for understanding how the early brain begins to code itself, establishing the roots of how we think and learn.

I like to think of the brain as having a basic operating system that has been encoded with myriad routines that help us parse information and engage with stimuli. In order to grasp this metaphor, it is necessary to understand what a routine is. From a computer science perspective, a *routine* is a portion of computer code within a larger program that performs a specific task and operates relatively independently. Essentially, a routine is a sequence of instructions that perform a task. Multiple programs can use the same routine, wherever that task needs to be performed.

Throughout our childhood, our brain encodes various routines accidentally as we develop and grow. Our social and cultural environment and experiences shape the way these brain routines become encoded. So, in the context of our computer metaphor, you could say that humans are born with a basic brain operating system similar to Windows OS or macOS.

Take the example of how a child acquires language. Children's operating systems come pre-programmed with an innate language acquisition routine. Language acquisition and development are complex, innately complicated processes that are challenging to describe. However, regardless of a child's social or cultural milieu, the ability to acquire language skills must be embedded in every child's brain as part of their basic operating system.

Like a world-class athlete's body, our brain needs professional training, too, if we want it to perform optimally.

When you consider that your baby brain is partially responsible for your current brain app, it's not surprising that it needs an upgrade. As the stories of Amelia and Elliot revealed, our brain and the ability to grow, learn, and adapt are critical assets. Knowing this, it's reasonable to wonder why we often don't give our brains the same reverence and support that professional athletes give their bodies. Think about it. World-class athletes hire coaches, scientists, doctors, physiologists, and nutritionists to support their bodies. If they hope to win gold medals, they know it will take a lot more effort than just getting some regular exercise and eating a plate of vegetables every day. Like a world-class athlete's body, our brain needs professional training, too, if we want it to perform optimally.

THE SCIENCE BEHIND COGNITIVE DEVELOPMENT

The idea of our brain app having developed in an *ad hoc* manner throughout childhood and adolescence is founded upon Jean Piaget's theory of cognitive development. Piaget was one of the first to reject the idea that intelligence is fixed. Instead, he proposed that children create increasingly complex mental models of their world as part of their cognitive development process.[iv] As children mature biologically, their ongoing interaction with their environment shapes and continually reshapes these mental models.

In psychology, the mental models our brain uses to organize knowledge and guide cognitive processes and behaviors are called *schemas*. Piaget defined a schema as a cohesive, repeatable action sequence that is tightly interconnected and governed by a core meaning.[v] Piaget's concept of schemas helps us understand how our brain codes routines during childhood.

Piaget's theoretical thinking framework also provides a solid base to enlighten our understanding of how a child's cognitive development impacts the adult brain. According to Piaget, all children pass through a series of four stages of cognitive development (see Table 1).[vi]

Table 1. Piaget's Four Stages of Cognitive Development

Stage	Age	Description
Sensorimotor	Birth to 18–24 months	The infant lives in the present. If the infant can't see an object, then the object does not exist.
Pre-operational	2 to 7 years	The child begins to understand that objects and events can be represented as mental entities or symbols, resulting in symbolic thought.
Concrete Operational	7 to 11 years	The child develops operational thinking and the ability to think logically by manipulating physical objects or pictures of them.
Formal Operational	Adolescence to Adulthood	Adolescents develop Abstract Thinking capability so they can follow a discussion or argument without having to refer to concrete examples.

Although some critics have since questioned Piaget's methodology, the chronological accuracy of each stage of cognitive development, and the impact of a child's social environment, Piaget's work is still considered profoundly impactful. Nearly a century later, we need to recognize two crucial points. The first is that, although we understand that all children go through the four stages in the same order, we now know that some children progress at different speeds than Piaget suggested. The second distinction is that we must balance Piaget's approach with that of his peer Lev Vygotsky, who held a different view. Vygotsky saw children learning from adults in a social setting as the paramount factor in a child's cognitive development.[vii] From my perspective, both Piaget's and Vygotsky's work are extremely valuable when they are framed as being complementary.

HOW PIAGET'S FOUR STAGES CREATE YOUR CURRENT BRAIN APP

Let's discover how the science plays out practically. As you were growing up, you went through each of Piaget's stages of cognitive development at your own speed and with your own unique milestones. As you progressed, your brain coded your brain routines automatically. This initial coding created the basis of your current adult brain app and still impacts it today.

The activities, games, hobbies, and play routines you engaged in as a child directly affected the efficiency and effectiveness of your current brain app and its related thinking capabilities. It's important to understand this happened subconsciously, with little or no intentionality on your part. Consequently, some of your Subconscious Thinking Habits were coded efficiently and others weren't.

INTERACTIVE DISCOVERY LEARNING IS MORE POWERFUL THAN JUST MEMORIZING

Piaget's work also introduced the concept of *discovery learning*, which is based on the idea that children learn best by doing practical activities. Rather than teaching children by spoon-feeding them information, Piaget thought it was more beneficial for children to learn by doing.[viii]

Learning through discovery is a powerful mechanism for recoding brain routines because it taps into the brain's inherent neuroplasticity.

Discovery learning is extremely valuable for adults and executives as well. This approach plays a prominent role in how we practically develop and improve our clients' brain app. We use a play-driven discovery approach that enables them to have organic *ah-ha* learning moments, so they learn proactively, instead of receiving information passively. Learning through discovery is a powerful mechanism for recoding brain routines because it taps into the brain's inherent neuroplasticity. *Neuroplasticity* is the brain's ability to rewire and physiologically change itself in response to environmental interactions. This is how we upgrade your individual brain app.

Piaget's concepts of *assimilation* and *accommodation* are also helpful to us, as they reinforce the importance of discovery learning. According to Piaget, *assimilation* occurs when a child processes new information into established cognitive schemas and *accommodation* occurs when a child revises (recodes) established schemas to incorporate additional information. These two processes are separate and quite different. The former requires a passive learning approach, whereas the latter requires an active learning approach.[ix]

Piaget saw interactive discovery learning as essential because complex problem-solving skills cannot be taught; instead, they must be discovered.[x] Simply providing problem-solving templates or formulas does not achieve much. Generally, the person will continue to struggle to solve complex problems, as it can't be done formulaically. For an individual to be efficient and effective at complex problem-solving, the brain routines that underpin these skills need to be optimally developed. Later in this book, it will become clearer why we focus on discovery learning techniques for optimal complex problem solving. For now, the key takeaway is that interactive discovery learning and the repetition of increasingly complex and difficult mental activities are required to recode the adult brain.

KEY TAKEAWAYS

- While most people acknowledge that their brain and their thinking capacity are two of their greatest professional assets, they readily admit they don't know how their brain works. That's because most people have never been taught how to think, learn, and adapt optimally.
- Your current brain app developed as a happy accident, driven by the activities, games, and hobbies you pursued as a child. Your brain app probably doesn't function optimally because it wasn't purposefully designed.
- Jean Piaget postulated that children progress through four stages of cognitive development at various ages. I posit that

our brain codes routines at each of those stages, and these routines then form the basis of our adult brain app.

- It is possible to upgrade your adult brain app. We do this by tapping into the brain's inherent neuroplasticity and purposefully recoding the brain's routines, which I call Subconscious Thinking Habits.

- Piaget introduced the concept of discovery learning which suggests that children learn best by doing practical activities that are designed to help them realize new concepts and ideas. Likewise, I use a discovery learning approach with adults to improve their subconscious thinking capability and enhance their brain app.

Chapter 2

HABITS: YOU CAN'T CHANGE WHAT YOU'RE UNAWARE OF

"Neurons that fire together, wire together."
—Donald Hebb

Habits are routines your brain has encoded so deeply through repetition that you now perform them automatically. Every time your brain responds to a cue, whether consciously or subconsciously, it reinforces the connections between neurons. These *neural pathways* become increasingly stronger the more often they repeat that response. When a response has been repeated enough times, it becomes an automatic habit. This is how the brain codes habit routines.

A habit can be good or bad. Our brain doesn't care either way. It simply registers a response to a cue. When the same response is repeated over time, whether consciously or subconsciously, the brain codes a new routine in due course. Because the brain strengthens neural pathways in response to repetition regardless of whether or not a given routine is supportive, individuals naturally end up with a mix of good and bad habits.

For this book, I have broken the concept of habits into two types: Conscious Mind Habits and Subconscious Thinking Habits. *Conscious Mind Habits* are those of which we are fully aware. These habits relate primarily to routine physical activities—such as brushing your teeth or your exercise regime. They can also relate to physical cravings and addictions.

We tend to create healthy habits, such as exercising, deliberately at first. Eventually, they will run on autopilot because they have become so deeply embedded that we no longer need to activate them intentionally. Less healthy habits, such as cravings for chocolate, are often created unwittingly. They, too, run on autopilot once they have been embedded as a routine—that's why they're so hard to change. Over time, Conscious Mind Habits become so well entrenched that it is extremely difficult to override them with willpower alone.

I coined the term *Subconscious Thinking Habit* to describe a brain habit that operates below our conscious awareness. Unlike Conscious Mind Habits—which relate to *physical* activities that we *are* cognizant of—Subconscious Thinking Habits relate to *mental* thinking functions that we *are not* cognizant of.

Remember our brain app from the previous chapter? To build on that same metaphor, you can think of your Subconscious Thinking Habits as the routines that make up your brain app. Brain habits underpin the way we process information, reason, learn, adapt, and behave.

As you learned in Chapter 1, your current brain app—and thus, your Subconscious Thinking Habits—developed in an *ad hoc* fashion as you progressed through Piaget's stages of cognitive development. Your brain coded these routines through the learning and play activities you engaged in as a child. Because you completed Piaget's stages by the end of adolescence, your Subconscious Thinking Habits had pretty much solidified by then too. However, in this book, I will explain how an intentional approach can help you to rewire and recode the brain habits that support your thinking functions as an adult.

Regardless of type, every habit follows a three-part cognitive pattern. In his book *The Power of Habit*, Charles Duhigg calls these patterns *habit loops*. Duhigg's model applies well to Conscious Mind Habits; however, the model I have developed for Subconscious Thinking Habits is slightly different. In this chapter, I will show you how both models work and explain the key differences between them.

Once you have a solid understanding of the two types of habits and their respective patterns, I will introduce you to an innovative framework I have developed to describe and categorize the brain's thinking functions. It consists of ten Subconscious Thinking Habits, which I have grouped by function into four categories. I call these categories the *Four Pillars of Subconscious Success*. We will cover all ten Subconscious Thinking Habits and their respective Pillars in depth, beginning in Part II of this book.

CONSCIOUS MIND HABITS

To gain a better understanding of how Conscious Mind Habits work, let's look at an example of an unhealthy habit, such as eating junk food. Many of us reach for unhealthy snacks without even thinking, as we have repeated this activity for so long that it has become reflexive. This is why so many people struggle significantly, especially in the initial phase of a new diet. Unfortunately, willpower alone is often not enough to override eating habits that have been deeply engrained over time.

We have all felt the struggle and pull of unsupportive habits when they govern our lives. But, in the same way, we have also likely experienced the benefits of developing supportive habits that run on autopilot—for example, when we religiously get up each morning and prioritize going for a run. By repeating this activity daily over time, we can develop a routine habit that will benefit our overall physical health. Our brain codes new neural pathways and wires in this new routine, making the habit automatic and, thus, easier to sustain long term with little to no conscious effort.

Conscious Mind Habits are so much broader than nutrition and exercise, though. They are part of our everyday lives, from a habit as simple as cleaning our shoes to one as complex as a gambling addiction.

HABIT LOOP MODEL

Let's return to Charles Duhigg's concept of a *habit loop*. Figure 1 illustrates Duhigg's model, which has three components:

Cue: the trigger that initiates a habitual behavior.

Routine: the physical behavior that follows the triggering cue.

Reward: reinforcement for the behavior.[xi]

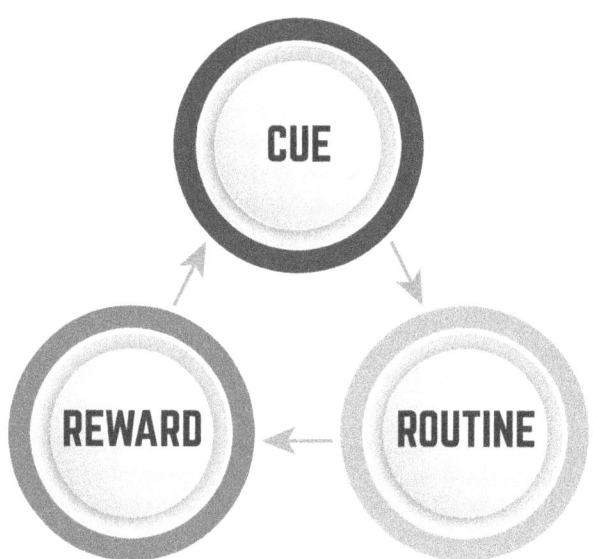

Figure 1. Diagram of Duhigg's Habit Loop

This neurological pattern is at the root of every Conscious Mind Habit. The same habit loop model applies to both our current behaviors and the desired behaviors we are consciously building.

Below is an example of how a habit loop works in the context of a well-established Conscious Mind Habit.

Cue: A trigger kickstarts the brain program associated with the habitual behavior.

Routine: The activated brain program launches into action and generates the associated habitual behavior automatically.

Reward: You receive a payoff as a result, which further reinforces the habitual behavior.

Now, let's take a look at a concrete example. Suppose you have a habit of reaching for chocolate when you're stressed. Here is the habit loop for that behavior.

Cue: You're feeling stressed.

Routine: You reach for a piece of chocolate without consciously thinking about it.

Reward: After consuming the treat, you feel more relaxed.

As I mentioned earlier, Duhigg expands his concept of habit loops to include *cravings*, a concept that I am sure is familiar to many of us. Duhigg posits that a habit can create a neurological craving for something we especially enjoy. Our cravings give our habits power. Clearly, our psychological cravings have revolutionized the marketing of consumer products.[xii]

Importantly, habit loops have a broader context that is separate from cravings. In a 2012 interview on *NPR Radio*, Duhigg said, "You can do these complex behaviors without being mentally aware of it at all. And that's because of the capacity of the basal ganglia: to take a behavior and turn it in into an *automatic routine* [emphasis added]."[xiii]

Conscious Mind Habits and their corresponding habit loops are fascinating in their own right. They also provide a great foundation for understanding Subconscious Thinking Habits.

SUBCONSCIOUS THINKING HABITS

Conscious Mind Habits operate above the conscious threshold—at least initially. And so, we are aware of them and their associated cues, routines, and rewards. Subconscious Thinking Habits, on the other hand, operate below our conscious threshold. Thus, our awareness of them is indirect. Subconscious Thinking Habits start to become more noticeable when they impact our performance negatively. For example, when people began moving into open office environments, some become aware of how difficult it was to focus effectively amidst all the distractions. This is still an issue for many people who work in open environments.

The challenge for most individuals is that their Subconscious Thinking Habits still function the same way they did in late adolescence. As you learned in Chapter 1, our metaphorical brain app develops throughout childhood and adolescence. Subconscious Thinking Habits evolve in an unintentional way as we mature and virtually stop developing by the time we become adults. As a result, many of us find ourselves struggling, especially as our lives and careers become increasingly challenging, complex, and demanding. Regrettably, this struggle will continue unless we intentionally upgrade our brain app and its routines.

Traditional problem-solving techniques tell you _what_ to do, but not _how_ to do it.

Imbalances and deficiencies in Subconscious Thinking Habits can cause the brain's routines to run slowly or glitch occasionally, just as computer operating system sometimes does. Consider, for example, the process of complex problem-solving. Have you ever noticed that even though there are many problem-solving techniques to choose from, some people still struggle to apply them? Usually, this is because the Subconscious Thinking Habit I call Analytical Thinking is running slowly or ineffectively.[1]

> *Knowing what to do is only half the battle. Subconscious Thinking Habits are the missing link that helps you figure out how to do it.*

We will get into the specifics of this Subconscious Thinking Habit later. However, for now, the takeaway is this: traditional problem-solving techniques tell you *what* to do, but not *how* to do it. Knowing what to do is only half the battle. Subconscious Thinking Habits are the missing link that helps you figure out how to do it.

> *The quality and timeliness of the output you can produce depends on the effectiveness and efficiency of your Subconscious Thinking Habits.*

The quality and timeliness of the output you can produce depends on the effectiveness and efficiency of your Subconscious Thinking Habits. Enhancing your Subconscious Thinking Habits supports you in optimally applying the knowledge you have learned.

SUBCONSCIOUS THINKING HABIT MODEL

I have adapted Duhigg's habit loop model to illustrate the neurological pattern for a Subconscious Thinking Habit. Unlike Conscious Mind Habits, which deliver a *physical* reward, Subconscious Thinking Habits deliver a *mental* output. Therefore, I have replaced Duhigg's original *Reward* component with *Output*. And because Subconscious

---

[1] In Chapter 3, I will explain that speed and effectiveness are, indeed, two very different brain performance metrics. Our Fluid Thinking assessment measures both of them.

Thinking Habits operate below our conscious awareness, I have replaced *Routine* with *Subconscious Routine*. You can see a diagram of my Subconscious Thinking Habit model in Figure 2.

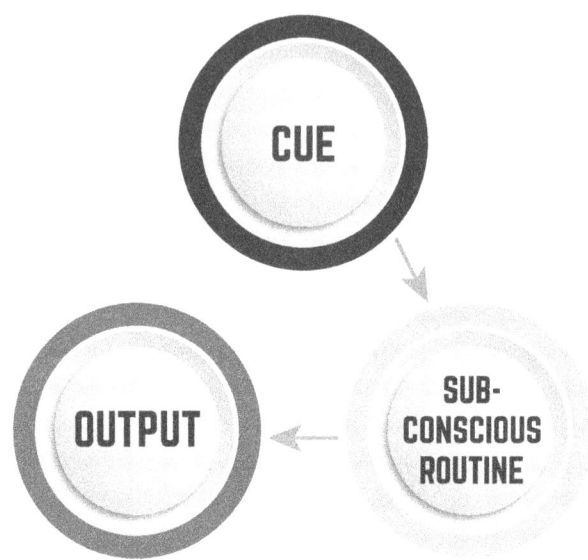

Figure 2. Diagram of a Subconscious Thinking Habit

Below is a description of each component.

Cue:	the information or stimulus that activates the *Subconscious Routine.*
Subconscious Routine:	the brain program associated with the relevant Subconscious Thinking Habit that processes the information subconsciously and automatically.
Output:	the mental output generated by the associated Subconscious Routine.

Have you ever struggled to maintain your focus while working on an important project? (For most people, this is a constant challenge.)

As you will learn a bit later in this chapter, one of your Subconscious Thinking Habits supports your ability to focus. When this habit is operating below the ideal level, it can hijack your capacity to control your attention.

Let's take a look at the mechanism for a Subconscious Thinking Habit in the context of a real-world example. If you've ever found yourself distracted by screen notifications, you will be able to relate to the following scenario:

Cue:	An email notification pops up on your screen, distracting you from an important priority.
Subconscious Routine:	Without thinking, you automatically open the email.
Output:	Because your brain is still operating on autopilot and you are not consciously aware of being distracted, you continue to respond to non-urgent emails, even though an important deadline is rapidly approaching.

THE FOUR PILLARS OF SUBCONSCIOUS SUCCESS

My approach to upgrading brains, and the framework I describe below, has evolved through my extensive work with executives and entrepreneurs, combined with detailed research and study in the fields of cognitive science and neuroscience.

The Four Pillars of Subconscious Success in my approach are:

- Pillar One: Controlling Attention
- Pillar Two: Complex Problem-Solving
- Pillar Three: Strategy, Planning, and Execution
- Pillar Four: Social Leadership

In the sections that follow, I explain each Pillar and describe how it impacts the thinking and behaviors of executives, leaders, and entrepreneurs. It is important to note that each Pillar builds on the previous one. When all Four Pillars and their associated Subconscious Thinking Habits operate in harmony, they drive success subconsciously, enabling leaders to optimize their own performance and that of their teams. However, should one or more Pillars operate suboptimally, this will significantly impact an individual's capacity to deliver the desired output.

Figure 3 illustrates the Four Pillars of Subconscious Success and their associated Subconscious Thinking Habits.

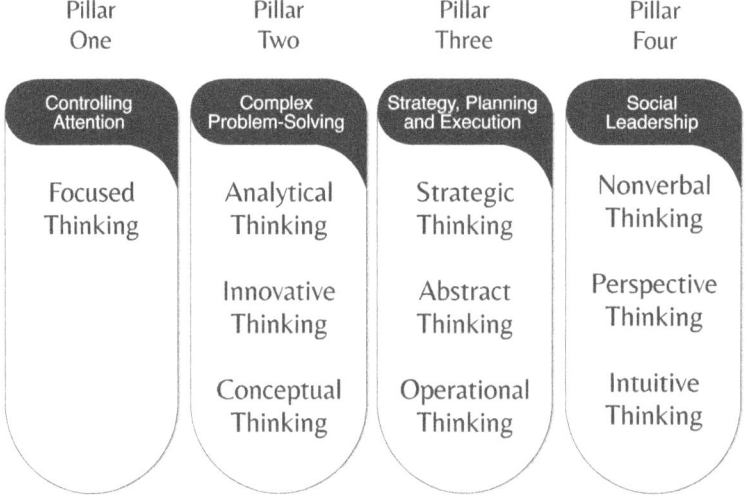

Figure 3. Four Pillars of Subconscious Success and Associated Subconscious Thinking Habits

---

It takes far more time, effort, and mental energy to compensate for less efficient Subconscious Thinking Habits than it does to develop them.

Interestingly, we have found that it takes far more time, effort, and mental energy to compensate for less efficient Subconscious

Thinking Habits than it does to develop them. People's lives usually improve significantly after they upgrade their brain app.

PILLAR ONE: CONTROLLING ATTENTION

Pillar One: Controlling Attention provides the foundational underpinning for our subconscious thinking and subsequent performance. This all-pervasive Pillar comprises the Subconscious Thinking Habit of *Focused Thinking*, which gives you control over your attention so you can leverage your focus optimally.

Lower Focused Thinking capability commonly manifests as lower output and productivity. When individuals aren't fully in control of their attention, it is difficult to remain focused on their top priority. The impact of lower focus is distractibility, procrastination, and poor time management. Individuals with lower focus often rush to meet deadlines, drift off during meetings, and need to re-read documents. Overcoming this derailer can bring about dramatic shifts in performance, productivity, and personal resilience.

We will discuss Pillar One in more detail in Part II of this book.

PILLAR TWO: COMPLEX PROBLEM-SOLVING

Pillar Two: Complex Problem-Solving comprises three very different styles of thinking, all of which are equally important to the complex problem-solving process. Together, the following Subconscious Thinking Habits ensure that the strategic value of solutions is maximized:

- *Analytical Thinking* supports the ability to break down complex situations into bite-size chunks as a precursor to defining a problem.
- *Innovative Thinking* underpins the ability to brainstorm and generate multiple potential solutions to solve the defined problem.

- *Conceptual Thinking* is used to test the soundness of each solution before identifying the optimum solution to the defined problem.

Creating ideal balance across this set of Subconscious Thinking Habits dramatically impacts the effectiveness of the problem-solving process. For this reason, optimized Complex Problem-Solving is a non-negotiable for anyone who spends a significant amount of their time solving complex problems and addressing complicated opportunities and risks.

The Subconscious Thinking Habits associated with Pillar Two impact a person's problem-solving speed *and* the quality of their solutions. When one or more of these habits is operating suboptimally, an individual might solve problems more slowly or generate less-than-ideal solutions (sometimes both).

Subconscious problem-solving deficiencies can be extremely costly in today's rapidly changing landscape. We can expect the need for advanced critical thinking and problem solving skills to grow exponentially as companies grapple with fundamental challenges such as climate change, global political unrest, COVID-19, and the Fourth Industrial Revolution whose staggering technological advances promise to fuse our physical, digital, and biological worlds.

We will cover Pillar Two in depth in Part III.

PILLAR THREE: STRATEGY, PLANNING, AND EXECUTION

Pillar Three: Strategy, Planning, and Execution follows naturally from Pillar Two. In the previous section, we covered the skills you need to solve a complex problem, and now we will cover the skills you'll need in order to implement the optimum solution successfully. Again, this Pillar integrates three very different thinking styles, all of which are equally essential for successfully executing strategic initiatives.

Pillar Three comprises the following Subconscious Thinking Habits:

- *Strategic Thinking* underpins big-picture thinking, strategic formulation, and communication.
- *Abstract Thinking* supports developing the strategic plan that's needed to execute a strategy and underpins the ability to delegate the various components of that plan clearly and effectively.
- *Operational Thinking* ensures that the delegatees execute their respective components of the strategic plan in a practical and collaborative manner to deliver a successful outcome.

Not surprisingly, a deficiency in one or more of these Subconscious Thinking Habits can significantly damage the quality of how solutions are strategically executed. Creating balance among all three habits in Pillar Three can prevent a lot of unnecessary rework, as you'll see in Part IV of this book.

PILLAR FOUR: SOCIAL LEADERSHIP

Pillar Four: Social Leadership covers the competencies needed to build rapport, trust, and followership. Unlike the Subconscious Thinking Habits that rely on hard, rational skills, the habits associated with Social Leadership rely on soft, sensing skills. They support leaders in building rapport, motivating people, and coaching their teams. And they help ensure that the individuals who will be charged with executing the strategy buy into the strategic plan and take full ownership of their assigned tasks.

Pillar Four comprises the following Subconscious Thinking Habits:

- *Nonverbal Thinking* underpins the ability to build rapport with others and read subtle nonverbal cues such as body language, facial expressions, and tone of voice.
- *Perspective Thinking* supports the ability to empathize and understand another person's perspective and feelings, a key component of emotional intelligence.

- *Intuitive Thinking* supports the ability to pick up environmental cues (e.g., reading a room). It also underpins your gut feelings and street smarts.

Social Leadership is the rounding Pillar, the polishing cloth you need to make success shine through. We call it the *ceiling breaker* because when you develop Pillar Four in tandem with the other Pillars, it becomes much easier to break through professional ceilings. When all ten Subconscious Thinking Habits are balanced, they have a dramatic impact on a person's professional potential and performance. Without strong Social Leadership, all the strategic pre-work can fall on the deaf ears of disengaged employees and co-workers because you have not previously cultivated relationships, nor developed appropriate levels of rapport.

Just like complex problem-solving skills, the soft people skills related to emotional intelligence and social intelligence—as well as self-management skills, such as active learning, resilience, stress tolerance, and flexibility—will become increasingly essential as we move toward the future.

In Part V of this book, we will explore Social Leadership more deeply.

WHAT LIES AHEAD

By now, I hope you now have a basic understanding of the Four Pillars of Subconscious Success and some insight into why they are so key to unlocking more powerful performance. Already, you can start to see that investing in developing your Subconscious Thinking Habits can lead to a new and improved brain app.

In Chapter 3, I will cover the science behind upgrading your brain app by tapping into your brain's inherent neuroplasticity. Critically, I will introduce my concept of *brain balance*, which challenges the conventional theory that alleges that individuals are either right-brained or left-brained, depending on which hemisphere of their brain is dominant. As you'll see, it is not only important, but also very necessary, for the brain's left and right hemispheres to be optimally balanced.

We will then do a deep dive into each of the Four Pillars of Subconscious Success and their associated Subconscious Thinking Habits. This journey will help you understand how inefficient Subconscious Thinking Habits can derail and hamper both personal and professional success.

Finally, I will explain how optimizing the efficiency and effectiveness all ten Subconscious Thinking Habits leads to brain balance. (I call this effect *Mental Chi.*) The end result: an empowering path to unlocking subconscious success.

KEY TAKEAWAYS

- There are two types of habits: Conscious Mind Habits and Subconscious Thinking Habits.
- Conscious Mind Habits are those of which you are consciously aware. These are typically related to physical or observable behavioral patterns. Conscious Mind Habits are triggered by a cue, which then activates the automatic habitual behavior routine that ultimately delivers a reward.
- Subconscious Thinking Habits are those of which you are unaware. These habits are related to automated information processing and subconscious thinking routines. They are triggered by a cue that activates a subconscious routine, which then produces an output. Because the entire process occurs below your conscious awareness, the output may be beneficial or counterproductive.
- My hypothesis is that Fluid Thinking (i.e., the ability to think, learn, and adapt effectively and quickly) is underpinned by a framework I call the Four Pillars of Subconscious Success, which comprises ten Subconscious Thinking Habits.

Chapter 3

BRAIN BALANCE

"I happen to be extremely left-brained; my instinct is to draw a chart rather than a picture. I'm trying to get my right-brain muscles into shape. I actually think this shift toward right-brain abilities has the potential to make us both better off and better in a deeper sense."
—*Daniel H. Pink*

The Chinese philosophy of yin and yang delves into the complementary nature of opposites, making it a rounded and rich metaphor for the brain. The two hemispheres are separate and yet intrinsically connected, just like the yin and yang. This counterintuitive connection between the left and right hemispheres of the brain creates the harmony that produces *brain balance*—a superpower you can leverage to achieve success, both professionally and in your personal life, too.

This chapter focuses on understanding why brain balance is the essence of subconscious success. I will highlight the cognitive science and neuroscience that underpins brain balance and learning capability. I will also explain that it is possible to leverage neuroplasticity to upgrade your brain app and create tangible, long-term benefits through the targeted development of your Subconscious Thinking Habits.

> **Note:** We will be discussing brain balance based on how the majority of individuals' brains work. By this, I mean we will explore how the left and right hemispheres of the brain operate for a right-handed person. If you're left-handed, fear not; everything we will cover still applies to you, but due to being left-handed, the function of your brain's hemispheres is reversed.

WHAT IS BRAIN BALANCE?

As I explained earlier, adult brain competencies are randomized across people, depending primarily on what activities they undertook when they were growing up. This *ad hoc* approach to cognitive development yields wide variations in the effectiveness and efficiency of each individual's brain app—the hallmark of an unbalanced brain. Consequently, cognitive capabilities vary significantly among individuals. Even those who share a similar background and education can have wildly divergent combinations of cognitive strengths and derailers. Through testing, we have found that most people struggle with at least one cognitive derailer. On average, individuals typically have three or four. This is not at all surprising, as it would be extremely unlikely for a person to have developed optimal brain balance purely by accident.

Once an individual reaches young adulthood, their brain tends to become more hardwired. Consequently, their adult brain app becomes more rigid and less adaptable in the way it thinks and processes information. Because those brain routines and thinking capabilities that were effectively coded in childhood continue to run efficiently, they require lower amounts of mental energy in adulthood. In contrast, those brain routines and thinking capabilities that were ineffectively coded in childhood tend to be quite glitchy and, therefore, require more mental energy.

Put simply, our childhood cognitive development drives thinking skills in adulthood. The cognitive strengths and derailers we had as children will remain evident during our adult years. Thus, the thinking routines we developed in childhood determine the quality of our adult brain app. To allow the derailers that developed in childhood to limit the success of our adult brain app can be extremely costly, both personally and professionally.

Until recently, science has viewed an individual's thinking capabilities as being largely unchangeable. If this were true, it would be impossible to upgrade your brain app. For many people, this would result in limited potential, inadequate performance, and a short-ened career trajectory. Fortunately, we now know it is indeed possible to upgrade your brain app—and achieve brain balance—by intentionally tapping into your brain's inherent neuroplasticity.

THE ROLE OF NEUROPLASTICITY

Neuroplasticity, or *brain plasticity* as it is also called, is the brain's ability to rewire itself over time through repeated mental and physical activities. This leads to changes in the brain's physical structure and functionality. Neuroplasticity supports the brain in adapting to new situations readily. In essence, this brings us back to Donald Hebb's famous articulation, "Neurons that fire together wire together."

Santiago Ramón y Cajal (1852-1934), a pioneer in modern neuro-science and the first person of Spanish origin to win a Nobel Prize, famously said, "Any man could, if he were so inclined, be the sculptor of his own brain."[xiv] Ramón y Cajal's statement was undeniably forecasting the concept of neuroplasticity. Remarkably, he predicted this many years before Polish neuroscientist Jerzy Konorski first used the term in 1948. [xv]

Ramón y Cajal's critical insight has been adopted in surprisingly different circumstances. For example, the military and professional sports have been capitalizing on the concept of deliberate practice (in the form of drills) for a very long time. History's greatest armies and athletes have consistently shown the value of developing subconscious routines through rigorous and consistent practice. The secret to victory often lies in training practices that embed routines into the brain. Effective routines, regardless of whether they are physical or mental in nature, become embedded into the subconscious so they can be executed with total ease, speed, and without having to think about them consciously.

A vital pivot in neuroscience was the more recent shift in the understanding of neuroplasticity. We have known for a long time that a child's brain is malleable; however, the idea that our brains remain plastic throughout our entire lives is relatively new. Until recently, scientists believed the brain would become hard-wired by the time a person reached young adulthood. They also thought that if the mechanistic nature of the brain were to be damaged, then its functioning and capability could not be repaired. Thankfully, as Dr. Norman Doidge explains in his book, *The Brain That Changes Itself,* the brain's neuroplasticity ensues well into old age.[xvi] Doidge advances the idea that science can proactively leverage the fertile nature of the brain's inherent neuroplastic capacity to generate new functionality or recover lost functionality. Indeed, his work presents some wonderful examples of how tapping into the brain's plasticity has produced extraordinary medical outcomes.

THE SCIENCE BEHIND BRAIN BALANCE

As a brain coach, I am passionate about developing my clients' brain balance and delivering sustainable improvements in their subconscious thinking routines and behaviors. However, the scientist in me gets even more curious about the science behind brain balance. While earlier theories focused predominantly on the left hemisphere, researchers have given much attention to both sides of the brain in recent decades, and our knowledge of the role of each hemisphere has broadened considerably. Over time, we have come to understand that the right hemisphere plays a crucial role in learning and in achieving brain balance.

In this chapter, we will look at the theories of two well-known authorities whose work is fundamental to understanding brain balance and its impact on leadership and learning.

SEPARATE YET CONNECTED

In his influential article titled "Planning on the Left Side and Managing on the Right," Henry Mintzberg notes that for right-handed people, the left hemisphere of the brain underpins logical thinking processes and processes information in a linear, sequential, and ordered manner. From Mintzberg's perspective, "...[T]he most obvious linear faculty [of the left hemisphere] is language." [xvii]

In sharp contrast, he notes that the right hemisphere of the brain operates in a more holistic and relational way, processing information in a parallel and simultaneous fashion. Mintzberg states, "...[T]he most obvious faculty [of the right hemisphere] is comprehension of visual images." [xviii]

Mintzberg's explanation of the respective roles of the left and right hemispheres supports his hypothesis that the specialization of the hemispheres is an important consideration for leadership. According to Mintzberg, successfully planning a sequence of steps is more a faculty of the brain's left hemisphere, whereas strategy and the important policy-level processes required to lead an organization are more the faculty of the right hemisphere.

Because the right hemisphere processes information in a nonverbal manner, "...our left hemisphere cannot articulate explicitly what our right hemisphere knows implicitly."

He also contrasts the explicit awareness of the left hemisphere's conscious, serial, and language-based thought processes with the right hemisphere's subconscious, relational, holistic, and nonverbal thought processes. Less is known about the right hemisphere's thought processes, which makes Mintzberg's insight especially valuable. Because the right hemisphere processes information in a nonverbal manner, "...our left hemisphere cannot articulate explicitly what our right hemisphere knows implicitly." [xix]

This perspective is essential to my work as well, as Subconscious Thinking Habits are predominantly the domain of the right hemisphere. The opposite faculties of the hemispheres inherently separate them, yet when combined and optimally developed, their connection and complementarity cannot be ignored.

A quick side note: while we attribute unique functionality and faculties to the left and right hemispheres of the brain, it is important to understand the role of the *corpus callosum*, which is a large bundle of specialized nerve fibers that resides beneath the cerebral cortex. The corpus callosum connects the two hemispheres of the brain, enabling communication between the left and right hemispheres. Thus, it integrates and rapidly transfers information between both hemispheres. The corpus callosum can also inhibit the transfer of information between the hemispheres when necessary, so a particular hemisphere can take more of a lead role when required.

THE BICAMERAL BRAIN

Elkhonon Goldberg, a clinical professor of neurology at New York University School of Medicine, is well known for his work on the *bicameral brain*.[2] Goldberg elegantly summarizes the traditional understanding of *hemispherical specialization,* stating, "…[T]he 'dominant' (usually left) hemisphere is in charge of language, whereas the 'subdominant' (usually right) hemisphere is in charge of nonverbal, particularly visuo-spatial[3] functions."[xx] This perspective reinforces Mintzberg's work and provides an important framework for understanding of the bicameral brain.

Goldberg sees the brain as having two divided and distinct hemispheres that work together but function and process information in very different ways. According to his *novelty-routinization theory*, the left hemisphere specializes in processes that are driven by well-established cognitive routines based on past strategies and experiences.

---

[2] The term *bicameral* literally means "two-chambered." In neuroscience, it refers to the two hemispheres of the brain and, specifically, the differential—and highly specialized—roles of the left and right hemispheres.

[3] The brain's visuo-spatial functions include capabilities such as spatial orientation, the ability to analyze visual stimuli, and the ability to manipulate images mentally.

In contrast, the right hemisphere specializes in novel cognitive challenges that cannot be resolved by relying on pre-existing cognitive routines. Thus, *cognitive novelty* requires an innovative and adaptive approach to thinking.

Figure 4 illustrates the functions of the left and right hemispheres based on Goldberg's novelty-routinization theory.

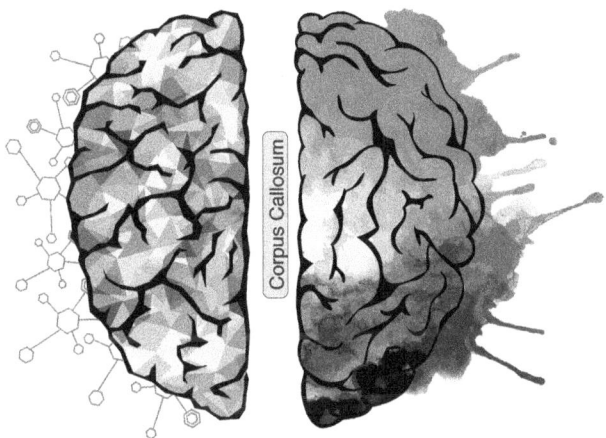

Left Hemisphere: Right Hemisphere:

Routinization   Novelty

Left Hemisphere	Right Hemisphere
1. Serial Processing	1. Parallel Processing
2. Language	2. Nonverbal & Spatial
3. Past Oriented	3. Future Oriented
4. Detail Oriented	4. Big Picture
5. Recalling Knowledge	5. Learning Agility
6. Routine Thinking	6. Agile Thinking
7. Explicit	7. Implicit
8. Logical Argument/ Book Smarts	8. Experiential/ Street Smarts
9. Intellectualize	9. Intuitive
10. Analytical	10. Synthesize
11. Rote Learning	11. Applying New Learnings

Visual Adaptation of Goldberg's Novelty - Routinization Theory

Figure 4. The Bicameral Brain

Interestingly, Goldberg's novelty-routinization theory of hemispheric specialization confirms that the neural pathways that underpin cognitive behavior can indeed change over time. Change occurs as an individual masters a cognitive task through repeated practice. Importantly, Goldberg found that this change can happen only unidirectionally, from the right hemisphere to the left.[xxi]

Goldberg's premises are consistent with our findings: the left hemisphere acts somewhat like a knowledge database from which an individual retrieves and uses their existing knowledge and subject-matter expertise. Conversely, the right hemisphere is more adept at exploring new and novel ideas, problems, or opportunities. The latter operates more like a computer operating system that controls the quality and speed at which new and novel information or situations can be processed and explored.

Through repeated practice, the cognitive novelty approach associated with the right hemisphere shifts to one of cognitive mastery, which is associated with the left hemisphere. Over time, the two hemispheres connect and collaborate to build cognitive routines. The right-to-left hemisphere activation shift occurs as the task being undertaken stops being novel and becomes increasingly familiar and routine. This shift is the hallmark of brain balance. It drives optimum performance.

Goldberg emphasizes that this right-to-left hemisphere activation shift has been measured and demonstrated in laboratories using "... multiple neuroimaging methodologies: fMRI, PET, and EEG."[xxii]

So, what does the shift from cognitive novelty to cognitive mastery look like in real life?

An excellent example is learning to drive. Initially, as you become familiar with everything that driving entails, you rely heavily on the right hemisphere. However, with a lot of practice, you eventually master the skill of driving so well that you can do it without even thinking about it. Indeed, driving becomes a cognitive routine because your brain can easily access this skill from the left hemisphere automatically, below the conscious threshold. When you have mastered driving, you can adapt to changes in traffic and weather conditions quickly, even on unfamiliar roads, and control your vehicle with complete ease.

HOW NEW SCIENCE CHALLENGES OLD APPROACHES TO LEARNING

Some reasonably important implications follow from Goldberg's novelty-routinization theory of hemispheric specialization. Specifically, his right-to-left hemisphere activation shift creates many questions regarding traditional education, training, and coaching. Let's explore how our understanding of learning has changed as a result of new discoveries in the field of cognitive science and neuroscience.

HAVE WE BEEN TRYING TO TEACH BACKWARDS?

Goldberg's research has shown that learning takes place unidirectionally, from the right hemisphere to the left. Yet educational institutions and training programs take a traditional approach to teaching relying almost exclusively on left-hemisphere functions such as language and memorization. So, does that mean we have been trying to teach backwards all this time? If that's true, it's extremely problematic. Let's look closer at this interesting quandary.

Have you ever wondered why two people can attend the same training program on the same day with the same facilitator, and yet experience very different levels of learning? Commonly, training program attendees will come away with varying degrees of ability to apply what they learned to effect behavioral change. This is a familiar dilemma for businesses, entrepreneurs, and individuals, and it comes back to the fact that traditional teaching methods take a left-to-right hemisphere approach—the exact opposite of what our brains need in order to learn optimally. Goldberg sums this problem up well when he says, "Indeed, two individuals may have vastly different degrees of mastery of the 'same' cognitive skills, which will be reflected in different degrees of their reliance on the right versus the left hemisphere."[xxiii]

We are still trying to teach backwards because we don't understand the underpinnings behind brain science. If we reversed our teaching approach, we would avoid so many speed bumps. Currently, we try to cram as much language-based information as possible into an individual's left hemisphere. In so doing, we bypass the right hemisphere entirely and fail to enhance and develop it intentionally.

When an individual's ability to learn has not been developed optimally, their brain will have difficulty keeping up. This will impact the quality and speed of all future learning, and the ability to apply those learnings. Relying predominantly on oral and written language for training leaves our left hemisphere overworked and our brain drained, as we are continually asking it to do things it wasn't designed to do (i.e., cognitive novelty). We could minimize this if we started to normalize approaches to learning that support the way our brain functions, rather than the reverse, but this is the start of a much larger conversation.

The real ROI on education, training, and development can be greatly increased by developing a person's Fluid Thinking and its related Subconscious Thinking Habits.

From my perspective, the real ROI on education, training, and development can be greatly increased by developing a person's Fluid Thinking and its related Subconscious Thinking Habits. This would improve both learning agility and the ability to apply new learnings quickly and effectively. Once this step is completed, the focus could then switch to providing content training and developing a person's domain knowledge more easily and quickly.

The course correction needed to create brain balance requires changing the way we deliver education, training, and coaching.

From a learning and development perspective, we need to stop revering the sequential and analytical nature of the left hemisphere at the expense of the holistic and more intuitive capability of the right hemisphere. In his 1976 article, Mintzberg lamented that management education has "…virtually consecrated the modern management school to the worship of the left hemisphere."[xxiv] He said, "I am calling for a new balance in our schools, the balance that the best human brains can achieve, between the analytical and intuitive."[xxv]

> *Brain balance is more than a concept or philosophy; it is a call to action to redefine radically how we educate and foster learning to create the next level of thinking our ever-changing global context demands.*

Brain balance is more than a concept or philosophy; it is a call-to-action to redefine radically how we educate and foster learning to create the next level of thinking our ever-changing global context demands. Piaget spoke these words in 1964, but they are even more true today:

> The principle [sic] goal of education in the schools should be creating men and women who are capable of doing new things, not simply repeating what other generations have done; men and women who are creative, inventive and discoverers, who can be critical and verify, and not accept, everything they are offered.[xxvi]

> *Unfortunately, our current status quo is like sending us to the gym, but equipping us to work out only the left side of our body and then wondering why we can do only half of what is required.*

For too long, education, training, and coaching have over-emphasized the left hemisphere through language and logic, failing to develop the right hemisphere. Unfortunately, our current status quo is like sending us to the gym, but equipping us to work out only the left side of our body and then wondering why we can do only half of what is required.

The distinguishing factors of the two hemispheres of the brain are becoming increasingly important as we move toward the future. Favoring the left hemisphere is limiting, especially in business. According to Mintzberg, the vast majority of the higher-order thinking competencies leaders require are in the realm of the right hemisphere.[xxvii] Clearly, relying too heavily on the left hemisphere compromises the quality of leadership performance. The best leaders can do it all because they have developed brain balance.

CHC THEORY OF COGNITIVE ABILITIES

The *Cattell-Horn-Carroll theory* (commonly abbreviated as *CHC theory*) is a model for analyzing the cognitive abilities that impact an individual's learning ability.[xxviii] Based upon the research of three psychologists named Raymond B. Cattell, John L. Horn, and John B. Carroll, this theory currently classifies cognitive skills within 16 broad abilities that have been traditionally correlated with academic achievement. Of the 16 CHC clusters, only two were initially proposed by Cattell in the early 1940s when he put forth his *Gf-Gc* theory. Both of these are very important to our discussion of brain balance:

- *Crystallized Intelligence* (abbreviated *Gc*) is the accumulation of all previously acquired knowledge. It involves the ability to recall and leverage pre-existing knowledge and skills. It is akin to book smarts and relies on subject-matter expertise, prior experience, and cognitive routines that were developed in the past.
- *Fluid Intelligence* (abbreviated *Gf*) is the raw intelligence we use to learn and adapt. It gives us the ability to reason, conceptualize, create mental models, mentally manipulate information, and solve new problems without relying on past experience and previously acquired knowledge.

Fluid Intelligence is akin to street smarts. It is also future-oriented, helping us to navigate uncharted waters and address issues we have never faced before.

During the period from 1965 to the early 1990s, John Horn extended Cattell's dichotomous *Gf-Gc* model by adding an additional six broad abilities. It then became known as the Cattell-Horn *Gf-Gc* theory.

From 1980 until 1993, John Carroll undertook very comprehensive empirical research regarding the structure of human cognitive abilities and developed his three-stratum theory, which proposed three levels:

- General cognitive ability (stratum III, the highest level)
- Broad cognitive abilities (stratum II, consisting of eight broad abilities including Fluid Intelligence and Crystallized Intelligence)
- Narrow cognitive abilities (stratum I, which are more specialized abilities underpinning the broader stratum II abilities)

In the late 1990s, the Cattell-Horn *Gf-Gc* theory and Carroll's three-stratum theory were integrated under a single taxonomy and framework which became known as CHC theory.

CRYSTALLIZED AND FLUID INTELLIGENCE IN CHC THEORY

To gain a deeper understanding of Fluid Intelligence, we look to the eloquent words of John Horn, one of the original architects of CHC theory:

> *Fluid abilities* (*Gf*) drive the individual's ability to think and act quickly, solve novel problems, and encode short-term memories. They have been described as the source of intelligence that an individual uses when he or she doesn't already know what to do. Fluid Intelligence is grounded in physiological efficiency and is thus *relatively independent of education and acculturation*.

The emphasis added is my own, as independence of education and acculturation is the key differentiator between Fluid Intelligence and Crystallized Intelligence. It is also the reason why Fluid Intelligence plays such a vital role in personal and professional performance.

According to CHC theory, our capacity for Crystallized Intelligence and Fluid Intelligence changes as we age. Crystallized Intelligence continues to increase until we reach old age, whereas Fluid Intelligence peaks in young adulthood and then declines. Figure 5 illustrates how these two cognitive abilities progress over a person's lifespan.

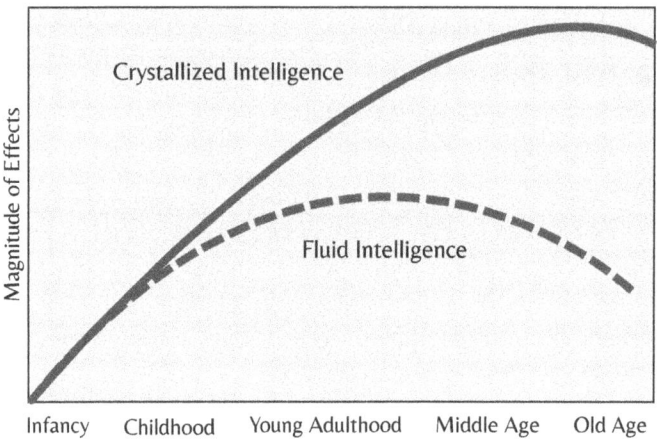

Figure 5. Crystallized and Fluid Intelligence in CHC Theory

CHC theory continues to evolve, with other researchers later adding to and expanding on Cattell's original work. It is important to note that the concept of neuroplasticity was not yet well-known when Cattell first proposed a distinction between Fluid and Crystallized Intelligence in his 1940s-era *Gf-Gc* theory. Thus, the researchers did not consider the idea that people might be able to continue to improve their Fluid Intelligence in adulthood. To this day, CHC theory focuses on measuring cognitive abilities rather than on enhancing and developing them.

Educators still use CHC theory framework as a basis for conducting cognitive assessments. However, there continues to be an overemphasis on language-based Crystallized Intelligence tests to assess people's explicit knowledge (i.e., knowledge individuals can express through language, either orally or written). So they rely on language skills to assess cognitive abilities. Tests that take a language-based approach can be problematic, especially when they are administered to individuals who lack proficiency in the language in which the test is written. Fortunately, test instruments would eventually evolve to become broader and more inclusive with the addition of nonverbal Fluid Intelligence assessments.

LANGUAGE-FREE ASSESSMENT OF COGNITIVE ABILITIES

In the 1980s, Dr. Helga A. H. Rowe was looking to measure and test the educability of children and adults from various backgrounds, including indigenous and aboriginal Australians. Rowe's work addressed a limitation in the testing protocol, as tests were predominantly English-language based. Obviously, this was a significant disadvantage for those who weren't fluent in English.[xxix] In addition, the verbal intelligence tests of that era focused primarily on book learning. This only widened the gap of perceived intellectual capability between those fluent in English and those who were not.

This gap would spur Rowe on a journey to find a more appropriate means of testing. She knew that a nonverbal testing approach would bypass the left-hemisphere-focused language bias and provide a neutral testing ground for everyone, regardless of their proficiency in English. Rowe's initial efforts were frustrating for her, as many of the existing nonverbal tests were extremely narrow and assessed only a limited number of cognitive abilities. Ultimately, she designed her own comprehensive, integrated Nonverbal Ability Test (NAT), which she founded on the concept of Fluid Intelligence.

By leveraging the principles of CHC theory and Fluid Intelligence, Rowe was able to develop a more comprehensive model that included ten dimensions related to fluid reasoning plus four dimensions of short-term memory.[xxx] These measures impact educability, learning capability, and adaptability.

Significantly, Dr. Rowe's ground-breaking progress in nonverbal ability testing is foundational to my own work. The ten Subconscious Thinking Habits I describe in this book are based on Rowe's dimensions of fluid reasoning. After many discussions with Dr. Rowe, I have adapted the original ten fluid reasoning skills to create a comprehensive model that is tailored specifically to the needs of business leaders, including business-oriented language instead of technical cognitive terms.

> **Note**: In my model, I use the term *Fluid Thinking* to focus on the more specific fluid reasoning aspects of Fluid Intelligence (i.e., the Subconscious Thinking Habits). It is also to take into account that we do not test short-term memory as a full Fluid Intelligence test does.[4] In addition, I also discovered that businesspeople find the term *thinking* more intuitive and easier to understand than *intelligence*.[5] Likewise, I refer to Crystallized Intelligence as *Crystallized Knowledge*, as the concept of "what you know" is more easily understood.

Not only do the Subconscious Thinking Habits underpin Fluid Thinking, but they are integral to brain balance and subconscious success. Indeed, I propose that Subconscious Thinking Habits are predominantly the domain of the right hemisphere of the brain. This connection is consistent with Goldberg's novelty-routinization theory, and it is the reason why we use a nonverbal approach to test Subconscious Thinking Habits. Certainly, Rowe's earlier

---

[4] The reason for this is because it would be difficult for a business executive to operate with suboptimal short-term memory.
[5] The term *intelligence* is often misunderstood and has some stigma attached to it.

work in eliminating language bias in educational testing has given us a rich gift to help level the playing field when identifying and developing professional talent.

Now that we have covered some of the most fundamental theories behind learning and cognitive testing, I would like to put forth my own hypothesis of how we think, learn, and adapt. In developing this framework, I have connected and built upon the research of many brilliant scientists. And so, the theory I offer you here humbly stands on the shoulders of giants.

FLUID THINKING DEVELOPMENT THEORY

The insights we learned from Rowe's research and our earlier discussions about Piaget, Mintzberg, Goldberg, and CHC theory have built the cornerstone for understanding how valuable fully developed Fluid Thinking is. Collectively, they underscore the vital role Fluid Thinking plays in creating the brain balance required for subconscious success, making a strong case for increasing the attention we give to enhancing our Fluid Thinking capability.

In the context of Goldberg's novelty-routinization theory, Crystallized Knowledge comprises knowledge that has become routinized.

Central to my Fluid Thinking Development Theory are the concepts of Crystallized Knowledge and Fluid Thinking, which are similar to Crystallized Intelligence and Fluid Intelligence in CHC theory, but with a few notable differences. In the context of my hypothesis, Crystallized Knowledge refers to how the brain organizes and applies pre-existing knowledge and skills in various situations. Significantly, we develop Crystallized Knowledge through experience, cultural socialization, and schooling. In the context of Goldberg's novelty-routinization theory, Crystallized Knowledge comprises knowledge that has become routinized. As such, it is a faculty of the brain's left hemisphere. You can think of Crystallized

Knowledge as a knowledge database that is stored in the brain, analogous to data stored on a computer hard drive.

A distinguishing feature of Fluid Thinking is the capacity to solve new and novel problems without having any prior knowledge or strategies to guide the solution. This flexible and adaptive quality facilitates how the brain learns new skills and how it applies those skills to solve novel problems in unfamiliar situations. Here too, we see a clear connection to Goldberg's work in the relationship between Fluid Thinking and the right hemisphere of the brain, which deals with cognitive novelty. In the context of our computer metaphor, Fluid Thinking is akin to a computer's operating system in that it runs in the background outside your awareness; however, you become very aware of it when it runs slowly or freezes at an inopportune time.

Figure 6 summarizes the differences between Crystallized Knowledge and Fluid Thinking.

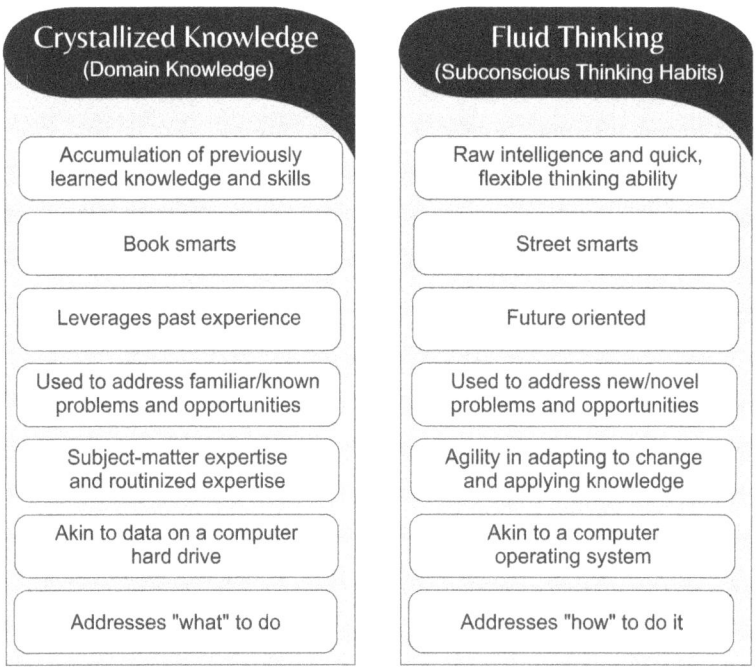

Crystallized Knowledge (Domain Knowledge)	Fluid Thinking (Subconscious Thinking Habits)
Accumulation of previously learned knowledge and skills	Raw intelligence and quick, flexible thinking ability
Book smarts	Street smarts
Leverages past experience	Future oriented
Used to address familiar/known problems and opportunities	Used to address new/novel problems and opportunities
Subject-matter expertise and routinized expertise	Agility in adapting to change and applying knowledge
Akin to data on a computer hard drive	Akin to a computer operating system
Addresses "what" to do	Addresses "how" to do it

Figure 6. Crystallized Knowledge versus Fluid Thinking

Interestingly, Fluid Thinking develops earlier than Crystallized Knowledge. As Rowe stated, "According to CHC Theory, *Fluid Intelligence is invested in learning throughout the school years to produce Crystallized Intelligence* [emphasis added]."[xxxi]

> *Fluid Thinking acts as the learning engine that produces a student's Crystallized Knowledge.*

In the context of my framework, Fluid Thinking acts as the *learning engine* that produces a student's Crystallized Knowledge—a fact that, regrettably, is not yet widely understood.

My theory also incorporates Piaget's work. Piaget thought that intelligence was connected to the capacity for *adaptation,* which is achieved through the assimilation of increasingly complex cognitive abilities as a child progresses through Piaget's four stages of cognitive development (see Chapter 1). He also considered that intelligence implies increasingly higher levels of cognitive organization (i.e., increased structural complexity), the capacity to invent trial-and-error behavior while also learning from those experiences, and the ability to anticipate consequences.

Piaget's concept of adaptation is very much aligned with the concept of Fluid Thinking and the novelty component in Goldberg's novelty-routinization theory. Understanding the interplay between novelty-routinization and how we progress through Piaget's four stages of cognitive development helps us understand how our brain initially encoded our Subconscious Thinking Habits and our current level of Fluid Thinking as we were growing up.

Because we are all confronted with the certainty of growing older, we must consider the impact of aging on Fluid Thinking. As I explained earlier in this chapter, normally, Fluid Thinking reaches its peak in early adulthood and then steadily declines as we age. During this process of atrophy, our capacity to deal with new and novel situations also declines. However, with regard to Fluid

Thinking, there is a noteworthy difference between my hypothesis and CHC theory.

Crucially, my hypothesis leverages the latest research in neuroplasticity. Modern neuroscience has shown that our brain has the capacity to grow and change well into old age. As a result of this new understanding, we now know that we can continue to develop our Fluid Thinking throughout adulthood. The dotted line in Figure 7 illustrates this potential for cognitive development.

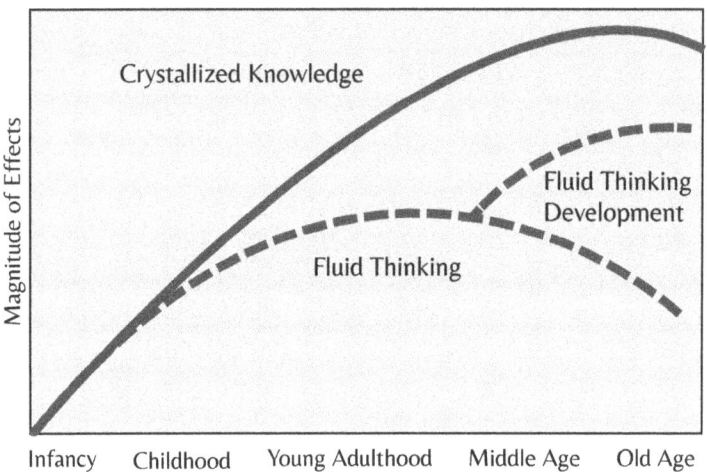

Figure 7. Fluid Thinking Development Theory

Why accept declining Fluid Thinking ability when we have a choice? Unlike our ancestors, we don't need to spend our entire adult lives struggling with the cognitive derailers we acquired in childhood. When we understand that optimal Fluid Thinking is not only possible but *necessary* at every age, we can undertake intentional, directed learning to develop it at any age.

In short, you're not stuck with your accidental brain app anymore. Now, you have the opportunity to upgrade it. Developing optimal Fluid Thinking is essential to brain balance. This is why it is so important for leaders to optimize all ten Subconscious Thinking Habits—these are the keys to achieving subconscious success.

RECONCEPTUALIZING EDUCATION, TRAINING, AND COACHING

I echo Mintzberg's call-to-action for a new and more balanced approach to learning. As you learned from the earlier discussion about CHC theory, our current approach to education relies primarily on developing a person's Crystallized Knowledge and then testing their ability to recall or demonstrate that Crystallized Knowledge. This type of learning creates an extensive knowledge database in the brain and focuses on improving an individual's Crystallized Knowledge. Unfortunately, this approach effectively limits educators' ability to benchmark and assess overarching thinking, learning, and application capability because it focuses on *what we know* rather than *how we think*.

Moreover, focusing just on learning new content fails to equip people to learn optimally because the role of Fluid Thinking in learning development is currently underestimated and often inadvertently sidelined. This unwitting underestimation is significant because failure to develop the right hemisphere of the brain—and, thus, its related ten Subconscious Thinking Habits—directly impacts a person's ability to learn and apply new Crystallized Knowledge.

The impact Fluid Thinking can have on an individual's potential is indisputably far reaching, with many facets of the brain's cognitive capabilities yet to be discovered. Here's some food for thought: Cattell found that Fluid Intelligence is a determining factor in the speed at which a person accumulates Crystallized Intelligence.[xxxii] So, it wouldn't be much of a stretch to speculate that a person with higher levels of Fluid Thinking could acquire (and apply) significantly more Crystallized Knowledge over their lifetime. Certainly, this is an area that is ripe for further exploration, particularly in the areas of education and addressing the World Economic Forum reskilling emergency.

HOW BRAIN COACHING WORKS

Now that you know why brain balance is so important, it is time to take a more practical look at how you can upgrade your brain app. Again, this book can only provide an understanding of our methodology because developing brain balance is a precise and individualized process. I restate this to manage expectations, as my goal is to start a broader conversation so the principles of cognitive science and neuroscience can be adopted into mainstream education and performance development. With that said, let me give you a taste of how it all comes together.

DISCOVERY LEARNING AND DELIBERATE PRACTICE

Tapping into the brain's neuroplasticity to enhance an individual's Fluid Thinking requires a targeted and personalized approach. This develops a person's Subconscious Thinking Habits so that tasks that were once difficult and time consuming become much easier and faster, significantly reducing the amount of mental effort and energy required to perform them. Simply put, optimally developed Subconscious Thinking Habits propel us into a state of automaticity. We achieve this by combining Piaget's concept of *discovery learning* with Professor K. A. Ericsson's concept of *deliberate practice.*[xxxiii, xxxiv]

Uniting these two approaches provides a unique blend and a solid foundation for cognitive development. By leveraging Piaget's idea of discovery learning, we create the ideal environment for individuals to discover and take ownership of their learning process and outcomes. Likewise, we use Ericsson's concept of deliberate practice to provide specialized training in the form of innovative brain exercises. These fun and increasingly challenging Fluid Thinking activities strengthen the brain routines associated with the targeted Subconscious Thinking Habits. This combination of novelty and routine development supports how the brain learns and how it enhances the Fluid Thinking needed to thrive.

Deliberate practice is more complex and multi-faceted than it appears. On the surface, it would seem to be simply intentionally practicing something, but it's more complicated than that. According to Ericsson, deliberate practice must include the following:

- It must have a specific purpose or goal.
- It needs to be focused.
- It needs to be in a well-defined field where it's possible to distinguish between an expert and a novice.
- The learner needs to receive feedback.
- The learner needs to be pushed outside of their comfort zone.
- The learner needs to work through temporary plateaus using new techniques and be creative.
- An experienced teacher or coach needs to design and deliver a tailored program, which includes demonstrating practice and learning techniques.

Understanding these characteristics helps establish the scope of deliberate practice and shows how it connects with discovery learning. This makes it easier to understand why we tailor our Fluid Thinking program—in short, it needs to be nuanced, specific, and precise. Arnold Palmer, a very successful professional golfer, shared an insightful and light-hearted comment that captures the core of deliberate practice. He said, "It's a funny thing, the more I practice, the luckier I get."

We typically start with the Subconscious Thinking Habit of Focused Thinking, as this helps you strengthen your capacity to focus and direct your attention. In turn, it elevates your capability to engage purposefully with deliberate practice and to optimize all future cognitive development.

OUR TRACR FLUID THINKING METHODOLOGY

Our Fluid Thinking Program is based on our *TRACR Fluid Thinking Methodology*, which I created by leveraging and building upon the work of Dr. Helga Rowe. After having many discussions with

Rowe, I developed a nonverbal Fluid Thinking test that measures and benchmarks your current Fluid Thinking ability. This test uses pictures and diagrams to assess the efficiency of all ten Subconscious Thinking Habits and ensuring that we are engaging the right hemisphere of the brain.

Figure 8 illustrates the steps in our TRACR Fluid Thinking Methodology. I explain each step in detail below.

Figure 8. TRACR Fluid Thinking Methodology

As the acronym implies, our TRACR Fluid Thinking Methodology comprises the following steps:

- **T**est—You complete our Fluid Thinking test, which takes about forty minutes.
- **R**eport—Then, we score your test and produce your Fluid Thinking Report, which is akin to a personal brain manual that identifies your cognitive strengths and derailers. This report includes a personalized road map of our Fluid Thinking development program that we tailor to your precise needs.
- **A**ct—Next, we put your customized program into action by coaching you through a series of challenging and fun Fluid Thinking activities, puzzles, and exercises. We design these brain workouts specifically to develop the Subconscious Thinking Habits that need improvement based on your personal test scores.

- Change—As you advance, the brain exercises become increasingly complex. The process of repeating progressively more challenging puzzles trains your brain to create and strengthen neural pathways. With repetition, your targeted Subconscious Thinking Habits become more efficient and effective.

  We also show you how to apply your enhanced Subconscious Thinking Habits in real life, so they become embedded in your brain and drive sustainable behavioral change and brain balance.

- Retest—When you have completed our brain coaching program, we retest your Fluid Thinking and compare the results to your initial benchmark so you can see how much your Fluid Thinking has improved.

It is important to note that our Fluid Thinking test measures both the effectiveness and the efficiency of thinking ability. *Effectiveness* relates to the quality of the thinking (i.e., high or low), whereas *efficiency* relates to the thinking speed (e.g., fast or slow). A Subconscious Thinking Habit can fall into one of four categories:

- **Optimal skill level**—highly effective (quality) and highly efficient (fast)
- **Moderate skill level**—highly effective (quality) and lower efficiency (slower)
- **Lower skill level**—lower effectiveness (quality) and lower efficiency (slower)
- **Overdeveloped**—lower effectiveness (quality) and higher efficiency (fast)

ASSESSING COGNITIVE COMPETENCE

In the 1970s, Noel Burch developed the conscious competence learning model, which explains how people learn and master new skills. In this model, an individual moves through four stages as they progress from incompetence to competence in a skill. Here is a summary of the four stages:

1. **Unconscious Incompetence**—The person has a blind spot and is unaware that they lack a specific skill.
2. **Conscious Incompetence**—The person is aware of a skill but lacks the ability to perform it.
3. **Conscious Competence**—The person has learned a skill well, but not well enough to be able to perform it without thinking about it.
4. **Unconscious Competence**—The person has mastered a skill and can perform it automatically.[xxxv]

We use the conscious competence learning model to navigate the process of identifying and overcoming cognitive derailers. Your personalized Fluid Thinking Report reveals where your ability currently lies within the context of the four stages of competence. The matrix shown in Figure 9 provides an overview of how we use this model to classify a person's cognitive strengths and derailers.

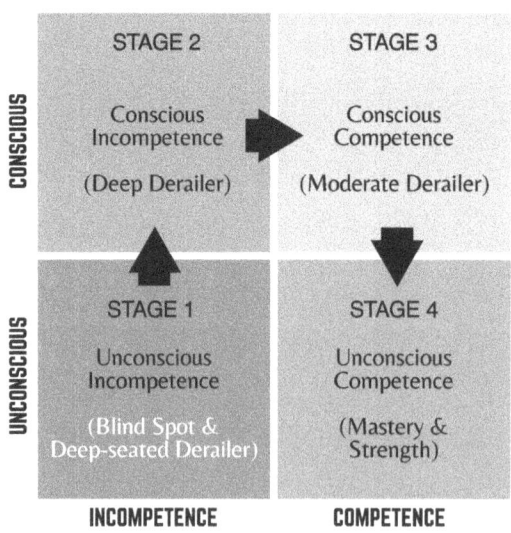

Source: Based on Noel Burch's Model

Figure 9. Conscious Competence Learning Model

In the sections below, I explain in more detail how our testing relates to each stage of the conscious competence learning model.

STAGE ONE: UNCONSCIOUS INCOMPETENCE

At Stage One, Unconscious Incompetence, the individual is completely unaware that they lack competence in a specific area. Thus, from our perspective, that person would have a deep-seated subconscious derailer that needs significant improvement. Often, I refer to these as blind spot derailers, as they take individuals by surprise and can have far-reaching consequences on their professional performance.

Here's an example of how a Stage One derailer might play out. The Fluid Thinking Report for an executive I'll call Max showed that he had low awareness of unwritten social rules; consequently, he was prone to crossing people's boundaries unwittingly. Although Max had agreed with most of the insights on his Fluid Thinking Report, he disagreed with this one. So, I suggested that he ask a few trusted business colleagues for input.

STAGE TWO: CONSCIOUS INCOMPETENCE

Unfortunately, Max didn't follow my advice to talk with some trusted associates at work. Instead, went home and asked his partner that night. His partner sat him down and, for over an hour, gave him a long list of examples of all the times Max had crossed unwritten social boundaries. By the time their conversation ended, Max had progressed to Stage Two. He was now very aware that he inadvertently offended people.

When an individual is at Stage Two, Conscious Incompetence, they are consciously aware that a deep Subconscious Thinking Habit derailer is significantly inhibiting their performance.

STAGE THREE: CONSCIOUS COMPETENCE

At Stage Three, Conscious Competence, a person begins to understand how to correct a Subconscious Thinking Habit derailer. Guided Fluid Thinking coaching and deliberate practice assist with this process. The person's behavior begins to improve; however, the process still requires a lot of concentration, mental energy, and conscious effort. We call this the work-in-progress stage. While the person definitely shows signs of improvement, the specific Fluid Thinking skill does not yet come naturally to them.

During Stage Three, we worked with Max to develop the Subconscious Thinking Habit that was causing this derailer. We also provided coaching to help him apply new social behaviors at work. Max made great progress as he continued to apply his new skill consciously and deliberately. Although he still slipped occasionally, he was able to learn from his mistakes, further improving and developing his conscious competence.

STAGE FOUR: UNCONSCIOUS COMPETENCE

When an individual has done a significant amount of deliberate practice on a particular the Subconscious Thinking Habit, the new, improved behaviors associated with that habit become second nature. At this point, the person becomes at ease with the desired behaviors and can perform them in almost any situation, regardless of outside stressors.

At Stage Four, Unconscious Competence, the derailer has been transformed into a strength through repetition. The person can perform the desired behavior competently without conscious thought. When a person can perform successful behaviors subconsciously, peak performance becomes reliable and automatic. This is the essence of subconscious success.

With continued practice, Max's new social behaviors became his new normal—much to the relief of Max, his partner, and his colleagues. He was able to see a difference in his colleagues' behavior toward him, too, because he no longer inadvertently offended people. Having mastered his new behaviors, Max became subconsciously competent at using them.

THE ROLE OF COGNITIVE COMPETENCE IN FUTURE SUCCESS

Brain balance is the essential piece of the subconscious success puzzle. All the science we have covered helps explain why brain balance is fundamental to achieving personal success.

As you read this book, you will ultimately need to decide whether brain balance is a need or a want. I believe it is a need, a great elevator of how we learn, how we craft cognitive competence, and how we approach the challenge of needing to adapt continually in our increasingly complex world. The two core reasons behind my position are the rapid progression of our digital landscape (particularly the Artificial Intelligence revolution that accompanies it) and the forecasted professional skills needed for our leaders to succeed in the future. Though there are many other reasons, these two are worth exploring.

The World Economic Forum's 2020 *Future of Jobs Report* highlights the top ten skills that will be required for business by 2025.[xxxvi] Interestingly, eighty percent of these skills are underpinned by, and related to, Fluid Thinking (and all ten Subconscious Thinking Habits). Only twenty percent of the skills identified are related to Crystallized Knowledge, and those still need optimized Fluid Thinking for sustained performance and success. The table in Figure 10 lists the skills the WEF identified. I have highlighted the cognitive territory of Fluid Thinking in a tangible business context, relative to the cognitive territory of Crystallized Knowledge:

TYPE OF Cognitive SKILL	*WEF Category of Skill	*WEF SKILL
Fluid Thinking	Problem-solving	• Analytical thinking and innovation • Complex problem-solving • Critical thinking and analysis • Creativity, originality, and initiative • Reasoning, problem-solving, and ideation
Fluid Thinking	Self-management	• Active learning and learning strategies • Resilience, stress tolerance, and flexibility
Fluid Thinking	Working with people	• Leadership and social influence
Crystallized Knowledge	Technology use and development	• Technology use, monitoring, and control • Technology design and programming

*Source: World Economic Forum The Future of Jobs Report, 2020

Figure 10. World Economic Forum's Top Ten Skills for Business by 2025

We will all face an enormous burden as we navigate the challenge of ongoing reskilling and upskilling. In order to keep up with the rapid pace, we will need to develop the right hemisphere of our brain through discovery learning and deliberate practice. If we fail to do that, we will struggle mightily with the frustration caused by slower information processing and glitches in our brain app.

60

The world is in a state of suspended animation regarding how we will choose to approach these reskilling challenges. This will be a great test of our collective capacity to adopt a more balanced approach to learning, training, and development. As we face the continuous learning journey ahead, we can leverage brain balance to propel us forward with a level of ease that many might find difficult to comprehend. Achieving subconscious success in the future will depend on how we approach developing the brain's capacity. Brain balance, which leads to Mental Chi, is the great elevator and differentiator. It underpins the ability to exploit fully the capability of an intentionally designed and upgraded brain app.

KEY TAKEAWAYS

- In most people, the left hemisphere is in charge of language, whereas the right hemisphere is in charge of nonverbal (particularly visuo-spatial) functions.
- We learn new skills through the novelty-oriented right hemisphere. Once we have mastered a skill through repetition, it is transferred to the left hemisphere as an automatic, subconscious cognitive routine (e.g., learning to drive a car). Balancing the capabilities of the brain's left and right hemispheres is the essence of subconscious success.
- In the CHC theory of cognitive abilities, Crystallized Intelligence is the accumulation of all previously learned knowledge. It is akin to book smarts, from my perspective. In contrast, Fluid Intelligence is the ability to solve new and novel problems without relying on previously acquired knowledge. It underpins adaptability, learning agility, and flexibility. From my perspective, Fluid Intelligence is akin to street smarts.
- In my Fluid Thinking Development Theory, I use the terms *Crystallized Knowledge* to refer to what we know and *Fluid Thinking* to refer to how we think, learn, and adapt in novel situations. Neuroplasticity is the brain's ability to rewire

itself over time through repeated mental and physical activities, and it is extremely important in enhancing Fluid Thinking.

- The World Economic Forum warns of a reskilling emergency that will require one billion people will need to be retrained by 2030 as a result of the Fourth Industrial Revolution. From my perspective, eight of the top ten skills the WEF identified are related to Fluid Thinking capability, while only two are related to Crystallized Knowledge.

- To ensure success in the future, we must enhance people's Fluid Thinking capability. The traditional left hemisphere, language-based approach is an ineffective and inefficient method for developing Fluid Thinking. It requires a right hemisphere, visuo-spatial novelty based approach.

PART II

PILLAR ONE

CONTROLLING ATTENTION

Pillar
One

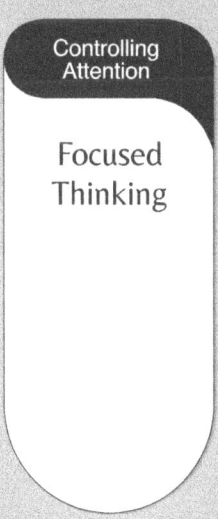

Chapter 4

YOUR BRAIN LOVES DISTRACTION

"An expert is someone who has succeeded in making decisions and judgments simpler through knowing what to pay attention to and what to ignore."
—Edward de Bono

There are never enough hours in the day. The increasing pressure of multiple demands can trap us into buzzing around like a bee, flying from one priority to the next, as we deal with frequent interruptions and struggle to maintain our focus in a sea of distractions. It is a battle to stay on task because distractions are everywhere. They can be external (environmental) or internal (mental). Half the time, we are unaware of how they impact us, and we react to them subconsciously. What makes things even worse is that our brains are wired to love being distracted. That means we crave distraction, especially when faced with complex, unpleasant, or unengaging tasks.

It is a wonder we get anything done. How can we ever succeed when most of us struggle so much with distraction, prioritization, and procrastination? Because we operate subconsciously to a large extent, we do not fully understand why we behave the way we do, particularly when a behavior doesn't support us. That means our brains are not consciously creating our success. But we cannot leave our success up to chance! That's why this first Pillar is so foundational. We need to identify an undesirable behavior before we can work on changing it.

There is only one Subconscious Thinking Habit associated with Pillar One: Controlling Attention. It is called Focused Thinking (see Figure 11).

Pillar
One

Controlling
Attention

Focused
Thinking

Figure 11. Pillar One: Controlling Attention

This habit is very broad, impacting multiple areas. For example, you need to be highly focused when analyzing detailed material, picking up new concepts in a meeting, developing new strategies and plans, delegating activities, and particularly when engaging with other people. One of our clients was concerned that they had short-term memory problems because they had difficulty remembering conversations. However, the root cause was that their mind was thinking of other things instead of concentrating on the conversation. Thus, the information was never encoded into their brain. No wonder they were unable to recall it!

Focused Thinking is critical to success, and almost everyone requires development in this area. In fact, approximately ninety percent of the people we test initially show low or only moderate efficiency in their Focused Thinking. This means they are moderately to highly distractible. Because Focused Thinking occurs at a subconscious level, people aren't even consciously aware that they have difficulty controlling their attention.

As comforting as it is to feel you are in control, conscious desire and willpower alone will never be enough to overcome our capacity to be distracted. This is because the root cause of distraction is connected to lower Focused Thinking capability. Therefore, regardless of how much intention and effort you put in, long-term immunity to distraction can never occur at a conscious level. While Conscious Mind Habits and willpower might help to treat the symptoms temporarily, why live with distraction symptoms when you could resolve the underlying cause by applying cognitive science principles?

Developing your Subconscious Thinking Habit of Focused Thinking helps increase your capacity to control your attention, allowing you to regain your mental energy and bring balance back into your life. To achieve this, we tap into the brain's inherent neuroplasticity and rewire the brain. So, we now have a way to gain control of our attention, rather than simply falling victim to distraction and procrastination time and again.

LIMA CHARLIE: AM I COMING THROUGH LOUD AND CLEAR?

Our ability to focus essentially comes down to our brain's signal-to-noise ratio. In layman's terms, the *signal-to-noise ratio* (SNR) refers to the level of relevant information (i.e., the *signal*) relative to the level of irrelevant information (i.e., the *noise* created by distractions).

Distractions generate the most noise, not only because they are so plentiful, but also because they often offer more excitement than the things we know we ought to be doing instead.

67

I often use a mobile phone as a metaphor when explaining the signal-to-noise ratio to our executive brain coaching clients. The ascending bars displayed at the top of the screen on your smartphone indicate the strength of your mobile cellular signal. When you see four or five bars, it means the signal is strong, so you will hear the other person loudly and clearly. However, if you were to roam to a location where the signal is weak, you would begin to notice some noise on the line. You might hear hissing, cracking, or static, and the other person's voice would become distorted. If the signal continued to get weaker, the call would eventually drop.

Like a cellular tower, our brain creates a signal for a top priority on our to-do list. For example, when we need to write a report, create a presentation, or prepare for an important meeting, our brain must first create a signal for that task. However, the never-ending barrage of distractions in our external and internal environment creates noise that overwhelms the signal. Consequently, we find ourselves sidetracked by time-wasting activities or doing low-priority busywork instead of focusing our attention on our highest priority. Then, midway through the afternoon, we start to realize we won't complete that high-priority task today as we had hoped, just as we were unable to complete it yesterday and the day before!

When our brain struggles to create a clear signal for our most important and highest priorities, our attention is drawn to noise. Distractions generate the most noise, not only because they are so plentiful, but also because they often offer more excitement than the things we know we ought to be doing instead. As a result, the signal begins to quiet down and gets lost in the uproar, making it difficult for us to concentrate on our top priorities and prompting us to focus on the things that are clamoring for our immediate attention.

For a task to be a top priority, it needs to be important. But many people fall into the trap of attending to matters that are much less important than their highest priority tasks. As deadlines approach, those top-priority tasks become increasingly urgent. When we allow high priority tasks to become urgent, we become like the mouse on a treadmill, always running. However, had we attended to the high-priority task sooner, it wouldn't have become urgent later.

In military parlance, "Lima Charlie" means "loud and clear." This popular expression applies to Controlling Attention because, in order to stay focused, our brains need a Lima Charlie signal that indicates what our top priority is. It all comes back to the signal-to-noise ratio. Our brains thrive on clarity. Without it, we will be constantly distracted by the noise. When there is so much noise that we cannot concentrate on our top priority, we go around and around in a maddening cycle. Einstein is quoted as saying, "Insanity is doing the same thing over and over and expecting different results." An imbalance in your brain's signal-to-noise ratio leads to a cycle that can make you feel as if you are going crazy. People commonly feel frazzled and mentally exhausted as a result.

It is critical to understand that you need to identify your top priorities in order to create a clear signal for your brain to focus on. However, it is challenging to do this when your brain has low signal-to-noise ratio capability. This is why we frequently see people behave as Alice did in *Alice's Adventures in Wonderland*:

> "Would you tell me, please, which way I ought to go from here?" said Alice.

> "That depends a good deal on where you want to get to," said the Cat.

> "I don't much care where," said Alice.

> "Then it doesn't matter which way you go," said the Cat.[xxxvii]

Like Alice, our brains are often unclear about our top priority. As the Cat said, if you don't care where you want to go, why does it matter which way you go? This is a good metaphor as, without a strong signal, your brain is far more susceptible to following the noise inadvertently, without even being aware of it at the time. When this happens, your attention controls your brain instead of your brain controlling your attention—a problem that highly efficient Focused Thinking can solve.

Like all your Subconscious Thinking Habits, Focused Thinking can be developed. Training your brain to become more focused is similar to lifting weights to strengthen your biceps. Both require specific types of exercises that need to be repeated over a period of time to attain the desired results. In our executive brain coaching program, we use a system of specially designed deliberate practice exercises based on the latest research in neuroscience. As ninety percent of our clients struggle with suboptimal Focused Thinking, almost everyone needs to work on developing this Subconscious Thinking Habit. Because Focused Thinking is so foundational and underpins nearly every other Subconscious Thinking Habit, developing your Focused Thinking first makes it easier to improve in other areas later.

It is one thing to understand why your brain is so easily distracted, but it is another thing altogether to be able to intercept a distraction attack and maintain your focus.

It is one thing to understand why your brain is so easily distracted, but it is another thing altogether to be able to intercept a distraction attack and maintain your focus. When you develop your Focused Thinking through deliberate practice, you can dramatically reduce your susceptibility to being distracted and improve your productivity significantly.

ALL NOISE, NO SIGNAL IS SURPRISINGLY EXPENSIVE

Due to distractions at work, the average person loses about 580 hours of productivity a year, which represents almost 28 percent of total working hours.

Besides being frustrating, the poor focus associated with a low signal-to-noise ratio carries serious financial implications. In 2020, *The Economist Intelligence Unit Limited* conducted a survey of 600 knowledge workers and published their findings. According to their report, "In Search of Lost Focus: the engine of distributed work," the average annual cost of lost focus on the job is roughly $34,000 per person, equating to approximately $391 billion per year for companies in the United States.[xxxviii] Due to distractions at work, the average person loses about 580 hours of productivity a year, which represents almost 28 percent of total working hours. Moreover, the group calculated that companies could gain as much as $1.2 trillion per year by improving their employees' focus and, thus, their productivity. This means that all the distractions, and the noise they create, reduce our job productivity by almost thirty percent and cost businesses over $1 trillion per year. Regardless of the substantial financial incentives, imagine how much more you would achieve if you could get up to an additional 580 hours of work done each year. Now, imagine what you could achieve in your personal life if you could reclaim all the time you lose because of distractions outside of work.

Although the "In Search of Lost Focus" report offers no prescriptive solutions for improving employee focus, we at enigmaFIT know that developing your Focused Thinking leads to substantial increases in productivity. In order to gain the 580 hours we lose each year, the average person who works 48 weeks a year would need to recoup about 12 hours of lost productivity each week.

That's about 2.5 hours a day, assuming a five-day work week. Our clients routinely report that developing their Focused Thinking enables them to gain one or two hours of productivity each day, often well before they have completed the entire program.

When your Focused Thinking is enhanced, your brain's signal-to-noise ratio increases. That means your brain can create a stronger signal, and it becomes much easier for you to stay on task. This is akin to giving Alice an address and a Google Maps app with spoken directions. Everything is Lima Charlie, from "turn right in 200 yards" to "your destination is on your left." Alice now has a strong signal. Knowing her destination and having clear directions, she can filter out the noise created by distractions and control her focus. Well-developed Focused Thinking enables Alice to control her attention by giving her conscious awareness of the distractions around her and letting her decide whether or not she wants to respond to them. All the while, Alice can keep in sync with her signal to achieve her top priority, which is to arrive safely at her destination.

In summary, when your brain is controlling your attention, your productivity, time management, and performance naturally increase.

PRIORITIES, PRIORITIES, PRIORITIES

If distraction had a sibling, it would be prioritization. Like most siblings, priorities constantly fight for attention. Adding to the complex family dynamics is the fact that priorities are not always clear, especially when distraction is having a tantrum. When your brain is torn between distraction and prioritization, it can seem like everything is in flux, and every priority is almost as important as the next. It can feel as though you're in a washing machine, spinning round and round. I called this the *whirlpool effect*.

TOMORROW IS THE MOST PRODUCTIVE DAY OF THE WEEK

If distraction and prioritization are siblings, then procrastination is distraction's best friend. It is like that friend who casually invites you to join them for a quick drink, only one drink turns into two or three and, before you know it, you've both lost track of the time. When we are distracted, it becomes tempting to procrastinate. We often abandon our priorities when presented with other options that are more fun and exciting.

Imagine having an angel on one shoulder and two devils on the other. Prioritization is the angel, while distraction and procrastination are two mischievous little imps. The latter are always trying to steal our attention. It is no wonder our brains have such a tough time staying focused on our priorities.

KEY TAKEAWAYS

- The Subconscious Thinking Habit of Focused Thinking underlies your brain's ability to control your attention.
- Controlling Attention essentially comes down to our brain's internal signal-to-noise ratio.
- Almost ninety percent of the people we test are shown to have low or moderate Focused Thinking capability.
- When your Focused Thinking is high, you are less likely to be derailed unwittingly by distractions. You also have little difficulty concentrating on your top priority. You're able to stay focused, no matter how many tempting distractions you encounter. Consequently, you rarely procrastinate.
- Our brain coaching clients recover between one and two hours per day when they improve their ability to control their attention. Plus, they are less mentally exhausted at the end of the day, as they have been considerably more productive.

Chapter 5

FOCUSED THINKING

"The most dangerous distractions are the ones you love, but they don't love you back." —Warren Buffet

Pillar
One

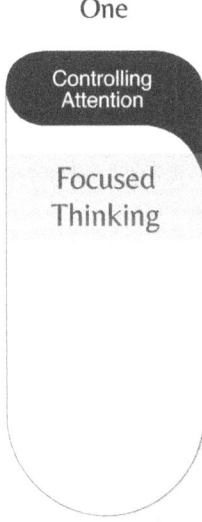

Controlling
Attention

Focused
Thinking

Does your attention control your brain or does your brain control your attention?

This is an insightful question, as it opens a doorway to discussing how the brain works and what we understand about optimizing it. This question can also be confronting, as it was for Elliott in Chapter 1, considering very few of us have any formal education regarding how our brain works. Yet, our capacity to generate income depends on optimizing our brain's performance.

Your brain loves distractions, but those distractions don't love you back because they take you away from your priorities in a vicious cycle that eats into your mental and personal energy. As I mentioned in the previous chapter, most of us suffer from this dilemma. We are buzzing from one thing to the next in our own way, lured by shiny objects.

But distraction and procrastination are no match for the Subconscious Thinking Habit of Focused Thinking. When you optimize your Focused Thinking, controlling your attention does not need to rely on a rush of adrenal hormones to get you over the finish line.

SUBCONSCIOUS THINKING HABIT MODEL FOR FOCUSED THINKING

Focused Thinking is central to optimizing personal productivity, team productivity, and leadership capability. Our brains use this Subconscious Thinking Habit to ensure we are directing our attention appropriately and keeping it focused on our most important priorities. This is especially necessary when we need to resist tempting distractions in our work environment ("Would you like to grab a cup of coffee?") or control our unintentional mind-wandering ("I wonder where I will go on my vacation this year…").

As you learned in Chapter 4, at enigmaFIT, the vast majority of people we test have low to moderate Focused Thinking. We will discuss how that imbalance negatively impacts our personal and professional lives later in this chapter.

If you have lower Focused Thinking capability, here is an example of what your Subconscious Thinking Habit might look like:

Cue: You have an important report to deliver in two weeks, and it is your top priority.

Routine: You subconsciously run your underdeveloped Focused Thinking routine.

Output: You procrastinate and get distracted frequently by lower-priority activities, which are easier and more interesting (and give you the illusion of being productive). Then, the day before the report is due, you end up working hero hours to finish it, often delivering at the last minute.

When Focused Thinking is lower, the brain is easily distracted by extraneous environmental work activity (the noise) and has difficulty staying focused on the top priority (the signal) due to the brain's lower signal-to-noise ratio.

FOCUS IN THE HUNTING AND GATHERING ERA— A HYPOTHESIS

I have developed a theory about the evolution of Focused Thinking. During hunter-gatherer times, humans spent about ten percent of their time actively hunting prey and about ninety percent of their time scanning their environment for threats and looking for prey to hunt. My hypothesis is that they needed to maintain a hard, narrow focus during the act of capturing their prey and a soft, peripheral focus when they were scanning their environment.

The world and the environment in which we live today has changed dramatically since then. Many people today are knowledge workers who think for a living. Because we operate in a digital workplace and perform highly complex tasks, I believe we now need a hard, narrow focus about ninety percent of the time. The rest of the time, we need a soft, peripheral focus.

Unfortunately, most people today are still in hunter-gatherer mode. We at enigmaFIT know this because ninety percent of the people we test are shown to have low or moderate Focused Thinking capability—that is, their brains operate predominately in a mode of soft, peripheral focus. That's why most people are so easily distracted by their own thoughts, environmental interruptions, and other noise.

Let me explain how I developed my hypothesis. According to *Scientific American*, our brain has not changed substantially over the last 10,000 years.[xxxix] It is roughly the same size and volume, having expanded and contracted only slightly over time in response to changing conditions brought about by intermittent periods of famine and disease.

I invite you to consider the macro factors that have been at play in Focused Thinking for the past 10,000 years or so. Our hunter and gatherer ancestors began farming roughly 10,000 years ago—a change that created a massive shift in how their brains needed to function. As hunters and gatherers, they had needed a soft, peripheral focus most of the time to survive. This allowed them to scan their natural environment quickly and effectively on a much broader scale in search of prey to hunt and to avoid becoming prey to other hunters. Only after spotting prey would our ancestors subconsciously switch to hard, narrow focus. Switching enabled them to zone in on their prey and work together as a group to capture it. As they hunted, a considerable surge of adrenaline and cortisol rushed through their brains, supporting their hard, narrow focus. I have theorized that our ancestors relied on adrenal hormones only for short periods of time—just long enough to capture their prey. The rest of the time, their brains maintained a soft, peripheral focus, which does not require sustained production of adrenal hormones.

Today, we need a completely different kind of focus than our ancestors did. Most of our days and many of our nights are spent looking at a computer screen that is barely an arm's length away. That means we need hard, narrow focus most of the time; however, our brain is still operating in hunter-gatherer mode with its soft, peripheral focus. Evolution hasn't quite caught up yet, which is the underlying dilemma.

The one area where having a lower and softer focus is preferable is when you are undertaking creative or innovative thinking (see Chapter 8) because it allows the brain to operate in more of a free-flowing mode. However, ideally, you want this to happen by making a conscious choice to take a soft focus, rather than being in the subconscious default mode of lower focus no matter what activity you are undertaking.

My hypothesis offers insight into the reason why over ninety percent of the executives we test have only low to moderate Focused Thinking capability. When we operate with a soft, peripheral focus, we are constantly distracted by noise and changes in our environment and react to these disturbances subconsciously. This instinctual behavior is why many people struggle to stay focused on their top priority. Fortunately, this can be easily overcome by tapping into the brain's inherent plasticity to rewire neural pathways. Anyone can achieve this using an expert coach who provides a deliberate practice approach.

WE LIVE IN A WORLD OF DISTRACTIONS

Much of what we read and try to incorporate into our lives is serious and important, but learning can be difficult when the material we are reading comes across as dry and boring. Our brains learn best by doing and thrive on fun, play, and being challenged. This is why our brain coaching approach embraces these learning principles to change Subconscious Thinking Habits successfully.

Many people have heard that you can improve your focus simply by switching off external distractions such as your phone, email notifications, instant messaging, etc. This advice is based on taking a Crystallized Knowledge approach and, although it might sound good in theory, it isn't always sustainable—let me explain. First of all, when you shut off external distractions, you are only treating the symptoms of lower Focused Thinking; you're not addressing the root cause, which originates in your subconscious brain. Second, even though you may know *exactly* what you need to do (that is, avoid checking your phone and emails), it's nearly impossible to do it for very long. Our brains simply can't resist glancing at our phones and devices. We tell ourselves we're just going to take a quick look. And then, before we know it, we are responding to emails and text messages, even though most of them are not urgent. Soon, even more distractions take us away from our highest priority, and we're not even consciously aware it's happening.

In contrast to taking a Crystallized Knowledge approach, enhancing Fluid Thinking, in general, and Focused Thinking, specifically, requires taking an active learning and experiential approach. There's a big difference between acquiring new knowledge and integrating what you learned. Integration requires your brain to rewire its neural pathways. This process takes time. That's why our clients do deliberate practice exercises over a period of several months to increase the efficiency of their Subconscious Thinking Habits.

Here is an example that's easy to understand. Almost everyone is familiar with the game of *Where's Waldo?*, which challenges players to find a character named Waldo who's been cleverly hidden in an artist's illustration. In the context of the brain's signal-to-noise ratio, you can think of Waldo as the signal and all the other people in the picture as the noise. Individuals with lower Focused Thinking find *Where's Waldo?* puzzles to be extremely frustrating. It takes them a long time to locate Waldo because their attention is constantly distracted by the other people in the picture.

We use scientifically designed deliberate practice exercises, similar to *Where's Waldo?* puzzles, to help you improve your Focused Thinking ability. As you practice solving increasingly difficult puzzles, over time, your brain learns to increase the Waldo signal and decrease the background noise. Eventually, your Focused Thinking becomes more efficient and effective because your brain's signal-to-noise ratio will have improved.

Although solving challenging and fun puzzles can improve your Focused Thinking, it's important to note that these types of activities are only the means through which we accomplish this goal. Finding Waldo is not the endgame. The endgame is to enhance your Focused Thinking ability and apply it, so you can reduce distractibility in every area of your life, whether it's work, family, social, play, etc.

We are all navigating myriad external distractions in our day-to-day lives. Some of the most common ones are related to technology: emails, phone calls, messages, social media memes, notifications, and pings—not to mention all the time we lose in Google Land. We are also constantly sidetracked by spur-of-the-moment coffee breaks, last-minute meetings, and the ultimate Godfather of distraction: "Have you got five minutes to discuss...?" In addition to these external distractions, our attention gets diverted by internal mental distractions when our mind wanders and when we daydream.

Let me tell you a few facts. First, it is not you, and you are not alone. Second, these distractions cannot be overcome using sheer willpower. Remember, your brain is still focusing the same way it needed to 10,000 years ago, so don't give yourself a hard time. Instead, let your brain know it's time to update the cognitive routines that underpin your Focused Thinking.

DISTRACTION: AN INTRINSIC CHALLENGE IN THE INFORMATION AGE

"What information consumes is rather obvious: it consumes the attention of its recipients. Hence a wealth of information creates a poverty of attention..."
—*Herbert A. Simon*

In 1971, the Nobel Prize-winning economist Herbert A. Simon, showed incredible insight when he stated, "What information consumes is rather obvious: it consumes the attention of its recipients.

Hence a wealth of information creates a poverty of attention…"[xl] We live in the age of information domination. We have more content than we can consume and less capacity to consume it than at any other point in history. Understanding that we have a poverty of attention is necessary because if we ignore that fact, we can become mentally exhausted by trapping ourselves into believing capacity is a choice and attention is a discipline. When we make these reductive conclusions, it is easy to understand why the World Health Organization (WHO) introduced and legitimized mental exhaustion by designating it as burnout syndrome in 2019.[xli]

The problem is that distractions—especially external ones—are often underestimated because they occur below our conscious threshold and largely go unnoticed. Hindsight acts as an uncomfortable mirror, as it reflects the consequences and negative effects of our compromised focus. As we reflect, we realize how and where distraction comes into play and how vital it is to master our focus.

It is important to acknowledge that there are many techniques that can improve focus for short periods of time; these help us cultivate a mental state of concentration temporarily. However, the nature of our day-to-day work and personal lives frequently pulls us out of this mental state. Through the rush of deadlines, videoconferences, meetings, emails, briefings, etc., we are subconsciously and unwittingly losing control of our attention. Without our conscious awareness, our minds begin to wander, and yet again, distraction has claimed our focus.

DOWN THE RABBIT HOLE

It is not my preference to be the bearer of bad news, but in this case, honesty is the best policy. We are not done talking about distraction yet. In fact, external distraction has a twin called *internal distraction*.

Remember Alice? If you are familiar with Lewis Carroll's story, you know that Alice ended up in Wonderland when she wandered off and fell down the rabbit hole. Curiously, research has shown that roughly fifty percent of the time, we wander away from the task at hand and fall down our own rabbit holes.[xlii] Our version of Wonderland is characterized by our minds' daydreaming, falling into overthinking, and thinking about things that are irrelevant to the task at hand, all of which derail our attention and productivity.

Our minds love to wander, but what we love can be in direct conflict with what is good for us. It is essential to understand that the mind is creative and wanders subtly. Unlike Alice, you will not be aware that you have fallen down the rabbit hole until you are jolted out of it. These internal distractions can take many forms.

For example, have you ever found yourself re-reading a passage in a book or an online article because your mind had wandered a bit, and you had not consciously taken in what was on the page? Do you ever find your mind wandering off in meetings, thinking about urgent tasks on your to-do list, daydreaming about your next vacation, or contemplating what you will eat for lunch? It's all part of the rabbit hole. But your mind doesn't flash a neon sign to help you avoid falling, which is why developing your Subconscious Thinking Habit of Focused Thinking is vital to reclaiming control of your attention.

PRIORITIZING PRIORITIES

Mirror, mirror, on the wall, which is the most important priority of all? Wouldn't it be nice if it were that simple? Regrettably, I am not in the rare magical mirror trade. However, I do have some proven methods that can get you the results you desire.

Prioritization is complex because it requires two critical skills:

- Understanding how to define and order priorities
- Controlling your attention

Our ability to prioritize well relies on another Subconscious Thinking Habit called Conceptual Thinking (see Chapter 9). Additionally, we need to have efficient Focused Thinking and a strong brain signal-to-noise ratio, as our top priorities are typically large, complex tasks that can feel overwhelming and tedious. So, even if our brain has created a very clear signal because we have prioritized effectively, distraction is just around the corner, waiting for an opportunity to steal our attention away from our top priorities.

While it's no secret that you need to use gym equipment to develop your body, very few people know that you can engage in specific exercises to develop your brain.

Although most of our clients have a cognitive understanding of this principle, they still find themselves falling into the same distraction patterns. That's because having a conceptual understanding of Focused Thinking is vastly different from developing it as a Subconscious Thinking Habit. Let me give you an analogy. Suppose you wanted a cut physique with low body fat and increased muscle definition. You could create a workout routine and spend an hour at the gym every day, but your body wouldn't change a bit if instead you spent that hour hanging out in the juice bar. You would need to get on the exercise machines and actually work out to get the results you wanted. Thus, having a conceptual understanding of Focused Thinking will not enable you to control your attention any more than hanging out at the juice bar at the gym will give you a cut physique. While it's no secret that you need to use gym equipment to develop your body, very few people know that you can engage in specific exercises to develop your brain.

FIRST, SECOND, THIRD—THE MYTH OF MULTITASKING

Efficiency (the speed of thinking) and effectiveness (the quality of thinking) continue to be linked to multitasking. The problem is that multitasking is a myth. Unfortunately, our culture continues to perpetuate this myth. Social norms create pressure to multitask, setting up unrealistic expectations that cannot be met and ultimately causing enormous stress. If anything, multitasking makes you even more unproductive.

In their article titled "Executive control of cognitive processes in task switching" published in the *Journal of Experimental Psychology: Human Perception and Performance*, Rubinstein, Evans, and Meyer unpack the myth of multitasking.[xliii] Their research shows that shifting between tasks even briefly can cost individuals forty percent of their productive time. Additionally, task switching wastes even more time when tasks are highly complex or unfamiliar.

So, while many of us multitask with the best of intentions, we are actually slicing and dicing our productive time and exacerbating the complexities of lowered Focused Thinking. The science keeps pointing us back to this foundational Pillar, highlighting why we need to learn how to control our attention. Buzzing from one lower priority activity to the next pulls us away from our top priorities, makes everything seem equally important and urgent, and leaves us in a state of brain drain.

Interestingly, individuals with highly developed Focused Thinking rarely even try to multitask because they know that multitasking is an unproductive way to work. Their brains are able to create a clear signal at the outset, and so they find it easy to stay focused on their highest priorities. By contrast, individuals with a lower signal-to-noise ratio (and thus, lower Focused Thinking) routinely try to multitask because they fail to understand that *activity* does not always mean *productivity*.

IF PROCRASTINATION WERE AN OLYMPIC SPORT, I WOULD WIN GOLD

Procrastination is one of the most common symptoms of lower Focused Thinking. After all, why do something today when you can put it off until tomorrow? That is the attitude of a procrastination champion.

All joking aside, the more complex and larger a task is, the more likely you will be to procrastinate. Our good intentions and best practices are no match for the lure of procrastination. When distractions team up with procrastination, the odds are not cognitively in our favor. We know our brain's signal-to-noise ratio is compromised, and because of this, our focus is easily derailed. But now we also know we can outwit these derailers by doing the brain work needed to develop a more efficient Subconscious Thinking Habit of Focused Thinking.

So, if the brain is so fantastic at procrastination, how do we get anything done? Entering the arena are the adrenal hormones, the game-changing, heavyweight, undefeated champions. Adrenaline and cortisol always save the day; however, depending on them for fuel and better focus comes with a high cost. And, in the long run, it is an entirely unsustainable approach to making deadlines. You can burn the midnight oil by working late into the evening and pulling hero hours, but the midnight oil will eventually burn out, and in the process, so will you. No matter how many times you promise yourself that next time will be different, it's unrealistic to think you will ever break this pattern unless you rewire your brain and develop higher Focused Thinking capability. I want you to pause and think about this basic fact. So many of our clients are frustrated because they're under the illusion that they should be able to control their attention. They blame themselves for lacking discipline and willpower, but nothing could be further from the truth.

YOUR BRAIN'S WIRING AFFECTS YOUR PERFORMANCE

Your brain's wiring determines how you respond to physiological and mental stress. Our understanding of this science is based on the work of Robert M. Yerkes and John D. Dodson, who published a paper titled "The Relation of Strength of Stimulus to Rapidity of Habit Formation" in 1908.[xliv] Their theory was considered breakthrough research at the time and later became known as the Yerkes-Dodson Law.

Yerkes was an American psychologist who undertook his Ph.D. at Harvard University in 1902, and later went on to become Professor of Psychology at Harvard. While initially working with mice and rats, he subsequently developed an interest in the psychological testing and measurement of humans. He is credited with undertaking the first wide-scale testing program during World War I when a psychological test was administered to approximately 1.7 million men. Yerkes was known as one of the foremost figures in the area of comparative psychology, which is a discipline that studies animals to learn about human behavior.

John Dodson was a master's degree student of Yerkes at Harvard University where they authored the above-mentioned paper together. Dodson went on to earn a Ph.D. in psychology from the University of Minnesota in 1918. While it appears that Yerkes and Dodson stayed in touch intermittently over the years, little more is known about Dodson's career.

According to the Yerkes-Dodson Law, performance varies relative to the level of physiological or mental arousal or stress a person is experiencing. Importantly, performance increases as stress increases, but only up to a tipping point, after which performance decreases rapidly.[xlv] As you can see in Figure 12, there is an optimum performance window during which our brain leverages stress to increase our focus. Adrenal hormones push us into peak performance mode, allowing us to move past procrastination. The pressure enables us to concentrate effectively so we can meet deadlines. Unfortunately, this hormonal boost comes at a substantial personal cost. The same graph also shows that we feel unmotivated when a task is tedious and there is too little stress, whereas too much pressure creates a mental state of anxiety and panic that significantly lowers performance and increases the potential for errors and the need for rework.

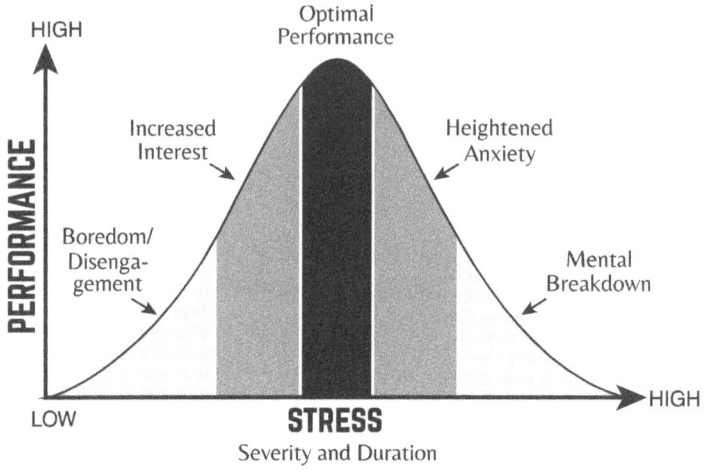

Legend:

Boredom/ Disengagement	Increased Interest	Optimal Performance	Heightened Anxiety	Mental Breakdown
• Bored • Distractable • Disengaged • Unmotivated	• Interested • Increasing focus • Becoming engaged • Increasing motivation	• In the zone • Highly productive • Very focused • Totally engaged • Very motivated	• Anxious • Mistake prone • Losing focus • Less engaged • Demotivated	• Panic • Exhausted • Defocused • Disengaged • Distressed

Figure 12. Yerkes-Dodson Human Performance Graph

Many people believe they work better under pressure, but it only seems that way because they are relying on adrenal hormones. When your Focused Thinking is well developed, you can work more effectively even without the pressure of an impending deadline. This means you don't need to flood your brain with adrenal hormones and put your mind and body in a state of significant stress in order to focus. Unfortunately, high stress levels over long periods of time lead to a deterioration in well-being known as "burnout," as well as decreased personal and professional performance. The World Health Organization (WHO) classifies burnout as an "occupational phenomenon" and recently revised their definition of this condition in the International Classification of Diseases (ICD-11). The ICD-11 defines burnout as follows:

> Burn-out is a syndrome conceptualized as resulting from chronic workplace stress that has not been successfully managed. It is characterized by three dimensions:
>
> - feelings of energy depletion or exhaustion;
> - increased mental distance from one's job, or feelings of negativism or cynicism related to one's job; and
> - reduced professional efficacy.[xlvi]

The good news is that everyone can enhance their Focused Thinking. Imagine what your life would be like if you could stop buzzing around and being disorientated by distractions, conflicting priorities, and procrastination. Well-developed Focused Thinking is a game-changer. It gives you the capability to operate at peak performance in a sustained manner, enabling you to produce more and higher quality work in less time. It develops your ability to fly above your current level of potential instead of simply buzzing in and out of it.

BIANCA: DERAILED BY DISTRACTION

With that said, let me introduce to you Bianca, our bee in a bottle. She is the star of the story in this chapter—one that looks at how we control our attention. Come buzz with Bianca and me as we fly into distraction, then onward to prioritization, and finally land at procrastination.

Bianca is an energetic and highly knowledgeable senior human resources executive who excels at connecting with people. Her colleagues playfully call her a bee in a bottle because she constantly buzzes around the office trying to do multiple tasks at once. She is a team player who is always available to help. Because her colleagues value Bianca's knowledge deeply, she is frequently interrupted by requests for five-minute consultations or impromptu chats over coffee. Unfortunately, her habit of buzzing around derails her from her top priorities. Despite all her activities, she is not achieving her productivity goals. Bianca suffers from *shiny object syndrome*[6]—that is, her attention leads her brain instead of her brain leading her attention.

Bianca is aware of her susceptibility to being distracted. The evidence has been piling up. Her lower Focused Thinking means more errors, leading to hours of rework and subsequent unproductive multitasking. Time pressures and deadlines compromise her communication, which in turn hinders her capacity to delegate early and effectively. As a result, Bianca works hero hours to meet her deadlines. All of this activity leaves her mentally exhausted and operating at the threshold of her capacity.

Frustrated, frazzled, and mentally drained from buzzing around and navigating shiny object syndrome, Bianca struggles to stay centered on her priorities. Consequently, her team's productivity and morale are down, too. In an attempt to refocus her attention, Bianca does what we all often do: she writes her priorities on a to-do list. Oh, how we cling to the famous, nerve-calming to-do list! Like hot chocolate on a cold day, it is temporarily comforting. Creating a to-do list declutters our minds so we can pause and feel more in control. Unfortunately, that calm and clear feeling is relatively short lived. When Bianca looks down at her list, she decides to go home and drink a bottle of wine—no, sorry, wrong story. What actually happens is that her comfort turns to

---

[6] Although *shiny object syndrome* is often associated with novelty-seeking behavior, we and many of our clients use this term to describe high distractibility associated with lower Focused Thinking, which leads to lower productivity and procrastination.

discomfort, as she understands the size and magnitude of all the tasks she needs to accomplish.

Although Bianca's list is comprehensive, precise, and prioritized— as fantastic as a to-do list can be—it is not long before distraction pulls her priorities into the activity vortex, exacerbating her lack of productivity. The end of the workday arrives too quickly as always, and the big-ticket items on Bianca's to-do list are still undone, leaving her even more demoralized. Day after day, she stays and works a little later. Although she wears her long hours like a badge of honor, she finds herself at the end of her capacity. On weekends, she collapses, barely recharging her batteries enough to enable her to buzz around again on Monday.

You might be wondering if Bianca ever takes advantage of the myriad resources that purportedly help with attention and focus. Would it surprise you to know that she has completed multiple time management courses? She had also tried switching off external distractions such as emails, phones, and social media.[7]

After trying multiple solutions that didn't work, it was becoming apparent that Bianca's capacity to control her attention needed im- provement. The larger, more complex, and more mundane a task was, the more susceptible she was to distraction and procrastina- tion. She was frustrated and annoyed by her habit of procrastinating whenever she needed to write a report, and she was always waiting until the last minute. So, Bianca opted to try a different tactic. She decided to isolate herself physically, thinking that would remove distractions. Finally, she thought to herself, she would beat pro- crastination and deliver her top priority.

---

[7] While these strategies can be helpful in the short term to treat the symptoms of lower Focused Thinking, they do not work in a sustainable way that brings ease and balance. They are sort of like sucking on a cough drop and hoping it cures tonsillitis. It will help temporarily, but it won't heal your tonsils because it's not addressing the root cause.

The next time an important report was due, Bianca decided to try a different approach. One week before the deadline, she cleared her diary for the entire day and committed to working from home, believing she would be able to focus better in a distraction-free zone. Bianca informed her executive assistant not to disturb her unless the matter was urgent. But when her day of isolation arrived, she found herself yet again derailed by distraction and procrastination. Her mind was constantly daydreaming, wandering off like Alice down the rabbit hole. Understandably, Bianca grew increasingly disappointed. Her plan wasn't working as well as she had hoped.

Time ticked on, and the deadline grew uncomfortably close. Bianca's stress levels increased, and her anxiety kicked into gear. Suddenly, on the last day, her focus became laser sharp. Working frantically, she finally finished the report at midnight. When the job was done, Bianca reflected on her day in isolation the week before and wondered, "Why was I suddenly able to control my focus at the last minute when I had been utterly incapable of concentrating earlier in the week?"

Unbeknownst to Bianca, she had tapped into her brain's secret weapon.[8]

Bianca's challenge is threefold:

1. It isn't easy to identify her key priorities because her to-do list is long, and everything seems equally important.
2. This lack of clarity means her brain has no clear signal on which to focus her attention.
3. With the lack of clarity, the volume of noise created by distractions is much louder.

---

[8] When the going gets tough, our bodies pump out adrenaline and cortisol. As we learned from our earlier discussion about the Yerkes-Dodson Law, when the deadline looms, our stress increases, and the consequent rush of adrenal hormones help us overcome distraction and procrastination.

This combination leaves her feeling powerless and unequipped to cut through the noise. Bianca remains in a state of flux until her adrenal hormones spike enough to enable her to push out results. She exhausts herself by trying to multitask from one task to the next, and rarely accomplishes her goals successfully despite her best efforts.

Like most people, Bianca struggles with lower Focused Thinking. In addition, her Conceptual Thinking is underdeveloped as well, and it is the reason why she has so much difficulty prioritizing tasks. Although Bianca's conscious tactics can be somewhat helpful, they all lead to the same cycle of distraction and procrastination. Bianca will be continually challenged in trying to control her attention unless she develops optimum Focused Thinking. Trying to maintain her focus will be like trying to deep dive into the ocean without an oxygen tank—difficult and sustainable only for a very short amount of time.

IMPACT OF LOWER FOCUSED THINKING

Often, minor distractions seem relatively harmless. After all, nobody got hurt while you were thinking about the Bahamas or deciding between a salad or a sandwich for lunch, right? While it's true that no serious injuries occurred while your mind was wandering in that meeting, you may have hurt yourself in a couple of ways. For one, you probably missed some of the information that was covered. When you miss important details, it impacts how your co-workers perceive you and the quality of work you produce.

Another common consequence of lower focus is *reactive listening*. When a person's Focused Thinking capability is low, they are not fully present in conversations and business situations. Their mind wanders, and with it, so does their ability to build rapport effectively. Even though they hear you talking, they are not listening in a focused way, so their responses are often more reactive than authentic. The consequences of a wandering mind build up, compromise the quality of work and professional relationships, and can significantly hinder professional progression. So, the rabbit hole is not great, and I think we can all agree that our mental Wonderland leaves us with some not-so-wonderful consequences.

A third consequence of underdeveloped Focused Thinking is unhappiness. In their article titled "A Wandering Mind Is an Unhappy Mind," Killingworth and Gilbert highlight that we spend 47 percent of our waking hours thinking about something other than what we are doing.[xlvii] As our minds wander, we become increasingly non-present, which comes at a high emotional cost, decreasing our happiness. Interestingly, their research showed that mind-wandering was the root cause of their subjects' unhappiness, again emphasizing the essential nature of developing this Subconscious Thinking Habit.

Don't make the mistake of underestimating the value of developing your Focused Thinking. The cost of wandering down rabbit holes is very high, both professionally and personally.

BIANCA: HIGHLY FOCUSED AFTER BRAIN COACHING

Completing our brain coaching program dramatically enhanced Bianca's Focused Thinking, and her brain's signal-to-noise ratio radically improved. With this came two important benefits. First, she can now quickly identify and intercept distractions that try to move her away from her key priorities. Second, the power to choose what she wants to focus on is now totally within her control.

When you optimize your Focused Thinking, you eliminate a subconscious pattern that derails your success. Well-developed Focused Thinking enables you to become the master of your attention and time. A brain that is free of both internal and external distractions is a brain that is free to create and execute with unparalleled productivity.

KEY TAKEAWAYS

- The economic cost of employees being distracted is significant, based on findings detailed in the "In Search of Lost Focus" report in *The Economist Magazine*. A survey found that the average person loses about 580 hours of productivity a year due to distractions, representing about 28 percent of total working hours. According to the report, this loss costs companies approximately $34,000 per employee per year, and companies could gain as much as $1.2 trillion annually by improving their employees' focus and, thus, their productivity.

- Other research shows that internal mental distractions occur because our minds frequently wander instead of concentrating on the task at hand. Losing focus through daydreaming decreases productivity and increases procrastination.

- People often try to treat the symptoms of lower Focused Thinking by eliminating external distractions. However, this approach is only temporary and not sustainable because it fails to address the root cause of lower focus, which lies in the subconscious brain.

- In seeking to overcome lower Focused Thinking, many people fall victim to taking a multitasking approach. However, research into the myth of multitasking shows that shifting between tasks even briefly can cost individuals forty percent of their productive time.

- When your Focused Thinking is optimized, you can overcome procrastination without the need to rely on adrenaline and cortisol to kick in to get you over the finish line.

- Well-developed Focused Thinking is a game-changer. It gives you the capability to operate at peak performance in a sustained manner, enabling you to produce more and higher quality work in less time.

- Enhanced Focused Thinking enables your brain to control your attention, rather than letting your attention control your brain.

PART III

PILLAR TWO

COMPLEX PROBLEM-SOLVING

Pillar
Two

Complex
Problem-Solving

Analytical
Thinking

Innovative
Thinking

Conceptual
Thinking

Chapter 6

INTRODUCTION TO COMPLEX PROBLEM-SOLVING

"We cannot solve our problems with the same thinking we used when we created them." —Albert Einstein

Problems are tricky beasts. You need to be crystal clear when defining a problem. If you aren't, you will likely solve an entirely different problem. The tasks of defining the core of a problem, creating multiple solutions, and evaluating and choosing the optimal solution are more complicated than we might appreciate. The brain needs to navigate a delicate balance between defining problems and finding ideal solutions.

Pillar Two: Complex Problem-Solving comprises three Subconscious Thinking Habits shown in Figure 13.

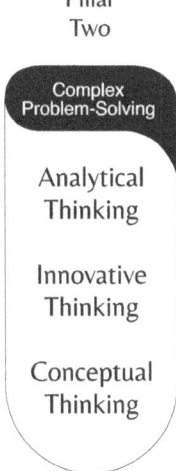

Figure 13. Pillar Two: Complex Problem-Solving

99

All three Subconscious Thinking Habits operate both independently and collaboratively throughout the entire problem-solving process to create the much-coveted lightbulb moment:

- **Analytical Thinking** is necessary to analyze and define the problem or opportunity accurately, as well as to articulate the criteria for a successful solution.
- **Innovative Thinking** is vital when brainstorming possible solutions to the defined problem or opportunity.
- **Conceptual Thinking** is required to evaluate each of the possible solutions and then determine the optimal one, ensuring it meets the criteria for success.

Traditionally, organizations create teams to solve complex problems. That's because we know that individuals bring different perspectives. But even more importantly, they possess varying levels of competency at different phases of the Complex Problem-Solving process. Some excel at defining problems, others thrive at brainstorming, while still others are fantastic at evaluating the solutions and selecting the one that has the most strategic value.

These varying levels of competency are based on the inherent cognitive capacity developed within each individual. It is uncommon for people to solve complex problems easily. Few people have naturally developed a balanced combination of Analytical Thinking, Innovative Thinking, and Conceptual Thinking. And yet, this balance is exactly what is needed for the eureka moment to occur.

Although a team-based approach to problem-solving can be very successful, it comes with a significant cost. Routinely involving teams in every decision takes more time and requires more resources than making decisions by yourself. It is indeed liberating when your neural pathways are developed and balanced in a way that allows you the freedom to tackle complex problems independently. Clearly, though, when a problem impacts a wide cross-section of people, it is important to solve it collaboratively. However, when each team member has optimal Complex Problem-Solving capability, you are more likely to reach the best possible solution more quickly.

From both a personal and professional perspective, the benefits of developing the three Subconscious Thinking Habits that support Complex Problem-Solving cannot be overemphasized. When cultivated, you achieve a new sense of mastery over your life.

BUT...AREN'T PROBLEMS SOLVED BEST BY TEAMS?

The complexity of team sports means your team is only as strong as your weakest member. If you are reading this, I am guessing you are already invested in personal excellence, so you are probably aware that the quality of teams in the workplace are often variable and unreliable. Most individuals who excel and rapidly progress in their career have a predisposition to fill in the gaps. When subpar work is submitted and or handed in late, they will fix the quality gap or do the work themselves to meet the deadline. The outcome of this rework is frustration in the short term. However, in the long run, this level of rework is unsustainable, particularly when a person is promoted to a higher level. Thus, the ability to solve complex problems easily lays the foundation for succeeding in more senior roles—and in life, in general.

Complex Problem-Solving as a team sport can be very effective, as long as a leader is managing the process by coaching from the sidelines. While it is important to know how to be an effective team player, it is equally important to cultivate a skill set that is just as effective off the field. It is difficult to have sustained career progression if you stay a player on the field. At some point, the transition from player to coach must take place to become a successful senior executive or entrepreneur. An off-field coach combines all three competencies and strategically delivers wins by understanding the nuances of the Complex Problem-Solving game. The question is, do you want to be playing the game on the field or orchestrating a great result from the sidelines?

SO, YOU WANT TO BE A LEADER?

Welcome to the big league. The demand for a new set of skills for success is evident, as the needs of the global business landscape are becoming increasingly unpredictable and volatile. Complex Problem-Solving is becoming a non-negotiable competency for future leaders. In 2020, The World Economic Forum published "The Future of Jobs Report," which cites complex problem-solving as one of the top three skills required for 2025.[xlviii] Additionally, of the top ten most-needed skills mentioned in the report, five relate to problem-solving:

- Analytical thinking and innovation
- Complex problem-solving
- Critical thinking and analysis
- Creativity, originality, and initiative
- Reasoning, problem-solving, and ideation

As our global business environment continues to encounter rapid change, the success of future executives, entrepreneurs, and students will rely on their capacity to think differently and solve new complex problems today and in the future. Honing the skills listed above will help future-proof your personal, business, and career trajectory.

THE SCIENCE BEHIND COMPLEX PROBLEM-SOLVING

In their article titled "Complex Problem-Solving: What It Is and What It Is Not" published in *Frontiers in Psychology*, Dietrich Dörner and Joachim Funke explain how to differentiate complex problems from simple problems and discuss the implications of solving complex problems.[xlix] They characterize simple problems as being well-defined within a closed space, whereas complex problems are not well defined, have open boundaries, and lack readily apparent solutions. They note we use *entirely different cognitive processes* to solve problems, depending on whether a problem is simple or complex. In Pillar Two, I will show you how these cognitive processes relate to the Subconscious Thinking Habits of Analytical Thinking, Innovative Thinking, and Conceptual Thinking.

The authors quote Dörner's earlier research, which was published in the journal *Simulation and Games* in 1980, on the intellectual difficulties people have when dealing with complexity.[1] From my perspective, complexity also affects the effectiveness and efficiency of our subconscious cognitive processes and conscious thinking. As we saw in Chapter 5, the research of Yerkes and Dodson showed that cognitive performance decreases significantly when individuals become overly stressed. Dörner found that when dealing with complexity in emergency situations, people tend toward:

- Decreased ability to self-reflect
- Diminished intellectual capacity when overstressed
- Increased action orientation with an accompanying increase in risk tolerance and readiness to violate the rules
- Reduced ability to develop and test hypotheses to deal with the situation at hand
- Lessened ability to contextualize goals

Dörner and Funke noted, "this phenomenon illustrates the strong connection between cognition, emotion and motivation ... the emergency reaction reveals a shift in the mode of information processing under the pressure of complexity."[li] From my perspective, this shift becomes exacerbated when dealing with complex problems, during events when people are under pressure, and in time-sensitive situations—particularly when one or more of the three Subconscious Thinking Habits that underlie Complex Problem-Solving are operating below optimal capability.

Traditional training can deliver knowledge acquisition (which is underpinned by Crystallized Knowledge), but not knowledge application (which is underpinned by Fluid Thinking).

Intriguingly, the authors referenced a 2017 study by Engelhart et al.,[lii] noting, "In their own experiment, the authors could show training effects only for knowledge acquisition, not for knowledge application. Only with specific feedback, performance in complex environments can be increased." *This is critically important because it's quintessentially the difference between Crystallized Knowledge and Fluid Thinking.*

As I explained in Chapter 3, traditional training can deliver *knowledge acquisition* (that is, Crystallized Knowledge), but not *knowledge application* (which is underpinned by Fluid Thinking). K. A. Ericsson developed the concept of deliberate practice and co-authored the 2017 paper by Engelhart et al. referenced above. So it is no surprise that knowledge application requires specific and expert feedback (the two core tenets of deliberate practice) for performance to improve in complex environments.

Much has been written about defining problem techniques, tools, strategies, etc. However, authors typically focus on *what to do* (Crystallized Knowledge), rather than *how to do it* (Fluid Thinking). Unfortunately, if your Analytical Thinking operates at low-to-moderate efficiency, you will have great difficulty analyzing and defining problems, irrespective of the quality of the problem-solving techniques and frameworks available to you.

THE FOUR STAGES OF COMPLEX PROBLEM-SOLVING

If you lack optimal balance among the Subconscious Thinking Habits associated with Pillar Two, you will probably struggle when confronted with the challenge of solving complex problems. Underdevelopment (or, in certain cases, overdevelopment) in any of these three areas impedes problem-solving, making the entire process slower and much less effective. It will take you longer than it should to arrive at the best possible solution, and you may have less confidence in the decisions you make along the way.

There are many complex problem-solving frameworks available today, and they all tend to be variations on the same theme. The framework I have developed is different in that it takes a cognitive perspective. It comprises the four stages shown in Figure 14. Each stage corresponds to a Subconscious Thinking Habit and presents its own unique challenges.

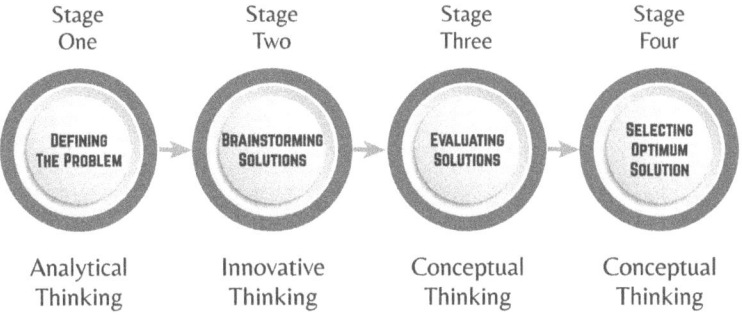

Figure 14. The Four Stages of Complex Problem-Solving

Once you fully understand these stages, it becomes easier to win—that is, to create effective and successful solutions to complex problems consistently. Let's take a closer look at what happens at each stage.

STAGE ONE: DEFINING THE PROBLEM (ANALYTICAL THINKING)

"A problem well stated is a problem half solved."
—Charles Kettering

The ability to define a problem successfully relies on the Subconscious Thinking Habit of Analytical Thinking, which supports rational and logical thinking. When your Analytical Thinking is highly developed, you can break down complex problems into smaller bite-sized components with ease. Thus, the key elements of the problem become much easier to identify. Breaking down complex issues provides a foundation from which a problem, and the associated criteria for a successful solution, can be accurately articulated and identified.

STAGE TWO: BRAINSTORMING SOLUTIONS (INNOVATIVE THINKING)

"Imagination is more important than knowledge. Knowledge is limited. Imagination encircles the world."
—Albert Einstein

We can generate numerous possible solutions using a process called *brainstorming*, which relies on the Subconscious Thinking Habit of Innovative Thinking. Unlike Analytical Thinking, which is based on logic, Innovative Thinking is based on a sensing and intuition. When your Innovative Thinking is highly developed, you are comfortable being presented with a blank slate and can develop new ideas quickly and organically. Your perspective is uninhibited, and you resist the temptation to fall into preconceptions that limit solutions. Likewise, you avoid succumbing to the urge to rely on past patterns of experience as the only building blocks for potential solutions. When your Innovative Thinking is optimized, creative ideas pop into your head quickly with little logical explanation because your brain is in a state of creative flow.

STAGE THREE: EVALUATING SOLUTIONS (CONCEPTUAL THINKING)

"True genius resides in the capacity for evaluation of uncertain, hazardous, and conflicting information."
—Winston Churchill

Stage Three of Complex Problem-Solving relies on the Subconscious Thinking Habit of Conceptual Thinking, which has a big-picture orientation. When highly developed, this holistic style of thinking pulls together disconnected pieces of information to create well-formed concepts, affording individuals the ability to understand quickly, clearly, and effectively what is going on and to act accordingly. Conceptual Thinking is a combination of both rational and logical thinking, with the addition of intuitive/sensing thinking when appropriate. Conceptual Thinking guides how you evaluate solutions against the criteria identified in Stage One and determines which solutions become prioritized and, ultimately, short-listed.

STAGE FOUR: SELECTING THE OPTIMUM SOLUTION (CONCEPTUAL THINKING)

"Every solution to every problem is simple. It's the distance between the two where the mystery lies."
—Derek Landy

The fourth and final stage of the Complex Problem-Solving framework is selecting the optimal solution. Again, Conceptual Thinking comes into play here, too. When your Conceptual Thinking is highly developed, initially, your brain quickly and intuitively evaluates the soundness of the various solutions before short-listing the best ones. Then, your brain employs the logic component of Conceptual Thinking to evaluate the shortlisted solutions before selecting the optimal solution. This rational aspect of Conceptual Thinking helps assess any unanticipated risks and determine whether the solution fits your organization's overarching goals and long-term strategies.

Once you have completed the evaluation and selected the ideal solution, it then becomes time to think through how the solution will be implemented successfully. This thinking process will be covered in Pillar Three: Strategy, Planning, and Execution.

KEY TAKEAWAYS

- Complex Problem-Solving comprises the Subconscious Thinking Habits of Analytical Thinking, Innovative Thinking, and Conceptual Thinking.
- You rely on Analytical Thinking to analyze information and use it to develop a comprehensive and accurate problem definition.
- You use Innovative Thinking to brainstorm multiple possible solutions.
- When your Conceptual Thinking is well-developed, you find it easy to evaluate solutions before choosing the one that has the highest probability of success.
- All three Subconscious Thinking Habits associated with Complex Problem-Solving must be optimized in order to coach your team from the sidelines successfully. If any are functioning below the optimum level, you will find Complex Problem-Solving to be difficult, time-consuming, and mentally taxing.

Chapter 7

ANALYTICAL THINKING

"Solved unless it is defined, a problem cannot be."
—Metaphorical Yoda

Pillar
Two

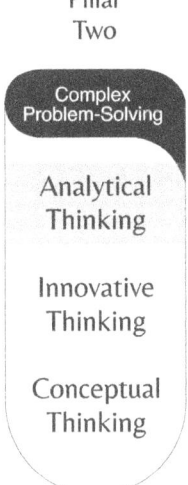

Metaphorical Yoda makes a solid point. How can a problem be solved if it hasn't been defined? Often, we are so pressed for time that we jump straight into solution mode before pausing to define the root cause of a problem. Typically, this results in solutions that are incompatible with the core problem—for example, the solution might address the symptoms but not the cause. It is annoying to admit, but most of us have lost time, sleep, and capacity because we failed to pause and think. We continue boxing with the shadows of misunderstood problems, wondering why we were getting taken out in multiple rounds—purely because we don't stop to break a problem down and define it in a detailed manner before we get back into the ring.

Great coaches understand that winning is secured off the field. The strategies, details, and drills they give their players beforehand ultimately determine their success on game day. Successful solutions are like an iceberg. Most of the work is entirely unseen; however, a mass of analysis and detailed thought stabilizes the solution under the surface.

The ability to pause and define problems before leaping into solution mode is a skill backed by one of the most influential thinkers in history. Albert Einstein is quoted as having said, "If I had only one hour to save the world, I would spend fifty-five minutes defining the problem, and only five minutes finding the solution." Personally, if the world needed saving, I would have a high degree of confidence in Einstein's capacity to come through with the next-level thinking necessary to give us a fighting chance. The key takeaway is that you must start by accurately defining the problem if you want your solution to succeed.

Unfortunately, most of us take the exact opposite approach to problems. If we are lucky, we might pause for five minutes to define the problem before we spend the other fifty-five minutes trying to solve it. Einstein had an incredibly analytical mind, so don't give yourself a hard time if you don't take to his approach naturally. Every brain is different, especially when it comes to the way we have developed our Subconscious Thinking Habits. For some, the thought of spending fifty-five minutes trying to define the problem is both daunting and overwhelming. Typically, this is due to having lower efficiency of Analytical Thinking, which inhibits the brain balance required to support us in dancing with the details, but not getting stuck in them.

SUBCONSCIOUS THINKING HABIT MODEL FOR ANALYTICAL THINKING

The Subconscious Thinking Habit model for Analytical Thinking is based on having the rational and subconscious capacity to pause, analyze, clarify, and define the root cause of a problem. When

Analytical Thinking is underdeveloped, it derails this process. People with low Analytical Thinking ability barely define a problem before jumping into solution mode. It can be frustrating to be aware of this behavior and yet be consistently unable to change it on a conscious level. It causes a lot of stress and leaves individuals oscillating between solutions, unable to make a confident decision.

If you happen to have lower Analytical Thinking ability, here is what your Subconscious Thinking Habit looks like:

Cue: You are given a problem to solve.

Routine: You subconsciously run your underdeveloped Analytical Thinking routine.

Output: You come up with an ill-defined problem and jump prematurely into solution mode.

When Analytical Thinking is lower, an inefficient trial-and-error approach is usually taken to solving the problem. The end result is wasted time and often lost opportunities and a less-than-ideal solution.

THE SCIENCE BEHIND ANALYTICAL THINKING

In their *Harvard Business Review* digital article titled "The Best Managers Balance Analytical and Emotional Intelligence," M. Smith et al. cite neuro-imaging research by their colleague, Professor Anthony Jack at Case Western Reserve University, regarding two major neural networks that operate in the human brain.[liii] The first is called the Analytical Network (AN), also known as the Task-Positive Network, which focuses on tasks and the analysis of quantitative data and information. The AN supports us to:

- Make sense of events and data from our environment
- Perform analytical tasks such as data analytics, financial analysis, etc.
- Solve problems and make decisions

The second major neural network is called the Empathetic Network (EN), which focuses on people aspects and qualitative observations from our environment. The EN supports us to:

- Optimize social engagement, actively listening and understanding another person's perspective
- Be open to new ideas, people, and emotions by continually scanning and sensing our social environment
- Deal with moral concerns or issues

The two neural networks have little overlap and are said to be antagonistic to each other—that is, they suppress each other. So, when your Empathetic Network is activated, your Analytical Network will be deactivated (and vice versa). Professor Jack perceives the Analytical Network and Empathetic Network as two opposing poles of reason. They both involve reason, cognitive activity, and information processing traits related to subconscious fast thinking.

M. Smith et al. note that "the most effective leaders do indeed use both and they are able to toggle back and forth between them in a fraction of a second." This is consistent with the way Subconscious Thinking Habits work—they all process information in parallel, quickly, and below the conscious threshold. In contrast, conscious thinking processes information at a slower rate and with conscious awareness, usually serially (i.e., one thought after the other).

The authors also contend that the Empathetic Network and the Analytical Network are engaged in an ongoing constant battle for brain dominance—after all, when one network is activated, the other is suppressed. This does not mean one is good and the other bad. Rather, they operate in balance, much like the concept of optimal brain balance, which I have been discussing. From my perspective, the Subconscious Thinking Habit of Strategic Thinking identifies which network is appropriate in the current circumstance and guides the process of toggling back and forth between the networks.

ANALYTICAL THINKING AND CAREER DEVELOPMENT

How does Analytical Thinking play out in the real world of jobs, careers, and career development? To get some input for this question, I turned to Indeed.com—which is a major worldwide jobs listing website—because they identify what capabilities and thinking skills employers across a wide range of industries and countries are looking for in job candidates. In an article on their website titled "Definition and Examples of Analytical Skills," Indeed.com's editorial team described the thinking skills needed to analyze complex issues and solve complex problems.[liv] Here are some key takeaways from the article, along with my perspectives on their conclusions:

- "Analytical thinking is a mental process that involves taking complex information or data and turning it into something that's easily understood by readers and listeners." I concur, as we use Analytical Thinking to make the complex simple by breaking complexity down into smaller, more digestible chunks that are easier to understand.
- "At the heart of analytical thinking is the ability to rapidly identify cause and effect relationships and devise potential outcomes." From my experience, the ability to identify cause-and-effect relationships is the key component of Analytical Thinking and of the problem definition stage of Complex Problem-Solving.
- The following analytical thinking skills are key for all job applicants:
  - Attention to detail
  - Critical thinking
  - Research and information analysis

      – Decision-making
      – Communication

I would add that the capability to define problems is probably the most important of all.

- Strong analytical thinking abilities make job applicants more attractive to employers because the job applicants require less supervision, make better decisions, and are less likely to make mistakes.

The authors also say that analytical thinking skills are used to "determine how to fix problems and come up with solutions." While I strongly agree that Analytical Thinking underpins the problem-definition stage, different thinking skills are required to generate solutions—namely, Innovative Thinking (see Chapter 8) and Conceptual Thinking (see Chapter 9).

DON'T CONFUSE THE SYMPTOMS WITH THE ROOT CAUSE

One of the most common issues with Complex Problem-Solving is the propensity for those with less efficient Analytical Thinking to get tangled up in all the various symptoms of a problem, rather than being able to cut to the chase quickly and determine the root cause.

In addition, when a large volume of data needs to be analyzed during the problem definition stage, those with lower Analytical Thinking ability can be overwhelmed by all the data. It takes them a considerable amount of time, effort, and mental energy to wade through the myriad of details. Consequently, they often find it very hard to define the problem. When they get stuck, they tend to back-off and procrastinate, especially if the situation is emotional or involves some type of conflict.

Can you relate to any of these traits? Let's take a closer look at how lower Analytical Thinking manifests in the workplace through the eyes of an executive who struggles with Complex Problem-Solving.

STAGE ONE: DEFINING THE PROBLEM

As mentioned in Chapter 6, Analytical Thinking underpins the first stage of the Complex Problem-Solving process (see Figure 15). Stage One, Defining the Problem, provides the basis upon which you will ultimately select the optimum solution to a complex problem.

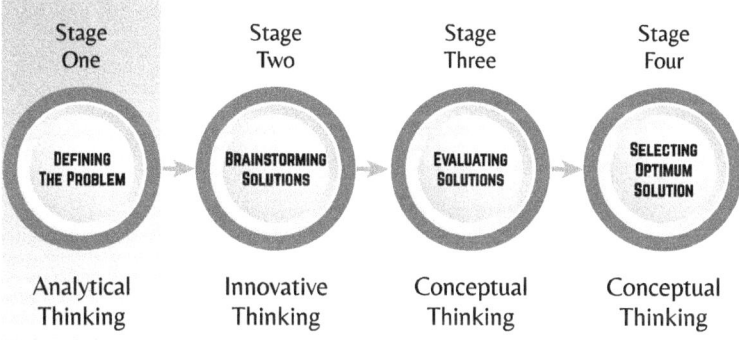

Figure 15. Complex Problem-Solving Stage One: Defining the Problem

When you do this stage well, the Complex Problem-Solving process starts with a solid foundation. In contrast, if you do it poorly, the process will start out on a rocky footing and participants will feel as if they are operating in a shifting-sands environment and continually second-guessing themselves.

To be an effective leader in today's rapidly shifting business landscape, you must be adept at solving complex problems. Commonly, individuals with lower Analytical Thinking become victims of the Peter Principle. This limits their career potential, allowing them to be promoted until they reach one level above their leadership competency. After all, if they can't even get to first base (i.e., Defining the Problem), they will be unlikely to score home runs.

DAVID: THE DEVIL IS IN THE PROBLEM DEFINITION

Meet David. He is your typical suit. A bright and tremendously knowledgeable leader in his field, he has received regular and fast-tracked promotions, leaping past his colleagues. He has been earmarked as part of the company's succession plan. We find David in a relatively senior executive position at a global multinational corporation at a comparably young age. His career has enjoyed pronounced success, his performance continues to exceed expectations, and his business unit's yearly double-digit growth is impressive.

You may be thinking David is an employer's dream, or that he embodies your current business aspirations. The only issue is that David has a problem. Although he is switched on enough to observe it, he cannot solve it, let alone define it. This is why we say the devil is in the definition. You can't solve what you can't define and effectively articulate.

David's issue is that his business unit's success is becoming increasingly dependent on him working harder and harder, leaving him a hop, skip, and a jump away from burnout. Those who have experienced burnout understand how it can flatline a career and a person simultaneously. What makes David's predicament more complicated is that working harder means he is not leveraging his team's abilities fully.

Regrettably, David has become trapped by working hero hours, which compromises his personal life as his professional workload creeps into family and personal time, taking a significant toll on David and his close relationships. Here again, we meet David pondering his problem and defining its symptoms without understanding its root cause.

Let's skip his internal monologue and land at the situational overview. Delegating is not going as planned. David's team is producing half-completed work, typically delivered at the eleventh hour. David is moonlighting as a magician, pulling rabbits out of his hat to meet major deadlines. While magic is a good party trick, the novelty is short lived. The pressure is amplified by David's rumination about the two potential causes of his continued need to work overtime.

Either David is ineffective or his team is. Regardless, either scenario could jeopardize his career progression. He has seen many a friend and colleague try to navigate in the wake of ineffective delegating. Frankly, regardless of whether it is David or his team that is ineffective, the end result is not desirable. Reconciling this problem is not something he wants (or is able) to do.

It's time for David to phone a friend, colleague, or mentor—two heads are usually better than one, unless the other head offers unpalatable advice. We find David like a Jedi, listening with equal parts respect and irritation to the words of his metaphorical Yoda who advises: "Solved unless it is defined, a problem cannot be." Interestingly, David's emotions flare disproportionately to the advice. As for many of us, this flare is triggered by a visceral desire to avoid analyzing the details, instead preferring to dive straight into fix-it mode, bypassing the definition stage and trying to go directly to the solution.

A few things are happening here. Initially, David believed the problem had been with his team. He had been tempted to fire one or two less-productive team members, hoping this would shock his team and then maybe the quality of their output would increase. Simultaneously, he thought about hiring a couple of new team members of a higher caliber. He postulated that, together, these actions would rebalance the workload and, ideally, improve the quality and timeliness of the work produced by the team. In

David's mind, this seemed to be an excellent solution. He thought maybe he was his own Yoda.

However, as David's emotions settled and his more rational sensibilities kicked in, some doubts began to surface. His solid solution had a concerning flaw. What if the new recruits are only of the same caliber as the ones he decides to let go? His current team had already gone through extensive interviewing, assessments, and onboarding of potential new team members, taking up more of his time and capacity. If the process was the same, wouldn't the outcome be the same, with a few months of extra hassle and even more pressure on him?

> *Rapidly, David found himself confronted by the thought that the real problem might be his leadership style.*

Rapidly, David found himself confronted by the thought that the real problem might be his leadership style. This realization left him stranded at Solution Station, clueless about which train to board, while our detail devil had a chuckle over all the chaos.

Interestingly, David's challenge isn't his lack of awareness of the problem, but the inability to define it, let alone solve it. His lower Analytical Thinking hinders his ability to define the problem accurately, so he never solves it properly. Although David is fantastic at chunking up[9] information and having big-picture vision, analyzing complex problems is always tricky terrain. He cannot quickly break down problems into bite-sized chunks. That's because David is neurologically wired to take a fire-aim-ready approach to problem-solving, which means he frequently comes up with excellent solutions to entirely different problems. Therefore, the problems often reoccur because the root cause is never addressed; understandably, this is highly irritating for David.

---

[9] "Chunking up" refers to moving from specific information or small details to larger and more general (or more abstract) ideas. By contrast, "chunking down" means moving from general ideas to specific details.

His irritation spills over into his team because David never clearly defines performance expectations. His team struggles because he fails to break things down effectively. He typically gives high-level verbal briefings that lack the specific information his team needs to produce the quality of work required. Additionally, his lowered Analytical Thinking means he tends to underestimate how much time and effort his team will need to deliver. David's high-level briefings and unachievable deadlines often leave his team confused, which significantly contributes to the burden of rework that invariably falls on David's shoulders. It is a vicious cycle, as David and his team dance around their frustrations. Worst of all, David is the only person who feels the consequences because he takes on the hero hours required to deliver the desired outcomes.

IMPACT OF LOWER ANALYTICAL THINKING

As David's example illustrates, one of the most challenging aspects of lower Analytical Thinking is that it increases your workload and burdens you every day. When this Subconscious Thinking Habit remains underdeveloped, it compromises various areas, and the effects compound rapidly. While these compromises can be kept at bay in the earlier stages of an individual's career, they immeasurably impact the sustainability of career growth if left unattended.

Everything that David experiences is absolutely normal and, in many ways, expected when you understand how Analytical Thinking impacts performance. When this Subconscious Thinking Habit is left underdeveloped, people just want to hunker down in Denial Town.

In the following sections, I outline the tangible impacts of lower Analytical Thinking on David's day-to-day operation. See if you can identify with David. Maybe he reminds you of someone you know?

AVOIDING DETAILS

Let's start at the very beginning. Big-picture thinkers like David have a predisposition to avoid details. To be blunt, they despise details. They would rather bury their head in the sand than deal with the mundane and energy-zapping nature of the small stuff. David's avoidance of leaping into the details of large amounts of data, long emails, briefs, and dreaded spreadsheets derail him from learning how to communicate essential information clearly and effectively. Instead, he prefers the high-level verbal briefing, as it is quicker and much easier to pull together. Although this approach worked for him early in his career when dealing with simpler problems, it rapidly yielded diminishing returns in his more senior role, as evidenced by his team's lack of output. It also started to impact his own performance because it interfered with his ability to analyze complex data to identify trends, opportunities, and risks accurately—all of which posed a threat to his career growth.

David isn't choosing this; his lower Analytical Thinking is the root cause, and everything else is a symptom.

AVOIDING CONFLICT AT ALL COSTS

Conflict resolution is grounded in detail, which is why people with lower Analytical Thinking tend to avoid situations that involve conflict. David dreads conflict. For him, analyzing all the conflicting pieces of a complex problem feels like looking for a needle in a haystack.

Likewise, David struggles with interpersonal conflict. He is beyond frustrated by his team. Although his frustration enrages him, he internalizes his emotions. Try as he might, David cannot figure out the underlying cause of the conflict.

PROCRASTINATION: JUST ANOTHER TYPE OF AVOIDANCE

Lower Analytical Thinking also impacts critical thinking and influences one's predisposition to procrastinate. These are costly derailers, in David's case, especially because he is in a senior position at a relatively young age. David is uncompromisingly pragmatic; so naturally, his attitude toward critical thinking is the same, meaning that he often takes information at face value. Because this tendency impacts his capacity to engage critically with data and details, he often misses the crucial nuances that are essential for deliverables.

The urge to avoid details is so strong that David procrastinates by engaging in less taxing activities. Who can blame him? Our brains love distraction, and often we do everything we can to avoid boring and monotonous tasks. So, it is natural that he would put things off, as he has not developed the Subconscious Thinking Habit needed to overcome this derailer.

TRAPPED IN INDECISION

Lower Analytical Thinking also derails decisiveness. If you're like David, you're always seeking certainty and additional information. David has an incessant need to research so he can get more clarity about a problem. It doesn't help that all that research just means he ends up with more details he needs to analyze.

When you get paralyzed by the details, it derails your confidence and allows self-doubt to creep in, making it difficult to make decisions confidently.

David mistakenly believes that the problem is a lack of information rather than his lack of capacity to analyze and synthesize the information he already has. He finds himself overwhelmed by the volume of data and increasingly less sure of how to proceed. It is a

121

classic case of information overload. When you get paralyzed by the details, it derails your confidence and allows self-doubt to creep in, making it difficult to make decisions confidently.

UNDERESTIMATING TIME AND EFFORT REQUIRED TO COMPLETE TASKS

The next derailing factor associated with lower Analytical Thinking is the overall difficulty with accurately estimating the amount of work, effort, and time needed to complete a task. People with lower Analytical Thinking are prone to lowballing. When this happens, they are already off to a compromised start. David is unaware that he frequently gives unrealistic deadlines to his team. This vicious cycle leads to mutual frustration, sometimes resentment, and often culminates in a lot of avoidable rework.

POOR DIRECTION LEADS TO POOR RESULTS

David's lower Analytical Thinking compromises his capacity to set performance benchmarks for his team. David assumes he and his team agree, so he briefs them based on an assumed level of knowledge. This is a recipe for disaster, because if your team members have the same levels of experience, expertise, and thinking as you have, they are more likely to be your peers and not your direct reports.

It's a nasty trap to assume everyone processes information the same way you do—especially if you are a big-picture thinker. Your team will fill in the gaps based on their own assumptions. Usually, the result will be deliverables that lack the desired quality and comprehensiveness, and then the boss and team members end up in a silent standoff. When clarity is lacking, poor performance often follows. This is how David and many others get derailed by their lower ability to analyze details and their lower ability to communicate clearly.

REDUCED READING COMPREHENSION

Do you use your highlighter like a lightsaber, fighting your way through complex documents, marking up all that is important through the power of neon yellow?

Like David, many people with lower Analytical Thinking experience the cycle of rereading complex and detailed information before they can understand the key concepts completely. You may use your highlighter like a lightsaber, fighting your way through complex documents and marking up all that is important through the power of neon yellow. As mighty as your intentions are, this approach typically leaves the page looking like a piece of abstract art that's dominated by neon yellow. Why does this happen? The brain struggles to identify the most important passages because everything appears equally important to a person with lower Analytical Thinking capability.

In addition, written documents contain extra detail to digest as compared to when someone is communicating with you verbally. Plus, when reading print, you can't ask clarifying questions in the moment.

BENEFITS OF HIGHLY DEVELOPED ANALYTICAL THINKING

As you can see, David's derailers are significant. But remember, they are only symptoms because the root cause is his lower Analytical Thinking ability. The good news is that, like all Subconscious Thinking Habits, Analytical Thinking can be developed through deliberate practice. Developing your Subconscious Thinking Habits can treat the root cause and leave you symptom-free—a liberating thought.

Complex Problem-Solving starts with accurately defining the problem, including the associated root causes. Highly developed Analytical

Thinking is the linchpin behind the ability to define problems, which is the precursor to developing an appropriate solution.

DAVID: DEFINING PROBLEMS MORE EFFECTIVELY AFTER BRAIN COACHING

David successfully completed our brain coaching program, and his Analytical Thinking improved significantly as a result. Let's see how his day-to-day experience at work and his career prospects improved. David is now:

- More comfortable with pausing and stepping back to define a problem and identify its root causes, rather than prematurely jumping into solution mode
- Better equipped to analyze details and gain valuable insights, rather than avoiding details whenever possible
- Proficient at chunking down information, quickly breaking tasks down into their component elements and readily identifying the starting point, thereby overcoming his procrastination
- Highly confident in his ability to estimate the scope of work and deadlines accurately, which also considerably enhances his capacity to delegate
- More rational and impartial when dealing with conflicts and problems that involve an emotional component
- Able to bottom-line issues quickly and confident in his decision making

In summary, David is leveraging his considerably enhanced Analytical Thinking to lead his team with more certainty and confidence. Now that his performance has improved considerably, he is well equipped to take on more senior roles.

KEY TAKEAWAYS

- Analytical Thinking is associated with the first stage of the Complex Problem-Solving process—namely, Defining the Problem.

- You rely on Analytical Thinking to analyze detailed and complex information before developing a comprehensive and accurate problem definition. People with lower Analytical Thinking typically jump into solution mode too quickly, resulting in an inefficient trial-and-error approach to solving problems.

- People with lower Analytical Thinking find it difficult to read and analyze a lot of detailed information quickly, so they try to avoid these types of tasks whenever possible. Also, they tend to overuse their highlighter pen because everything seems equally important.

- Lower Analytical Thinking negatively impacts the ability to make decisions confidently, estimate work effort accurately, delegate effectively, and deal with conflict logically. It also increases the tendency toward procrastination.

- Indeed.com suggest that strong Analytical Thinking abilities make job applicants more attractive to employers because those applicants require less supervision, make good decisions quickly and effectively, and are less likely to make mistakes.

Chapter 8
INNOVATIVE THINKING

"Innovation distinguishes between a leader and a follower."—Steve Jobs

Pillar
Two

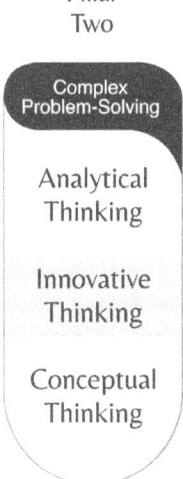

Innovative Thinking is an interesting Subconscious Thinking Habit because difficulties can arise not only when it is too low, but also when it is too high. Ideally, it has to be balanced. Innovative Thinking can be a double-edged sword, as it offers both strengths and derailers when it is under- or overdeveloped.

When Innovative Thinking is too low, it can lead an individual to be very process- and operationally driven. In contrast, when it is too high, it can lead to exceptional creativity, but with the lack of the practical capacity needed to implement ideas effectively. Both under- and overdevelopment can significantly impact a career trajectory and cause a great deal of frustration for the individual, their colleagues, their teams, and their organizations.

Innovative Thinking is underpinned by your subconscious capability to recognize patterns. When pattern recognition is high, Innovative Thinking capability is lower. While high pattern recognition can be a strength in certain operational roles, it is often a liability in leadership positions that require the ability to manage unpredictability and adapt quickly to change. Conversely, when pattern recognition is low, Innovative Thinking tends to be overly high, making it challenging to moderate your creativity and turn your myriad innovative ideas into practical solutions.

Innovative Thinking can be harder to grasp than the other Subconscious Thinking Habits because it is more multifaceted. This difficulty is partly because creativity and innovation are often perceived as being connected to an individual's personality. However, these are not personality traits. When people judge innovative capacity relative to personality, they often assume the person cannot change. In reality, anyone can become more innovative if they develop their Subconscious Thinking Habits optimally and understand how to leverage pattern recognition appropriately. When the brain has balance in this thinking capability, it can perform at peak level.

SUBCONSCIOUS THINKING HABIT MODEL FOR INNOVATIVE THINKING

Innovative Thinking is a very different style of thinking compared to Analytical Thinking. Analytical Thinking is based on a hard-nosed, laser-focused, rational, and logical process of breaking down complex problems and information into smaller, simpler, and more easily understood components. In contrast, Innovative Thinking is a much softer, sensing, semi-focused style of free-form thinking. Think of your state of mind when you are at your most creative. Is it when you are walking in the fresh air in the forest? When you're looking out over a beautiful water view? When you're luxuriating under a relaxing, warm shower while your mind is in a state of free flow? Or, perhaps some other approach works best for you? Whatever it is, I'll bet it's not when you are working at your desk in front of the computer!

I encourage our clients to sleep on significant problems or opportunities overnight when time allows. They are always amazed when their brain presents very creative and innovative solutions upon awakening in the morning.

As you can see in Table 2, the Cue/Routine/Output model for this Subconscious Thinking Habit presents itself differently depending on whether your Innovative Thinking is underdeveloped, overdeveloped, or balanced.

Table 2. Impact of Different Levels of Innovative Thinking

	Underdeveloped	Overdeveloped	Balanced
Cue	Your boss asks you to brainstorm solutions to a defined problem.		
Routine	You subconsciously run your **underdeveloped** Innovative Thinking routine	You subconsciously run your **overdeveloped** Innovative Thinking routine.	You subconsciously run your **optimized** Innovative Thinking routine.
Output	You experience difficulty creating novel ideas to address the situation and tend to regurgitate old solutions.	You generate myriad creative solutions to the defined problem, but tend to favor the off-the-wall solutions, which often aren't pragmatic.	You generate myriad creative solutions that are pragmatic and easy to implement.

In this chapter, we will see how unbalanced Innovative Thinking manifests in real life through the stories of Adrian and Michelle, each of whom has unique challenges because of their varying levels of development. Then later, we'll see how much better Adrian and Michelle perform when they have ideally balanced their Innovative Thinking capability by tapping into their brain's plasticity using a deliberate practice approach.

THE SCIENCE BEHIND INNOVATIVE THINKING

In their *Harvard Business Review* digital article titled "Why Constraints Are Good for Innovation," authors Acar et al. reviewed 145 empirical studies on the effect of constraints on creativity and innovation.[lv] They found that when no constraints were placed on creative and innovation processes, people became complacent and followed the path of least resistance, i.e., they chose the most intuitive idea rather than investing time, effort, and energy into developing better ideas. However, when constraints were too restrictive, employees became demotivated.

In contrast, providing appropriate constraints enhanced people's focus and creativity and led them to review information from a wide variety of sources, resulting in novel and creative solutions for new products, services, or processes. The authors found it is important to frame constraints as creative challenges, rather than inhibitors.

The authors also note that the key to fostering creativity and innovation is to orchestrate constraints that provide guidance and motivation for the innovative thinking process without restricting the employees' creativity and motivation.

Their findings reinforce my approach to Complex Problem-Solving, namely:

- You must be very specific during the problem definition phase, as this sets the framework for thinking through the problem and the associated constraints, and for defining clear criteria for successful solutions.
- You need a balanced, *just right* level of Innovative Thinking to generate creative solutions that are both fit for purpose and easy to implement, while leveraging past experience to avoid reinventing the wheel.

INNOVATIVE THINKING AND MINDLESSNESS

In their article titled "Sometimes Mindlessness Is Better Than Mindfulness," Burgoyne and Hambrick note that while mindfulness is often useful, it is counterproductive when a state of mindlessness would work better.[lvi] They discuss *automaticity*, which cognitive psychology defines as the automatic thoughts and behaviors that occur without our conscious attention.

Burgoyne and Hambrick referred to a study they had undertaken to investigate piano skill acquisition in beginners. The authors found that a novice's ability to focus their attention could predict their ability to learn to play "Happy Birthday" on the piano. The key point is that when a novice is learning a new skill, their ability to stay focused during the learning process drives the quality of their performance. This underscores the importance of ensuring your Focused Thinking (see Chapter 5) is functioning at a high level, particularly when learning new skills.

In contrast, the authors noted that, for people with well-practiced expertise and high levels of automaticity (e.g., a skilled golfer taking shots), paying too much attention to a task can be counterproductive. They cited research by Yannick Balk and his colleagues who deliberately induced performance pressure by videotaping the participants' golf shots and telling them their scores would be posted in the clubhouse for everyone to see. These golfers performed significantly worse than the control group. From my experience, this is not unexpected, as the Yerkes-Dodson Law shows performance plummets when people are subjected to excessive pressure and stress (see Chapter 5).

However, the golfers in Balk's control group leveraged automaticity. They were encouraged to think of a song they knew by heart, which distracted their brains. Keeping their attention focused on the song kept them from overthinking how they played the golf shot. Also, unlike the test group, the researchers did not subject the control group to performance pressure by filming the participants and posting their scores in the clubhouse. As a result, the control group played golf subconsciously and automatically—in a state of mindlessness. This is why the control group's scores were better than those of the test group.

Subconscious Thinking Habits are examples of automaticity.

This research reinforces my own work in the area of optimal Innovative Thinking. From my perspective, Subconscious Thinking Habits are examples of automaticity. I have found the brain will produce the most creative and innovative potential solutions to complex problems when it is in a state of mindlessness, as compared to when it is hyper-focused and overly mindful. Innovative Thinking requires the brain to be semi-focused. When the mind wanders, Innovative Thinking is free to operate subconsciously and automatically.

DO PEOPLE WITH ADHD HAVE A CREATIVE ADVANTAGE?

Attention Deficit Hyperactivity Disorder (ADHD) is a neurological disorder marked by distractibility, impulsivity, and hyperactivity— all of which can have a variety of impacts on their academic results, employment, and social relationships. However, in her article titled "The Creativity of ADHD," researcher Holly White notes that the same distractibility can give people with ADHD an edge when it comes to creative original thinking.[lvii] She also says, "ADHD may be an advantage and beneficial when the goal is to invent something very new, without being locked into, and constrained by old models, conventions and traditional ways of thinking."

From my perspective, White's conclusions reinforce the idea that being in a state of low focus and mindlessness, which she mentions is common in some people with ADHD, enhances the ability to think creatively and brainstorm innovative solutions. However, it is important to note that ADHD is a heterogeneous disorder, which means it presents differently in different people. Many people with ADHD focus intently on things that interest them but find it difficult to maintain focus when they are bored. For example, they might hyper-focus on hobbies, certain school activities, or screen activities such as video games.

Again, the Yerkes-Dodson Law may come into play here, too. Recall from Chapter 5 that when a person is demotivated or bored, their adrenal hormone levels are lower, which negatively impacts their cognitive performance. So, it seems reasonable that for a person with ADHD, when their interest in a topic increases, their adrenal hormone levels will also increase, thus leading to enhanced focus and cognitive performance.

CAN ALCOHOL IMPACT CREATIVITY?

And now, here's some left-field research. While, as a cognitive scientist, I do not recommend using alcohol to optimize your Subconscious Thinking Habits, research shows it can improve Innovative Thinking when taken in limited amounts. In a *Harvard Business Review* article titled "Defend Your Research: Drunk People Are Better at Creative Problem-Solving" author Alison Beard shares highlights from her interview with Professor Andrew Jarosz of Mississippi State University.[lviii] They discussed a research study by Professor Jarosz involving twenty male subjects whose blood alcohol levels approached legal intoxication. The men were given a series of word association problems to solve. Not only did those with mild intoxication provide a greater number of correct answers than the sober control group, but they also solved the problems faster. To me, this sounds counterintuitive, wouldn't you think? Let's explore this further by examining the conversation between Beard and Professor Jarosz from Beard's *Harvard Business Review* article.

HBR: So alcohol doesn't slow us down mentally after all?

Professor Jarosz: It still does, but we think creative problem-solving is one area in which a key effect of drunkenness—*loss of focus*—is a good thing ... When we asked participants how much they relied on strategic thinking versus sudden insights to solve the problems, the intoxicated people reported solving via insight on 10% more problems than their sober counterparts did.

My interpretation is that although sobriety is extremely important to Focused Thinking (see Chapter 5), being slightly tipsy may assist the creativity associated with Innovative Thinking. Using alcohol reduces focus, which allows the mind to wander and enhances creativity. Although I would not recommend this approach to enhancing creativity, the results of decreased focus and its impact on Innovative Thinking are consistent with what I have already covered in this chapter.

HBR: What about drugs?

Professor Jarosz: I couldn't comment on that. But studies have shown that people with specific types of brain damage do better on certain creative tests ... Those findings make sense to me because they go back to the impairment of focus. Even tea drinking has been shown to enhance creativity.

My interpretation of this is that the ritual of drinking tea induces relaxation, which is conducive to increased creativity because it puts the mind in a wandering state.

HBR: Why did you decide to study this? An attempt to justify your own drinking habits?

Professor Jarosz: I was more interested in investigating the potential for improving problem-solving skills. There's an old tale of Archimedes' "Aha!" moment in the bath, and I've always wondered what causes people to have sudden flashes of insight.

From my perspective, people are always looking for Archimedes' "Aha!" moment when solving problems. However, they don't realize those moments depend on having balanced Innovative Thinking as well as a soft focus when brainstorming potential solutions.

HBR: Have scientists found that alcohol yields any other mental benefits?

Professor Jarosz: One paper, "Lost in the Sauce," by Michael Sayette at the University of Pittsburgh and coauthors, reported that people under the influence are more susceptible to mind wandering, which could be helpful in some scenarios but harmful in others.

Again, my interpretation is that the key takeaway here is mind wandering can be an important component in optimizing creativity and Innovative Thinking.

HBR: And those moments led to better, faster performance?

Professor Jarosz: In this case, yes. Instead of doing a very focused, goal-directed search for the answer, they engaged in what neuroscientists call "spreading activation." If you looked at an fMRI of their brains, you might see different areas lighting up, indicating that they were *subconsciously* [emphasis added] activating all the recesses of their memories for the right words.

I agree with Professor Jarosz. From my perspective, the key was that the participants *subconsciously* accessed their memories when searching for the correct answers, rather than being limited by a conscious logical process.

STAGE TWO: BRAINSTORMING SOLUTIONS

Remember from Chapter 6 that after defining the problem in Stage One of the Complex Problem-Solving process, we move to Stage Two, where we brainstorm potential innovative solutions (see Figure 16).

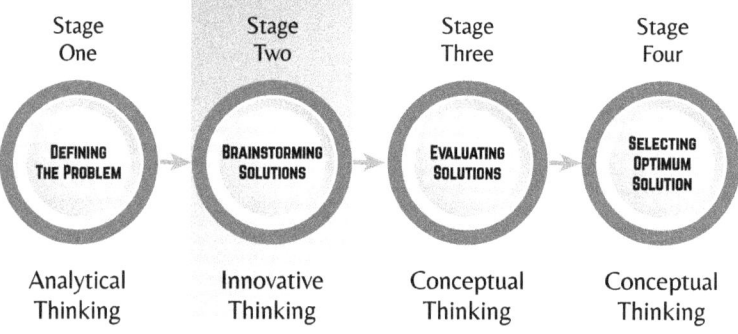

Figure 16. Complex Problem-Solving Stage Two: Brainstorming Solutions

As mentioned earlier, articulating the agreed-upon constraints for potential solutions at the beginning of a brainstorming session enhances the quality of the innovative solutions you can generate. Constraints provide clarity and focus for the brain, which in turn optimizes creativity during brainstorming. This is also why it is paramount to define the problem clearly in Stage One. Otherwise, as the research has shown, people tend to take the path of least resistance and identify obvious, low-hanging solutions rather than undertaking a comprehensive and productive approach to brainstorming.[lix]

ADRIAN: TRIED AND TRUSTED WORKS BEST

We all know an Adrian. He is highly competent and as reliable as the sun. In our context, Adrian is a respected vice president of operations for a global food brand. Adrian is exceptional in his area of operations and in the quality of his deliverables. He has been at the company longer than some of the junior employees have been alive. Epitomizing the status quo, his long tenure with the company has allowed him to tap into the patterns of company politics. However, Adrian lacks agility and adaptability, and he is not particularly innovative. Consequently, he greets new opportunities that require change and flexibility with an Ebenezer Scrooge-like "Bah! Humbug!"

Adrian also approaches brainstorming with a Scrooge-like attitude. His appreciation for creativity is skeptical at best, and his general perspective is, *if it isn't broken, why fix it?* Brainstorming sessions are confronting for Adrian, as he often draws blanks where colleagues see solutions, resulting in him internalizing feelings of inadequacy. His negative feelings have compounded over time, making it easier for us to understand his "bah humbug" attitude. The only way he can contribute to brainstorming sessions is to rework old, tried-and-true ideas. Adrian has difficulty reconciling the changing context of new problems and pairing them with the knowledge he has gained from past experience. When he comes up with somewhat creative ideas and tries to implement them, he usually misses the mark because he has difficulty recontextualizing his ideas for the new environment.

Adrian's black-and-white thinking creates some dissonance with his peers because his leadership style lacks flexibility. He is well-known for his "my way or the highway" approach to leadership, which often drives promising, innovative team members to leave his business unit. On the other hand, Adrian is a powerhouse when it comes to developing systems and procedures. He thrives when dealing with work that involves a high level of pattern recognition. Here, he excels because he is able to leverage his past experience and his ability to identify and process patterns.

Unwittingly, his capacity to recognize patterns is a critical factor in Adrian's strong ability to identify his organization's unwritten social and corporate rules—a strength that has protected him from breaking these rules. Indeed, it helped him anticipate a colleague's behavior ahead of time, as he can often predict behavior based on the patterns of previous interactions. Often, Adrian is bemused at how people telegraph their actions without even realizing it. Additionally, his keen pattern recognition ability makes Adrian a swift learner who quickly masters new technologies as they are implemented. He is able to learn these new systems with far less effort than his colleagues.

Though there are some clear upsides to Adrian's proclivity towards patterns, he has some definite shortcomings, which mainly relate to how he navigates life and work. Adrian is continually blindsided by change and is relatively risk averse. That's because the patterns that contribute to his performance are based on predictability. Unfortunately, in this constantly changing business landscape, Adrian often struggles to see what is coming over the horizon. He finds creativity uncomfortable because it lacks consistency, and this discomfort naturally limits his progression beyond operational-style roles.

MICHELLE: SHOOTING FOR THE MOON AND THE STARS

Enter Michelle, the complete opposite of Adrian when it comes to Innovative Thinking. You probably know someone like Michelle, too, but it is highly plausible that you like her more than Adrian. Given the choice of which of the two to work for, Michelle is typically the first pick. She is the quintessential head of creative for the same global food company where Adrian works. Michelle is effervescent, utterly engaging, and full of vision. Working with her can feel like you have landed on the moon and are playing a game of imagination with the stars, one brainstorming session at a time.

Michelle is forward-thinking, always proactively looking to improve things, and often hosting brainstorming sessions to address a situation, problem, or opportunity. She thrives on bringing people together to create novel solutions to problems. As an innovative and creative thinker, her flexible approach to leadership is inviting to her peers. Michelle embraces change and encourages it from her team, having an open-door policy that allows her team to approach her about ways to optimize the business unit and the organization overall. Her attitude attracts people to her business unit, as they want to work with a manager who embraces creativity and innovation.

One of the greatest strengths Michelle brings to the table is her perspective: the capacity to take a clean-slate view of any problem. This means she is open to everything, holding no preconceptions, which makes space for embracing the new. For Michelle, nothing is off the table. However, this imaginative disposition comes at a cost—or, more precisely, an underdeveloped capacity to leverage her past experiences and use pattern recognition to her advantage. This means Michelle is predisposed to reinventing the wheel instead of applying the lessons learned from past experiences. This propensity creates large amounts of avoidable rework. It takes her significant mental energy to learn new systems, and reading manuals proves unfailingly confusing.

Michelle's infectious personality and dynamic nature afford her a lot of grace from her peers; likeability tends to do that. However, it does not erase the fact that she unwittingly oversteps social and corporate boundaries regularly. It is critical to understand that these infractions are subconscious because the excitement of change propels her to the moon with an intergalactic force. Nevertheless, this force often leaves a blazing trail behind her, usually with colleagues like Adrian.

ADRIAN AND MICHELLE: CLASH OF THE MANAGEMENT TITANS

All jokes aside, the tales of Michelle and Adrian are reasonably common. We find Michelle on her way to the moon, fueled by creative energy. In the hustle and bustle, she finds herself chatting with Susan, a member of Adrian's team. Michelle invites Susan to collaborate and asks Susan to help her do some research. It is just a small amount of research, and Michelle knows Susan has excellent subject-matter expertise in this specific area. Susan jumps at the opportunity, as she has long wanted to work with Michelle and engage her more creative side. However, there is a slight problem. In her enthusiasm, Michelle neglects to ask Adrian for permission to collaborate with Susan.

Unfortunately, this situation turns into a much bigger problem because Adrian has Susan working on an important and time-sensitive project. Regrettably, this is not the first time Michelle has overstepped the corporate boundaries with Adrian's team. Highly annoyed, Adrian has a private and honest, yet respectful, conversation with Michelle. He expresses his deep frustration, highlighting that Michelle frequently operates outside the corporate social boundaries. Additionally, Adrian expresses he is disappointed by the lack of common courtesy Michelle had displayed by going around him to collaborate directly with a member of his team. Adrian continues, commenting that this has happened several times, and that he is over it, as are many of Michelle's colleagues. He asserts that she needs to review her behavior and be open to changing it, as it is interfering with the deliverables and deadlines of other departments.

Michelle, confused, takes this feedback to her partner later that evening and inquires if she is prone to overstepping boundaries. A slow smile creeps across her partner's face, which she knows too well means a yes. Together, they unpack her behaviors, and Michelle is perplexed and shocked. Until now, she'd had no awareness—not even a hint—of the unintentional, yet genuine, offense she causes to her colleagues when she oversteps unwritten corporate social boundaries. Finally, she realizes that her agility, adaptability, and brilliant Innovative Thinking come with a few blind spots, especially around setting appropriate boundaries.

Michelle mulls it all over and connects some of the high-level dots, understanding it was not the first time she had been unaware of unhelpful behavioral patterns. Indeed, she had worked hard to overcome her shortcomings with problem-solving and no longer jumped into solution mode before defining the problem. It had taken a lot of intention to distance herself from her reputation of solving the wrong problems. Michelle wondered what else she might be unaware of while she spent her time in the clouds, musing with the stars...

IMPACT OF UNBALANCED INNOVATIVE THINKING

So what happens during Stage Two when you don't have a well-defined problem and clearly articulated constraints? Let's explore this from the perspectives of Adrian and Michelle.

Adrian would be lost at sea because his brain needs structure to process information and think through things optimally. Brainstorming potential solutions was difficult enough for him already because of his lower Innovative Thinking. So, Adrian would have felt sidelined, and the team would have missed out on leveraging his extensive operational expertise and company history.

Michelle, with her high Innovative Thinking, would have been bouncing off the walls with unrealistic, left-field solutions, as she did not have a clear frame of reference. Note that it is important to encourage the generation of left-field ideas during the brainstorming process because those left-field ideas often lead iteratively to a better solution that is also more practical. Unfortunately, without an appropriate framework, a lot of participants in brainstorming sessions feel they are spinning their wheels unproductively.

The key message: if you want to optimize the outcome of your brainstorming session, always begin with a well-defined problem statement. In addition, you need to agree upon the constraints in advance, so all the creative capability and energy can be harnessed and channeled to yield the best possible solutions.

A good, old-fashioned compare-and-contrast approach is most helpful in understanding what happens when this Subconscious Thinking Habit remains unbalanced. We will start with Adrian and the supportive and derailing impacts of his underdeveloped Innovative Thinking, which are summarized in Table 3.

Table 3. Behaviors Related to Underdeveloped Innovative Thinking

Supporting Behaviors	Derailing Behaviors
Highly competent at developing processes and systems	Lack of vision
Excellent execution skills	Black-and-white thinking and lower creativity
Fast learner	Inflexibility and uncomfortable with change
High compliance with social and corporate guidelines	Lower adaptability and lower thinking agility
Strong process skills	More risk averse

Table 4 recaps the supportive and derailing impacts of Michelle's overdeveloped Innovative Thinking. As you can see from these two lists, Adrian and Michelle are virtually exact opposites in their approach. Is it any wonder they clash?

Table 4. Supporting Behaviors Related to Overdeveloped Innovative Thinking

Supporting Behaviors	Derailing Behaviors
Visionary	Poorer execution skills
Thinks outside the box and very creative	Slower learner
Flexible and comfortable with change	Lower compliance with social and corporate guidelines, and unwittingly crosses boundaries
Higher adaptability and higher thinking agility	Weaker process skills
More risk tolerant	Less adept at proactively identifying risks

You can now understand why we approach Innovative Thinking with a balanced attitude; otherwise, the outcome can be staid or chaotic. If your Innovative Thinking is lower, like Adrian's, you risk getting too close to the sun and burning out of creative ideas rapidly. If it is overdeveloped, like Michelle's, you risk spending too much time musing with the moon, never returning to reality. Ideally, you want to be positioned perfectly between the two.

THE GOLDILOCKS EFFECT: WHEN INNOVATIVE THINKING IS "JUST RIGHT"

Do you remember *Goldilocks and the Three Bears?* Here is a quick refresher on Robert Southey's 1837 classic children's story. In the original version, Goldilocks was a not-so-polite older woman. In the updated and best-known version, the old woman was replaced by a young girl named Goldilocks. She was wandering through a forest and broke into the home of the Three Bears: Papa Bear, Mama Bear, and Baby Bear. She went on to try out their porridges, chairs, and beds. After Goldilocks sampled everything, she found that Baby Bear's porridge, chair, and bed were *just right*. Goldilocks fell asleep, and then when the bears came home, she bolted into the forest. Frankly, this children's story is a little strange for my taste, but the *just right* element has always stuck with me. It guides a lot of my work with my clients, as *just right* is the goal of brain balance.

The stories of Adrian and Michelle illustrate how Innovative Thinking needs to have that *just right*, balanced quality.

PAPA BEAR'S UNDERDEVELOPED INNOVATIVE THINKING

Adrian's Innovative Thinking is underdeveloped because his pattern recognition is too high. Going back to the bears, Adrian is Papa Bear, whose porridge was too hot and his bed too hard, much like the rigidity of Adrian's management style. Adrian's tendency to rely on past experiences is a double-edged sword: although this trait is an asset to him when solving problems that allow him to leverage familiar patterns, he has difficulty solving new problems when there are no pre-existing patterns to leverage. However, his pattern recognition gives him the capacity to navigate the operational nature of his role. Deep down, he is aware of his avoidance of creativity, as his experiences with it have frequently been negative. Adrian has internalized those experiences and has developed a self-defeating orientation towards Innovative Thinking.

MAMA BEAR'S OVERDEVELOPED INNOVATIVE THINKING

Michelle is the opposite of Adrian, with overdeveloped Innovative Thinking and lower pattern recognition capability. She faces very different challenges. Always energized by creativity, Michelle thrives on fresh thinking and creatively engaging with complex problems. However, because her pattern recognition is lower, it isn't easy to use her past experience to ground her creativity. Therefore, although she generates many innovative ideas, she has significant trouble translating an idea into a pragmatic solution. The constant reinventing of the wheel is rather irritating to her colleagues because, frequently, the ideas and solutions they produce are replaced a month later with yet another new initiative. Michelle's brain loves ideation but not implementation, which in turn impacts her output.

Arguably, Michelle could be like Mama Bear whose porridge was too cold and her bed too soft. This comparison makes sense, as she was likely inspired and left her porridge while it was hot. Although her inclusive management style was fantastic, Michelle's softness around execution means she has not found her *just right*.

BABY BEAR GETS INNOVATIVE THINKING "JUST RIGHT"

This brings us back to Baby Bear, whose porridge and bed are *just right*, exactly where Innovative Thinking should be. When it is optimally balanced, this Subconscious Thinking Habit brings the creativity needed for brainstorming solutions and also the pragmatism to implement them.

As I said earlier, balanced Innovative Thinking is like Goldilocks's Baby Bear. No one is aiming to be Baby Bear, so let's uncouple the two and zero in on the *just right* part. Take a moment to process where you feel you fit. Do you identify more with Adrian or Michelle? Or maybe you are a bit of both? Possibly you are already in balance. If so, embrace it.

BENEFITS OF BALANCED INNOVATIVE THINKING

Let me define what balanced Innovative Thinking looks like, as someone who has helped leaders across the globe create the balance needed to embrace innovation. Balanced Innovative Thinking results in individuals who have the following characteristics:

- Visionary
- Highly adaptable and agile
- Embraces change
- Open to calculated risks
- Full of creative ideas
- Quick and efficient learner
- Pragmatic and practical

Simultaneously, people with balanced Innovative Thinking also embrace processes and systems, are highly aware of patterns, are quick to learn, and have a sharp mind that is oriented toward seamless execution. They also embody the social and corporate finesse needed to mentor others and are comfortable leading in any situation.

Don't be daunted by a definition. It is very possible to find the middle ground. Some do it naturally, and some need to develop it. Either way, be the bear you want to be. In this case, tiny but mighty, and most importantly, *just right*.

ADRIAN AND MICHELLE: WORKING TOGETHER AFTER BRAIN COACHING

Adrian successfully completed our brain coaching program, and his underdeveloped Innovative Thinking improved dramatically as a result. Let's see how his day-to-day experience at work and his career prospects were enhanced:

- Despite his somewhat unapproachable nature, what I have not yet told you about Adrian is that once someone has fully explained a new initiative to him and he has bought into its benefits, he goes all in. Significantly, after the brain coaching, it was Adrian who came up with and drove a lot of innovative initiatives—which were also very pragmatic.
- In addition, once the wheels of a new initiative were in motion, his ability to leverage experience made him fantastic at thinking through the step-by-step implementation process to balance out his improved Innovative Thinking.
- Whereas his previously skeptical, "bah humbug" personality made him unapproachable, with his enhanced Innovative Thinking, he warmly and enthusiastically welcomed new ideas and was now very approachable.
- While Adrian was previously in a quite senior operations role, his prior underdeveloped Innovative Thinking

prevented his next career step. However, his enhanced Innovative Thinking rounded out his executive abilities and propelled him into an even more senior role as the head of a business unit.

- Adrian came to love and enjoy his newly developed flexibility, adaptability, and agility, while also wondering where these traits had been hiding throughout his career. He was more satisfied with his work, and now really enjoyed mentoring the younger executives, rather than his previous approach of snarling at them when they wanted to introduce new ideas. And funnily enough, the younger executives liked Adrian's "new and improved" leadership style.

After Michelle completed the Fluid Thinking Program, which included deliberate practice exercises to balance out her overdeveloped Innovative Thinking, she noticed some significant thinking, leadership, and behavioral changes, including:

- Despite Michelle's genuinely infectious personality, she struggled with corporate and social boundaries. While her peers mainly forgave her, it was not always forgotten. However, with her newly balanced Innovative Thinking, Michelle was now very consciously aware of unwritten corporate and social boundaries, and more appropriate and respectful in her dealings with work colleagues.
- Michelle was better able to anticipate, identify, and mitigate risks. In fact, she learned that risk analysis forced her brain to look at things from a different perspective, which usually led to even better innovative solutions, and ones that were significantly more practical.
- An enjoyable and unexpected side benefit of Michelle's newly balanced Innovative Thinking was that she was substantially more comfortable thinking about processes. And with her enhanced pattern recognition, she could learn new systems more easily, effectively, and efficiently.

- She also became increasingly comfortable with fully thinking through how her innovative initiatives would be implemented. And she was surprised by how much satisfaction she got from seeing her initiatives being executed, rather than leaving projects half-finished and jumping to the next exciting thing.

- While her social infringements and somewhat cavalier approach to risks and processes were previously stalling her professional growth, with her newly balanced Innovative Thinking, she was now seen as ready to be promoted. However, she enjoyed the marketing role so much that she chose to stay in the role for a while longer, but it was very comforting now to be seen as ready for promotion.

Are you wondering how Adrian and Michelle's relationship changed after they had both done the brain coaching program? As you can imagine, it became more harmonious, collaborative, and productive. The reason for this is that their Innovative Thinking was now optimized and balanced. This meant that Adrian was more open, adaptable, agile, and creative, and so they were both able to enjoy doing the "Innovative Thinking dance" together. In addition, Michelle was more grounded, practical, and risk aware, so she and Adrian could get on the same page quickly in creative initiatives, which were more targeted and easier to implement. Plus, Michelle was more respectful and appropriate when dealing with Adrian's team members.

KEY TAKEAWAYS

- Innovative Thinking corresponds to Stage Two of the Complex Problem-Solving Framework. It facilitates the ability to brainstorm and generate solutions that are highly creative, strategic, and pragmatic.

- When Innovative Thinking is underdeveloped, a person tends to be very inflexible and black-and-white in their thinking. People with lower Innovative Thinking find it difficult to adapt to change and generally dislike brainstorming sessions, as they find it very challenging to come up with genuinely innovative ideas.

- When Innovative Thinking is overdeveloped, a person tends to be very spontaneous and can generate many creative initiatives in no time flat. Unfortunately, their ideas are often not very practical. These individuals like to move on to the next idea rapidly, rather than thinking about the more boring (from their perspective) process of implementation.

- Underdeveloped and overdeveloped Innovative Thinking aren't entirely bad. Both imbalances have associated strengths and derailers. Ideally, Innovative Thinking needs to be balanced—neither overdeveloped nor underdeveloped. When your Innovative Thinking habit is *just right*, you are highly creative, visionary, agile, risk tolerant, and open to change, while also being quite pragmatic and practical, a quick learner, and very aware of social and corporate boundaries.

Chapter 9
CONCEPTUAL THINKING

"It is just human nature to take time to connect the dots. I know that. But I also know that there can be a day of reckoning when you wish you had connected the dots more quickly." —Al Gore

Pillar
Two

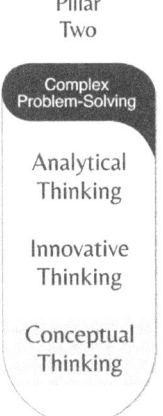

Complex Problem-Solving

Analytical Thinking

Innovative Thinking

Conceptual Thinking

Remember Jack Be Nimble from the nursery rhyme? We would all choose to be nimble like Jack, but sometimes nimbleness is not an option. When your Subconscious Thinking Habit of Conceptual Thinking is less efficient, it can feel as if you are running a race in which everyone else got a head start because they were able to connect the dots more quickly and insightfully. Not everyone struggles with this, but we have found that approximately one third of our clients need development in this area so they can keep up with their peers with ease. That said, it is essential to note that extremely high levels of Conceptual Thinking can also inadvertently hinder how you lead your team and your overall social leadership skills.

At its core, Conceptual Thinking is the ability to identify different categories and groupings of information, and then classify those disparate pieces of information into the appropriate categories or groups. As we will see in this chapter, Conceptual Thinking underpins the third and fourth stages of the Complex Problem-Solving process. Once you have defined the problem in Stage One (see Chapter 7) and brainstormed a multitude of potential solutions in Stage Two (see Chapter 8), you are ready to evaluate and prioritize your list of potential solutions (Stage Three), and then choose the one that has the highest likelihood of success (Stage Four).

A solid foundation in Conceptual Thinking helps us accurately determine what pieces of information fit together based on their common features, while also helping us determine where to place pieces of information that have entirely different features. It is the bedrock of how we grasp new content, connect the dots, and ultimately how nimble our thinking is and how quickly we can respond to new and unanticipated situations and questions.

Individuals with high conceptualization are typically big-picture thinkers who can quickly identify and evaluate issues, opportunities, and potential solutions. They are agile and rapidly connect the dots, allowing them to be confident in their decision-making process. They have developed optimal Conceptual Thinking, meaning they create well-formed concepts from smaller, disparate pieces of information. In contrast, high Analytical Thinking capability enables you to break down large, complex issues into smaller, bite-sized chunks swiftly. In many ways, Conceptual Thinking and Analytical Thinking are like two sides of the same coin, i.e., you use Analytical Thinking to chunk down information when defining complex problems, whereas you use Conceptual Thinking to chunk up information into well-formed concepts and solutions.

SUBCONSCIOUS THINKING HABIT MODEL FOR CONCEPTUAL THINKING

You need highly efficient Conceptual Thinking to be able to sort through the various solutions quickly and nimbly, before selecting the optimum one. Someone with high Conceptual Thinking ability can do this with relative ease, as the optimum solution tends to pop out from the rest.

By contrast, for someone with a lower level of Conceptual Thinking ability, this process can be quite torturous. Most of the solutions will appear to be quite viable to them, so their brain will find it very difficult to prioritize one solution above the rest.

Let's take a moment to pause and identify how the Subconscious Thinking Habit of Conceptual Thinking plays out when it is underdeveloped.

Cue: Your boss asks you to evaluate a range of solutions and identify which one optimally meets the solution criteria.

Routine: You subconsciously run your underdeveloped Conceptual Thinking routine.

Output: You find the process very difficult. It takes a long time to evaluate and prioritize the solutions. You also have lower levels of confidence in your recommendations.

However, when ideally developed, this habit makes you both nimble and quick, like Jack from the nursery rhyme. When confronted with the task of evaluating a list of possible solutions, you find that the best one practically picks itself.

THE SCIENCE BEHIND CONCEPTUAL THINKING

In 1955, *Harvard Business Review* published Robert Katz's article titled "Skills of an Effective Administrator." It was updated and republished in 1974.[ix] Katz's article is seen as a classic and is just as pertinent today as it was when first published. The article was one of the first to identify the importance of strong conceptual skills that underpin the Subconscious Thinking Habit of Conceptual Thinking. I think of it as a golden oldie, like a great hit on the music charts. It is a timeless piece of writing.

Katz proposed a model that encompasses the three crucial, yet very different, types of skills an administrator requires to be successful. Note that the word *administrator* would be equivalent to a manager or an executive in today's context. These skill sets are:

- **Technical Skills**—Katz identified that these skills require understanding and proficiency related to the methods, processes, procedures, and techniques needed for a particular specialty. Additionally, this specialized knowledge needs to be paired with analytical ability to use effectively the tools required for a specific role. These skills encompass what we commonly call the *subject-matter expertise* or *domain knowledge* needed to be proficient in a particular role—or, using my terminology, their Crystallized Knowledge.
- **Human Skills**—Katz identified these skills as the individual's capacity to work effectively within a group dynamic, as a team member, and to build an impactful and cooperative team when in a leadership role. (I refer to these as social leadership skills, which I cover in depth in Pillar Four: Social Leadership.)
- **Conceptual Skills**—Katz identified these skills as the individual's ability to see the organization holistically. It is the capacity to recognize the various parts of an organization, see how they depend on each other, and understand that the impact of change is never isolated. It is the power to visualize the connection between the enterprise and the industry. So, an executive has the ability to look wider and understand the links to the community and the economic, social, and political factors at play. It is the capacity to

know that the success of any decision relies on the quality of big-picture thinking and the quality of detailed execution.[lxi] In today's terminology, it's the ability to connect the dots quickly, effectively, and insightfully.

Katz was quite perceptive. He commented on thinking patterns related to executives and leaders. In his updated article from 1974, he made an interesting retrospective observation regarding *Conceptual Skills*. He asserted that Conceptual Skills are entirely dependent on specific ways of thinking. Katz believed these ways of thinking were learned early in life and difficult to change after adolescence—and that they were innate. This observation is similar to Piaget's theory regarding the development of foundational cognitive tools such as Conceptual Thinking and Analytical Thinking in children (see Chapter 1).

This golden oldie article is a classic, as Katz's observations were made before the concepts of brain plasticity and deliberate practice became well understood. Conscious and intentional efforts are needed to tap into the brain's plasticity to rewire and rewrite Subconscious Thinking Habits such as Analytical Thinking and Conceptual Thinking.

By now, I hope it is getting clearer why Conceptual Thinking is a big deal, and why it is such a vital Subconscious Thinking Habit to optimize. Both the ability to connect the dots and big-picture thinking are truly needed to go from being a player on the field to becoming an off-field coach in the game of Complex Problem-Solving.

STAGE THREE: EVALUATING SOLUTIONS

Recall from our discussion in Chapter 6 that we use Conceptual Thinking in the final two stages of Complex Problem-Solving. We are now at Stage Three, where we evaluate solutions (see Figure 17). This stage follows brainstorming, and it is when you compare the proposed ideas against the solution criteria you outlined when you defined the problem.

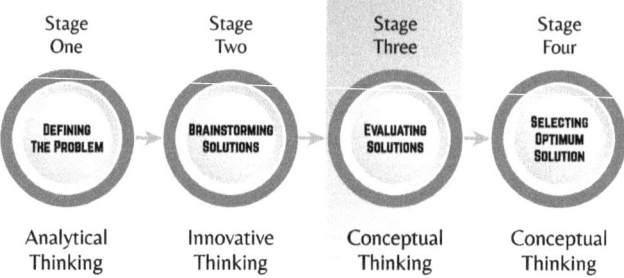

Figure 17. Complex Problem-Solving Stage Three: Evaluating Solutions

Individuals with higher Conceptual Thinking have relatively little trouble creating categories and sorting through the solutions. Their nimble minds are able to work quickly without getting fatigued when confronted with this task. However, when Conceptual Thinking is lower, this task becomes particularly difficult and time consuming. The brain struggles to chunk up and pull together smaller bits of information—typically resulting in a lack of confidence, indecisiveness, and high stress.

STAGE FOUR: SELECTING OPTIMUM SOLUTION

We are now in the fourth and final Complex Problem-Solving stage, which is to select the optimum solution from the handful of options that made the short list (see Figure 18).

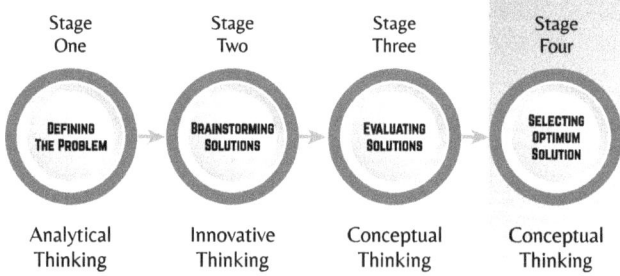

Figure 18. Complex Problem-Solving Stage Four:
Selecting Optimum Solution

When an individual has lower Conceptual Thinking, their brain has too many choices in the final selection stage. They are confronted with what seems like several great options, any of which could be chosen as the optimal solution from their perspective. Although the nominated solutions might be very different, they will all appear equally viable.

A person with lower Conceptual Thinking will struggle to get a clear signal as to which solution has the highest probability of success. They might try to connect the dots rationally. They might intuitively try to sense which one has the most strategic value. And they might even strain to compare each solution logically to the organizational goal and context. But because of their lower level of Conceptual Thinking, they will find it very challenging to discern the soundness of each solution. The person will have difficulty considering those big-picture perspectives, as none will readily come to mind.

Individuals who wrestle with challenges like this prefer to tackle Complex Problem-Solving in a team environment. For this reason, they are unlikely to get promoted to the most senior leadership position.

LEI: RIDING THE UNDERDEVELOPED CONCEPTUAL THINKING ROLLERCOASTER

Let me introduce you to Lei. He is the director of information technology at a manufacturing company. Lei is extremely diligent and always approaches his work with an attitude geared toward excellence. While he has many positive traits, Lei struggles in a few areas that compromise his overall performance. Specifically, his thinking speed seems to lag in comparison to that of his peers, as new ideas and concepts take him relatively longer to comprehend. When meetings or conversations are moving fast, he often feels a bit uncomfortable and left behind, always needing to play catch-up.

Lei's manager sees a lot of potential in him and is keen to see him grow personally and professionally. His manager has selected him to be part of an important committee. The committee's job is to analyze and review a product range that is losing market share. Their brief is to examine critically what is happening, brainstorm ideas, evaluate solutions, and ultimately deliver the optimum solution both in a report and as a presentation to the CEO and senior leadership team. His manager believes this is an excellent way for Lei to build rapport with his peers in other business units and develop his capacity to look at situations from a broader and more holistic perspective. Lei welcomes the opportunity with a smile; but on the inside, he feels a growing dread.

When you go on a rollercoaster ride and plunge down a big dip, your stomach drops. It can be terrifying, and that is how we find Lei feeling. Although he enjoys brainstorming, Lei's compromised ability to grasp new concepts quickly means he struggles significantly with tasks like evaluating solutions, writing reports, and presenting. Naturally, being assigned to a committee designed to do just that is an unwelcome thought for Lei. However, taking the assignment in stride, he decides to go in with a diligent attitude and take copious notes so he can review them later and get up to speed on his own time. He sits back and writes frantically as the committee zooms through analysis. Lei rarely asks any questions, not wanting to expose his lower conceptualization ability. When the meeting ends, Lei exhales a sigh of relief. He survived.

At the following meeting, his peers nominate him to write the report, as they were impressed by his diligent notetaking last time. Yet again, Lei's stomach drops. No one knows how hard report-writing is for him, nor how long it takes him. Connecting the dots, in general, is tricky terrain for Lei; but the idea of connecting them for the senior leadership team is an entirely different and very daunting task in his mind. Thankfully, the committee has done a great job of analyzing why the product range is losing market share, so Lei can pull all the information together nicely.

Having the problem clearly defined paves the way for brainstorming mode, which makes Lei more comfortable. Here, he shines. Because Lei's Innovative Thinking capability is highly developed, he offers the committee a multitude of new ideas and innovative solutions. He does so well that the committee agrees it's only fair that Lei lead the solution evaluation and recommendation process and present it to the CEO and senior leadership team. For Lei, this turn of events feels like being on a rollercoaster that won't stop. It slows for a minute and then, out of nowhere, comes another huge dip. His emotions are mixed. While he is delighted to be complimented so highly and trusted by his peers, he cannot ignore the anxiety swelling inside him, as he knows only too well that this could go very wrong.

Lei struggles to cull a list of ten solutions down to the three that the committee will review with him at the next meeting. He works long and hard, agonizing over what to prioritize, straining to figure out which solutions best match the identified criteria for a successful solution. Finally, he narrows down the list. Relief pours over him now that he has completed the task, as Lei had let some of his normal workload slip in the process. His typically messy desk is a bit of a disaster zone in the wake of trying to get everything perfect.

When the committee comes together again, they collectively evaluate the potential solutions. They also discuss the big-picture aspects and long-term strategic perspectives to ensure the solution they select aligns with the overarching organizational goals. Lei finds himself intrigued by these broader perspectives; a few of the what-if scenarios they discuss had never even crossed his mind. Collectively, they select a solution and reiterate that Lei should have the privilege of writing up the report and presenting their findings.

Valiantly, Lei presses on, ignoring his internal moans and groans. He knows how much he struggles with report writing. Their structure and layout are challenging for him and his writing requires heavy editing. More importantly, working out how to communicate ideas and concepts succinctly and clearly is a difficult process for him. Adding to the pressure is that, along with the report, he has been charged with the task of developing a presentation. Lei knows that presentations usually require him to think on his feet, and that is not his strong suit. He much prefers to stay in his lane, where his technical expertise never steers him wrong.

After agonizing over his project for days, Lei finally pulls together a first draft. The committee helps him edit the report and polish his presentation. Little do his colleagues know how much rework Lei has been shouldering, as the perfectionist in him demands that everything be just right.

In the days leading up to the presentation, Lei spends excessive time rehearsing and invests an inordinate amount of personal time in getting everything perfect. When the big day finally comes, Lei's presentation is mainly smooth sailing until halfway through, when the CEO interrupts with a question. The question takes Lei by surprise, as he has not rehearsed an answer to this seemingly random question. Again, his stomach drops, and he freezes like a deer in the headlights. Scrambling, he tries to answer, but he stumbles over his words and starts to confuse everyone. Thankfully, one of his fellow team members steps in and responds to the question. Pulling himself together, Lei continues with the presentation. With the help of his colleagues, every question is answered, even the ones Lei had not thought of in advance. Overall, everything goes surprisingly well. Relief floods over Lei when he finally gets off the rollercoaster.

Later that evening, while relaxing, he thinks over what he could have done or said differently. During this process of reflection, he is surprised by the great answers he is able to come up with now that the meeting is finished and the pressure was off. He chides himself for being unable to think on his feet during the presentation.

It was painfully evident to Lei that his brain seemed to have some uncontrollable delay switch, and he worried that the problem might be more obvious than he thought to his colleagues. After all, they had affectionately nicknamed him "Mr. Leave It with Me," as he often needed time to pause to reflect before getting back to someone. He needed more time than his business peers to think things through properly, and so he was always playing catch up. Unfortunately, he noticed that he was also less organized than his peers, with a very visibly cluttered desk. For Lei, everything just seemed to be a little bit harder and to take a little bit longer as compared to his peers, and this was something he sincerely wished he could change.

IMPACT OF LOWER CONCEPTUAL THINKING

Compromised, lower Conceptual Thinking comes with a few unwelcome side-effects beyond those we have already discussed. These side-effects keep people on the field and derail them from their dreams of becoming an off-field coach because next-level leaders need to have excellent Complex Problem-Solving skills and balanced Subconscious Thinking Habits.

As we saw earlier, Lei struggled with many derailers associated with lower Conceptual Thinking. For him, the process of evaluating the ten solutions the committee had proposed was like riding a rollercoaster, but not a fun one. It was the kind that throws your head into a spin as you fly upside down, go round and round, and creep up to great heights only to plummet down at top speed.

As Lei considered the pluses and minuses of the ten solutions, he became overwhelmed and was unable to decide where and how to start. The dots were so disconnected that it took him a long time to prioritize and evaluate each solution. Indeed, had he not been part of a committee that approached the project like a team sport, it is questionable whether he would have ever made a confident choice. He probably would have flip-flopped and second-guessed himself until the deadline, and maybe even long after it had passed.

When you're in a situation like this, your adrenal hormones are skyrocketing under pressure, and your anxiety further impairs your cognitive performance. This means your abilities to focus, use your working memory effectively, and solve problems are greatly reduced—precisely at the time when you need these capacities most. As we discussed in Pillar One: Controlling Attention, this is due to the negative impact of higher levels of stress on cognitive performance, as illustrated by the Yerkes-Dodson Law.[lxii]

Ideally, Lei would have naturally relied on his Conceptual Thinking to prioritize solutions. However, because his Conceptual Thinking was underdeveloped, every solution appeared equally important and equally likely to solve the problem. He found it difficult to group and categorize information quickly. So, it would have taken him a long time to create categories for high probability, moderate probability, and low probability of success, and then sort the data accordingly.

Below, we will look at the derailers associated with lower Conceptual Thinking and connect them back to Lei. As we examine them, notice any that are relatable. Do these traits remind you of a colleague, boss, friend, or maybe even yourself?

POOR PRIORITIZATION

Lower Conceptual Thinking can impact an individual's overall capacity to prioritize activities, not just solutions. It is challenging for them to identify which activity is most important, especially when facing the pressure of a deadline. Commonly, they suffer from squeaky wheel syndrome, where they allocate their attention relative to the noise that surrounds them—the more noise that something (or someone) makes, the more attention it receives, even if it isn't the highest priority. This is a particularly cumbersome trait when Focused Thinking (see Chapter 5) is lower, too.

Lei took a long time to think through issues, and that's why he had difficulty in readily prioritizing and categorizing the committee's solutions.

SLOWER LEARNING SPEED AND LOTS OF NOTES

Those with lower Conceptual Thinking often find company training programs, academic programs, and meetings challenging because a large amount of information needs to be absorbed and processed in real-time. When someone is slower at processing information, it can be confusing, as they can't grasp new concepts quickly enough in the moment to understand completely what is going on. An individual with lower Conceptual Thinking will compensate for this by taking copious notes to review later so they can fully grasp what was covered. This note-taking can be problematic when peers view it as diligence as in Lei's case, because then even more gets added to your workload.

DIFFICULTY CONNECTING THE DOTS

Individuals with lower conceptualization ability struggle to connect the dots and chunk up information. As we saw in Lei's case, it was hard for him to make sense of complex and disparate pieces of information. Though he might have understood each small piece of information, pulling them all together into well-formed strategic concepts was extremely difficult for him. Lei could not readily connect the dots.

INDECISIVENESS

Indecision is a hallmark of lower Conceptual Thinking. It is typical for those individuals to need more time to think through decisions. Additionally, when making decisions, they usually experience a lot of internal second-guessing and confusion, as they lack confidence in their decision making. Luckily for Lei, he had a team environment and could leverage the abilities of his peers with higher Conceptual Thinking.

EVERYTHING TAKES LONGER

Tasks take appreciably longer when Conceptual Thinking is underdeveloped. Individuals find their response time is significantly longer than that of their colleagues. They require more time when responding to complex emails or generating a complex report. Mentally organizing all the pieces of information in their head takes far longer, which delays writing. Once written, significant rework and editing are needed to create the necessary structure and flow.

Remember Lei's favorite phrase? "Leave it with me" is a fallback position; it allows you to buy some time to understand a situation fully before making decisions. This can become a difficult trait for executives because the number of decisions requiring answers can build up quickly, and then the executive becomes a bottleneck and a roadblock to productivity.

UNCLEAR COMMUNICATION, PARTICULARLY WHEN DELEGATING

Individuals navigating lower Conceptual Thinking often get confused or struggle to communicate clearly to their managers, peers, and teams. Communication can be jumbled, disorganized, lacking in clarity, and lengthy, often leaving others confused. Unfortunately, less efficient Conceptual Thinking also impacts how individuals delegate, as the lack of clarity can lead to frequent interruptions from team members seeking ongoing clarification regarding their delegated tasks.

As we discussed in Chapter 7, lower Analytical Thinking inhibits the ability to break down a task, which hinders the ability to explain the various components of a delegated task clearly. However, lower

Conceptual Thinking also creates issues with delegation, as people with lower Conceptual Thinking tend to speak in generalized terms and answer questions indirectly. Their language is often fluffy and imprecise when delegating tasks. Plus, their communication can be very convoluted and, therefore, difficult to parse.

SLOWER AT THINKING ON YOUR FEET

People with lower conceptualization have difficulty thinking on their feet, which makes it extremely challenging to think coherently under pressure during a presentation or a meeting. If they are asked a hard question that they hadn't been expecting, they will find it arduous to come up with an erudite answer in the moment. Rather than answering the question directly, they will waffle on, leaving their colleagues puzzled and confused. Lei experienced this when the CEO asked a question he had not prepared for—his mind froze, and he couldn't produce an appropriate answer.

Lower Conceptual Thinking also leads to overthinking. Those who struggle with lower conceptualization frequently find themselves coming up with the perfect answer hours after a meeting has ended and the opportunity has long passed.

PERFECTIONIST TRAITS

When your Conceptual Thinking is underdeveloped, it's easy to fall into the trap of thinking everything has to be done right. Lei and individuals like him take a long time to pull everything together. For them, confidence is only found through rework, rehearsal, and knowing everything perfectly. It is a nasty trap, as in the business world it is uncommon for things to go exactly according to plan. So, being thrown off by changes can be a major hindrance.

CLUTTERED WORKSPACE AND POOR ORGANIZATION OF INFORMATION

This clutter and lack of organization comes back to the underlying Conceptual Thinking capability (i.e., how individuals categorize and classify information). Lei's mind was cluttered, and so was his physical space, his desk, and the way he organized his information. Lei, like many others, struggled to categorize information systematically, making it consistently challenging to locate information quickly and create order in his workspace.

UNEXPECTED PROBLEM ASSOCIATED WITH HIGH CONCEPTUAL THINKING

Let's go back to Jack Be Nimble for a moment. What if you are Jack, and you are too nimble and too quick for others to keep up with you? When Conceptual Thinking is extremely high, it can significantly impact social leadership skills. Again, we are returning to the principle of brain balance and how it is essential to get off the field to successfully coach your team. A coach is only as good as their capability to lead their team's thinking and actions in order to win.

Unfortunately, coaches and executives with very high Conceptual Thinking get frustrated when team members with lower Conceptual Thinking can't keep up. The main reason for this is because individuals with very high Conceptual Thinking process information much faster than others. So, it is common for very high conceptualizers to leave their teams behind, inadvertently assuming that everyone is on the same page when, unfortunately, they often aren't. This creates tension when you are managing a team. This frustration can inadvertently show up as sarcasm or contempt for those who cannot get on the same page as quickly as the coach or executive would like. When this happens, the person can be unaware that they are speaking to others in a derisive manner.

There's no doubt that extremely high Conceptual Thinking has a few perks, such as a fast learning speed, big-picture vision, confident decision-making, ease of prioritization, and a knack for thinking on your feet. But these desirable traits can also have a cost. Very high Conceptual Thinking can create glitches in your social leadership ability if you're unaware. Typically, the result is a disconnect between the brief given and the work that is submitted.

Additionally, people with very high Conceptual Thinking don't suffer fools gladly and are generally impatient with those who have lower Conceptual Thinking capability. Adding insult to injury, these people often finish other people's sentences and can come across as arrogant and rude. When conversations or meetings are going too slowly, it is incredibly frustrating and irritating for them. To compensate, they try to speed things up, which further alienates their colleagues and strains relationships.

Very high conceptualizers often come across as the smartest people in the room. However, it is not the difference of intellect that is frustrating to them, but the relative difference in the brain information processing speed of others. To bring balance to their leadership style, they need to slow down their interactions with slower conceptualizers, so they can bring people along on the journey with them, instead of leaving them behind. If this social leadership aspect is not addressed appropriately, it becomes a career limitation for very high conceptualizers who cannot find a way to communicate with others effectively and connect with people so that they willingly follow. If a better balance is not developed, it can be very polarizing to their peers and team members. If you stand on the "mountain top" and see wonderful opportunities while your team members are stuck in the "valley" below, it generates feelings of confusion instead of fellowship.

Understanding your Subconscious Thinking Habits is the first step in changing them.

Where do you see yourself on the spectrum? Did you chuckle and say, "Oops, that's me!" Have you sneakily connected the dots and seen this behavior in your colleagues or team members? Either way, there is no wrong answer because understanding your Subconscious Thinking Habits is the first step in changing them.

BENEFITS OF HIGHLY DEVELOPED CONCEPTUAL THINKING

When Conceptual Thinking is high, we find it to be very complementary to Analytical Thinking, assuming the latter is also well-developed and is a key component of creating brain balance. This balance is the green zone where the brain easily assesses the solutions relative to the purpose, contextual risks, benefits, etc. This allows you to connect short- and long-term issues effectively relative to your organization's strategies and goals while also having a broad enough perspective to identify which issues are inside and outside of your control.

When you have developed an appropriate balance of Analytical Thinking, Innovative Thinking, and Conceptual Thinking, you find that those much-coveted eureka moments arise spontaneously. Complex problems become less daunting and they are a lot easier to solve.

LEI: ORGANIZED AND DECISIVE AFTER BRAIN COACHING

After Lei completed the Fluid Thinking Program, which included undertaking the associated deliberate practice exercises to improve his Conceptual Thinking, he observed many positive thinking, leadership, and behavioral changes, including:

- Improved ability to evaluate quickly potential solutions to complex problems.
- Enhanced capability to prioritize and short-list the solutions having the highest probability of solving a complex problem, and the ability to select the optimum solution with ease.
- Faster information processing in the moment, particularly in meetings, where he finds he can stay present during the discussion. And because he no longer furiously takes notes, he can generate and share many fresh ideas during meetings.

- Quicker and better at connecting the dots in real-time, rather than having to reflect on a problem only to come up with great ideas many hours later, long after the opportunity to share them has passed.
- Considerably clearer and more succinct at communication and delegation as a result of his newfound abilities to create mental models rapidly and map out what he wants to communicate in advance. These abilities also make it easier for him to write reports and develop presentations more quickly and with considerably less stress.
- Drastically less perfectionism, which saves a significant amount of time because he is better at identifying when he has reached the point of diminishing returns. Plus, he is much quicker and more confident in his decision-making.
- Significantly less rework and confusion. Because he can think more efficiently, communicate more clearly, and delegate more effectively, he no longer takes a trial-and-error approach.

KEY TAKEAWAYS

- We use Conceptual Thinking in Stages Three and Four of the Complex Problem-Solving Framework.
- People with lower Conceptual Thinking are typically slower learners with poorer communication and organization skills. They struggle with tasks that require prioritizing and connecting the dots. Because of their lower efficiency at conceptualizing, they have difficulty thinking under pressure and when confronted with unanticipated situations. They can also struggle with perfectionism.
- People with higher Conceptual Thinking are generally fast learners, prefer to focus on big-picture issues, are confident decision makers, prioritize easily, and are comfortable thinking on their feet under pressure.

- When your Conceptual Thinking is well developed, you find it easy to evaluate solutions and choose the one that has the highest probability of success.
- Although people with high Conceptual Thinking enjoy many advantages, when this Subconscious Thinking Habit is excessively high, it can undermine social leadership ability, as the person can inadvertently come across as arrogant and disdainful. Extremely high conceptualizers rarely suffer fools gladly.

PART IV

PILLAR THREE

STRATEGY, PLANNING, AND EXECUTION

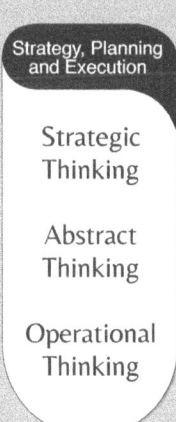

Pillar
Three

Strategy, Planning
and Execution

Strategic
Thinking

Abstract
Thinking

Operational
Thinking

Chapter 10

INTRODUCTION TO STRATEGY, PLANNING, AND EXECUTION

"Strategy without execution is a daydream.
Execution without strategy is a nightmare.
Either without talent simply doesn't exist."
—*Adapted from a Japanese proverb*

In Part III of this book, we took a detailed look at the process of effectively defining a problem, brainstorming multiple solutions, and then selecting the optimum solution. And so, we saw that Pillar Two: Complex Problem-Solving is all about determining what needs to be done to address a problem.

Now that we know *what* we're going to do, the focus shifts to *how* we will optimally implement our chosen solution. This is the process of strategic thinking. Pillar Three addresses how our brains strategize, plan, and ultimately execute solutions to achieve the desired outcome.

Pillar Three: Strategy, Planning, and Execution comprises the three Subconscious Thinking Habits in Figure 19.

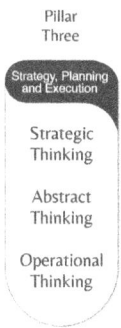

Figure 19. Pillar Three: Strategy, Planning, and Execution

Below is a description of each Subconscious Thinking Habit:

- **Strategic Thinking** is used to formulate a strategy for how we will accomplish the desired outcome and create a clear path forward, particularly when navigating through uncharted waters.
- **Abstract Thinking** is needed to develop a step-by-step plan for how to implement our chosen strategy. This plan includes determining what tasks need to be done, as well as the sequencing of the tasks and their associated timelines. It also includes deciding which tasks will be delegated to which team members.
- **Operational Thinking** enables each team member to determine how they will pragmatically execute their delegated task, keeping in mind that tasks need to be implemented collaboratively and in alignment with the overall strategy.

BUILDING BRIDGES

I understand all this might sound a bit too theoretical, so let's look at a concrete example of these three Subconscious Thinking Habits in action. Imagine how they would come into play if you were building a bridge over water. First, you would use your Strategic Thinking to create the strategic approach for designing the bridge. Second, you would rely on your Abstract Thinking to develop the high-level plan and timeline for building the bridge. And finally, you would employ your Operational Thinking capability to execute the strategy and plan, pragmatically constructing a sturdy bridge that will ultimately enable people to get across the water.

It is all relatively simple when you package it as a real-life example. Still, the interaction between these Subconscious Thinking Habits can be complex, as there needs to be tight integration among three very different thinking styles. Additionally, what makes this combination of thinking capabilities difficult is the need for high competency in all three areas to be effective.

Understandably, when you are building a physical structure like a bridge, you have a team to whom clearly defined tasks and timelines have been delegated. However, in business, these lines of separation between tasks and team members are not always so obvious. This issue is further complicated when the Subconscious Thinking Habits associated with Strategy, Planning, and Execution are unbalanced.

At enigmaFIT, we have found most of our clients have overdeveloped Operational Thinking. When extremely high Operational Thinking is combined with lower levels of Strategic Thinking and Abstract Thinking, the result is a person who is too hands on. Such leaders are not comfortable stepping back and undertaking the strategizing and planning processes. Instead, they leap into action.

Imagine how ineffective it would be for the captain of a ship to spend most of their time in the engine room instead of up on the ship's bridge, which is where they need to be to lead the crew and navigate the ship so it can get to the destination safely and on time. If the captain were constantly running to the engine room to fix problems instead of sending a crew member below deck to handle them, then no one would be steering the ship. Regardless of whether you are overseeing the construction of a physical bridge or navigating a metaphorical ship in business, you require a clear direction and strategy—along with associated plans and timelines and effective communication and delegation.

Possibly the best example of this is an orchestra conductor, who is responsible for the sound and quality of the music produced—yet the conductor doesn't play a single note. The conductor's desired outcome is to bring the score to life through every member of the orchestra. To achieve this, conductors must leverage their skills to lead, guide, and conduct the musicians to provide an exceptional music experience for their audience. Imagine how much strategizing and planning is involved to ensure the best possible execution and performance.

INTRODUCTION TO THE 4S STRATEGY METHODOLOGY

Strategy is the critical component in creating success. Because the process of Strategy, Planning, and Execution can be challenging, we have developed the 4S Strategy Methodology to describe it. Our methodology is illustrated in Figure 20.

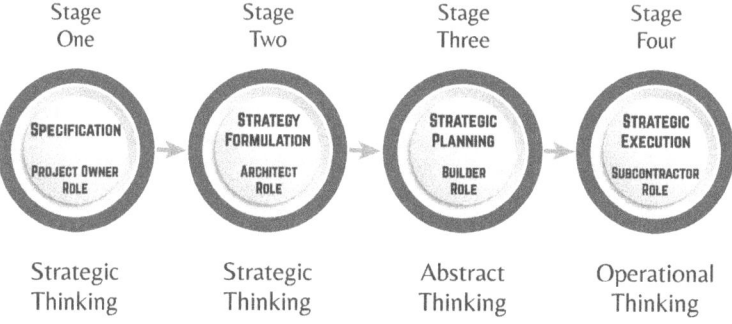

Figure 20. 4S Strategy Methodology

A brief overview of the four steps in the 4S Strategy Methodology follows. I will cover each one in more depth in the next three chapters.

1. **Specification**. First, you must clearly define and specify the outcome you desire to achieve. This step relies on Strategic Thinking.

2. **Strategy Formulation**. Next, you formulate a clear strategic path for how you will deliver the desired outcome. This also relies on Strategic Thinking.

3. **Strategic Planning**. In this step, you develop a high-level plan for implementing the key modules of the strategy. This includes addressing the order in which the various modules of the strategy are to be completed and a plan for delegating each module to the appropriate person. The habit of Abstract Thinking underpins Strategic Planning.

4. **Strategic Execution**. Finally, each team member creates a detailed plan for the practical execution of their delegated

module or smaller task. This step depends on Operational Thinking.

Individuals engage with the strategic process differently due to their varying levels of competency in the Subconscious Thinking Habits in Pillar Three. This is why it can be so challenging to strategize, plan, and execute successfully.

THE FOUR STRATEGIC ROLES

As you can see in Figure 20 above, each stage of the 4S Strategy Methodology is associated with a unique role or "hat." They are the Project Owner, Architect, Builder, and Subcontractor, respectively. In subsequent chapters, I will use the analogy of building a home to explore the 4S Strategy Methodology. As many steps take place between deciding to build a home and moving in, you need to take a multi-dimensional strategic approach to achieve your desired outcome. First, I will describe these four strategic roles in the context of our home-building analogy, and then I will explain how they apply to business-related initiatives.

KEY TAKEAWAYS

- Pillar Three: Strategy, Planning, and Execution comprises the Subconscious Thinking Habits of Strategic Thinking, Abstract Thinking, and Operational Thinking.
- Well-developed Strategic Thinking enables you to create a clear specification for the desired outcome, formulate a solid strategy, and pave a clear path forward to deliver the desired outcome.
- You rely on Abstract Thinking to develop a high-level implementation plan, which includes determining what modules and tasks need to be done when, and by whom.

- You use Operational Thinking to develop a pragmatic and detailed implementation plan for executing your assigned module or task(s).
- The 4S Strategy Methodology serves as a model for the Strategy, Planning, and Execution process. It includes four steps: Specification, Strategy Formulation, Strategic Planning, and Strategic Execution. Each of these steps is associated with a unique role or hat.
- It can be very challenging to strategize, plan, and execute initiatives successfully because individuals have varying levels of competency in the three Subconscious Thinking Habits associated with these functions.

Chapter 11
STRATEGIC THINKING

"Strategy is a style of thinking, a conscious and deliberate process, an intensive implementation system, the science of insuring future success." —Pete Johnson, American jazz pianist (1904–1967)

Pillar
Three

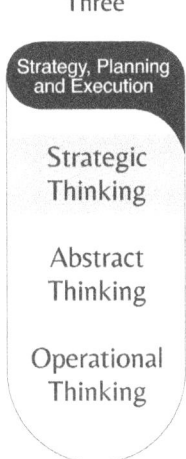

Strategy, Planning and Execution

Strategic Thinking

Abstract Thinking

Operational Thinking

Strategy and success go together like a hot cup of coffee and a freshly baked muffin. However, you need to know what strategic thinking is and how to apply it in order to achieve success.

It is essential not to confuse corporate strategy with personal Strategic Thinking. Many educational institutions teach corporate strategy theory. Once you learn it, it becomes part of your subject-matter expertise (i.e., Crystallized Knowledge). However, that doesn't necessarily mean you can apply that learning to develop an innovative strategy to address an issue you have never encountered before—this is the domain of Fluid Thinking. Knowledge alone is not enough to create the strategic behaviors needed. That's where the Subconscious Thinking Habit of Strategic Thinking comes in.

Knowing what to do is different from knowing how to do it.

Many executives have a solid understanding of corporate strategy; however, to be truly successful, they must also develop their Subconscious Thinking Habit of Strategic Thinking. That's because knowing *what* to do is different from knowing *how* to do it. Strategic Thinking is the ability to apply your existing knowledge to a completely new and different situation that's unlike any you have faced in the past.

The ability to think strategically continues to be a highly coveted skill in the corporate world. Employers regularly screen for it during job interviews, and it is a non-negotiable skill for senior executives and C-suite roles. In his *Harvard Business Review* article titled "Hiring: 6 Ways to Screen Job Candidates for Strategic Thinking," John Sullivan states, "In a 2013 Management Research Group survey, when executives were asked to select the leadership behaviors that were most critical to their organizations' future success, 97 percent of the time they chose being strategic."[lxiii] That is a very salient statistic, as it captures the necessity for strategic thinkers and shows that senior executives view strategic thinking as an essential capability to achieve success.

THE ROLE OF STRATEGIC THINKING IN 4S STRATEGY METHODOLOGY

In Chapter 10, I introduced the 4S Strategy Methodology, which breaks the strategic thinking process down into four discrete stages. As the Subconscious Thinking Habit of Strategic Thinking underpins the first two stages of our methodology, this chapter will cover both of these in depth:

	Role (Hat)	Goal
Stage One: Specification	Project Owner	Defining the desired outcome
Stage Two: Strategy Formulation	Architect	Deciding on the approach or design needed in order to deliver the desired outcome

To help you gain a deeper understanding of how your Strategic Thinking habit works, we will return to our analogy of building a home, and I will ask you to imagine yourself in each of the above roles. Ready? Okay then, put on your Project Owner hat, and let's get started.

4S STRATEGY METHODOLOGY: STAGE ONE—SPECIFICATION (PROJECT OWNER ROLE)

Congratulations, you have just bought a lovely level piece of land to build your dream home. Now, it's time to begin thinking about the Specification for your new home (see Figure 21). In this scenario, let's assume you already have a trusted Architect, Builder, and Subcontractors available to bring your vision to life.

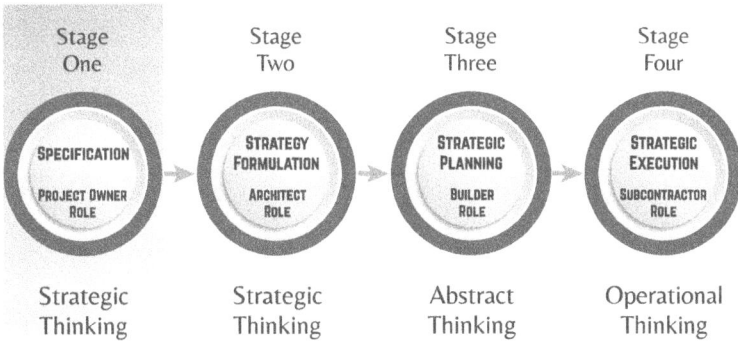

Figure 21. 4S Strategy Methodology: Stage One—Specification (Project Owner Role)

Before you can start developing the land, you need to pause and get clarity regarding your desired outcome for your dream home. You need to think through details such as the number of bedrooms and bathrooms, the design and location of living and dining areas, storage options, the size of your garage, etc. Do you want an outdoor space for entertaining? Should your home have an open living space or possibly multiple living spaces? You must consider every aspect before you can fully understand what you want in your dream home.

Once you have a clear vision for your dream home firmly in mind, you meet with your Architect. Together, you review every detail. After the briefing, the Architect designs your new home and comes back to show you the plans. Immediately, you see a problem. Although the multiple living zones and open living space on the ground floor are laid out exactly as you envisioned, the four bedrooms you asked for are all located on the second floor. Sheepishly, you tell your Architect that one bedroom needs to be downstairs to accommodate an elderly relative who visits from time to time and uses a wheelchair. The Architect processes this new information, internally frustrated because not knowing this detail in advance has wasted time and created additional work that could have been avoided. Now, they have to go back to the drawing board, as the home needs to be redesigned based on this new piece of information.

So, who was at fault here? Was it you as the homeowner (Project Owner) because you didn't specify what you needed with enough clarity? Or was it the Architect because they didn't ask enough questions? It is irrelevant because no matter where you assign blame, the core problem is the lack of specific, clear, and mutually agreed-upon specifications, which resulted in a large and unnecessary amount of rework. Unfortunately for both parties, this will cost time and money and cause emotional frustration.

WHY THE SPECIFICATION DOCUMENT IS SO IMPORTANT IN BUSINESS

Put your Project Owner hat down, and let's look at how the lessons learned as a homeowner impact day-to-day business. Often, executives and teams don't pause to think through thoroughly a strategy's desired outcome. Once they decide on the optimum solution to a problem or opportunity, they jump straight into execution mode. This fire-aim-ready approach misses the mark. If you gloss over the documentation of the Specification, or bypass it altogether, you can be virtually certain that significant rework will be required later. Rushing is a common mistake.

Documenting the Specification is extremely important. It forces your brain to create a clear and precise vision for the project, and everyone on the team will receive a consistent version of it. In contrast, if you have only a fuzzy vision of the project and shoot from the hip, you might verbalize your vision inconsistently, as you will probably explain it a bit differently each time. A written Specification document provides an opportunity for your colleagues and team to reflect on the project, ask clarifying questions, and develop an agreed-upon final Specification with much higher buy-in and group ownership.

4S STRATEGY METHODOLOGY: STAGE TWO— STRATEGY FORMULATION (ARCHITECT ROLE)

Let's return to our dream home analogy for a moment. This time, imagine you are wearing the Architect hat. Now that you know the homeowner's desired outcome, it's time to decide on your approach.

The Architect role corresponds to the Strategy Formulation stage of the 4S Strategy Methodology (see Figure 22). As the Architect, it is your job to use your Strategic Thinking to bring this home to life by creating a mental model of it before it can be constructed. Again, you need to pause and think through the different parts of the home and how everything will be connected in the floor plan. You need to assess the space and the placement of rooms so the home will flow seamlessly. Additionally, you need to anticipate any risks in the building process and proactively mitigate them.

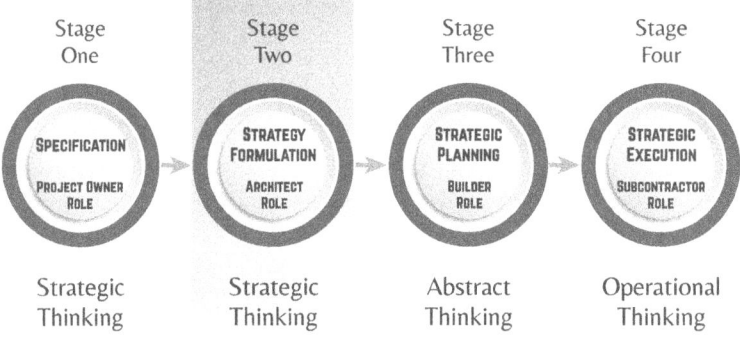

*Figure 22. 4S Strategy Methodology: Stage Two—
Strategy Formulation (Architect Role)*

Once you decide on an approach, you will create a strategic framework that will support your ability to communicate your design clearly to the homeowner (who is the Project Owner in our analogy) and also to provide clarity to the Builder. Your strategic framework and design will be used together as the road map for building the home.

I think we could all relate to the frustration the Architect would have felt when they were excitingly communicating their design and strategic framework to the homeowner for the first time, only to be sheepishly told about the elderly relative who stays occasionally. We can imagine the Architect thinking something like, "I wish you would have told me that during the briefing process rather than now, because a large amount of my time has been wasted and this will take considerable rework, which will delay the project." This is why it is so important for the Project Owner to think through their vision clearly and develop the written Specification document before engaging with the Architect.

THE VALUE OF STRATEGY FORMULATION IN BUSINESS

In business, the role of the Architect is daunting to most people because it requires a very high level of Strategic Thinking. Many leaders find the idea of stepping back to think through a strategic approach less comfortable than taking action, even when that action might be counterproductive to delivering a successful outcome.

Through our scientifically designed test that evaluates the effectiveness and efficiency of all ten Subconscious Thinking Habits, we have found that executives with low to moderate Strategic Thinking capability typically also have overdeveloped Operational Thinking. (As you will see in Chapter 13, the latter results in an excessively hands-on approach.) Leaders who possess this unbalanced combination are more comfortable with an *ad hoc*, plan-as-you-go approach because that's the way their brain works. But when they do not first pause to create a strategic framework, they struggle to communicate the path forward clearly and succinctly to their team members. In a day-to-day business environment, this shortcoming means that leaders too often get distracted by minor problems and try to micromanage all execution elements. While they understand that creating a road map would highlight risks and minimize rework, they find the task of creating a roadmap difficult and time consuming.

Leaders who struggle with Strategy Formulation tend to jump into action and work things out on the fly. In their minds, creating road maps and communicating key steps is a waste of time—precious time they could be using to get the job done. They expect their teams to be able to take an idea and "just run with it." Consequently, their teams often feel unguided. Lacking clear direction, team members continually ask for additional clarity so they can execute their tasks. This ongoing barrage of questions tends to frustrate leaders with underdeveloped Strategic Thinking capability. Because they do not understand why everyone is so confused, they assume their teams are overthinking things and unwilling to roll up their sleeves and get to work.

It is this mindset that creates a career ceiling for people with lower Strategic Thinking. Their roadblock is their inability to specify the desired outcome and formulate a strategic path forward for themselves and their teams. As individuals' careers progress, their success increasingly relies on their teams' capacity to execute their strategies. They need to leverage their teams by pausing and engaging with the first two stages of the 4S Strategy Methodology. Without these components, a proper plan cannot be developed, let alone executed. To put it simply in the context of our home-building analogy, until your Strategic Thinking capability is enhanced, the plot of land will never have a structurally sound home built on it.

SUBCONSCIOUS THINKING HABIT MODEL FOR STRATEGIC THINKING

When your Strategic Thinking is optimally developed, it is much easier to think through your desired outcome and create the initial project Specification. And because you find Strategy Formulation simpler and quicker, you can create a clear road map to help your team invest in the strategy. Also, you can communicate the strategic road map in a more coherent way, creating the buy-in that is essential to the successful execution of the strategy.

Here is an example of how an underdeveloped Strategic Thinking Habit plays out in business:

Cue: You need to develop a strategy in response to a new opportunity for your organization.

Routine: You subconsciously run your underdeveloped Strategic Thinking routine.

Output: You find it difficult to specify and define the opportunity and have trouble formulating a strategy to optimize the opportunity. While you may have a vague strategy in mind, you have difficulty communicating details to your team.

THE SCIENCE BEHIND STRATEGIC THINKING

Our clients consistently report that their Strategic Thinking abilities improve significantly after undertaking our Fluid Thinking program. We know the Subconscious Thinking Habits associated with Strategy, Planning, and Execution can be developed because we assess our clients' Strategic Thinking, Abstract Thinking, and Operational Thinking capabilities both before and after brain coaching. We often observe dramatic improvements in the test scores of those who have completed our program, and their ability to apply Strategic Thinking improves as well.

Additionally, we draw confidence from Michael D. Watkins. In his *Harvard Business Review* article titled "How to Think Strategically," he states:

> "Are great strategic thinkers born or made? The answer turns out to be 'yes.' Yes, individuals sit somewhere on the spectrum of innate talent, and yes, you can develop that talent."[lxiv]

Watkins refers to *cognitive reshaping*, which he describes as a process of repeated mental exercises that cultivate and create new mental habits. From a cognitive science perspective, I would add that it is vital to tap into the brain's inherent neuroplasticity through deliberate practice to improve the Subconscious Thinking Habit of Strategic Thinking.

THE KEY DIFFERENCE BETWEEN STRATEGY AND PLANNING

Many people confuse and conflate strategy formulation with strategic planning; they are not the same thing. While both skills are complementary, they require vastly different thinking styles, so clarifying the difference is a vital piece of the puzzle. Within the context of our 4S Strategy Methodology, Strategy Formulation is underpinned by Strategic Thinking, which is our current focus; however, Strategic Planning is underpinned by Abstract Thinking, which we will explore in Chapter 12.

Professor Henry Mintzberg has written extensively on the topics of strategy formulation and strategic planning. In his influential article, "The Fall and Rise of Strategic Planning," he says, "Planning cannot generate strategies. But given viable strategies, it can program them, make them operational."[lxv] Importantly, he compares and contrasts strategic thinking and strategic planning as follows:

> "Planning has always been about analysis—breaking down the goal or set of intentions into steps, formalizing those steps so that they can be implemented almost automatically, and articulating the anticipated consequences or results of each step ... Strategic thinking, in contrast, is about synthesis. It involves intuition and creativity."

This thinking is synergistic with my perspective, as it reinforces that the Subconscious Thinking Habit of Strategic Thinking is big-picture oriented and considerably more holistic, complex, and integrated than planning.

If leaders struggle to infuse their strategies with energy, the vital momentum needed to create success is lost. Insightfully, Mintzberg asserts that human beings sometimes simply stop thinking. A simple but slightly confronting insight, as I am sure we can all relate to switching off mentally when we get caught in the hustle and bustle. However, running on autopilot can have costly effects on professional growth.

THE IMPORTANCE OF STRATEGIC THINKING IN BUSINESS

Although the ability to think strategically is in high demand, it can be challenging to capture what it looks like in an everyday context. According to John Sullivan, Ph.D., who is a professor of management at San Francisco State University and an internationally known HR thought-leader, strategic thinkers add value in the following ways:

- Are forward-looking
- Take a big-picture perspective
- Are externally focused
- Have a global view[lxvi]

In essence, strategic thinkers help organizations prepare for the future through their capacity to see opportunities and mitigate risks, while also being able to identify emerging trends by leveraging global awareness. Intriguingly, Sullivan's definition of strategic thinking not only leverages the Subconscious Thinking Habit of Strategic Thinking but also considers other habits such as Focused Thinking (see Chapter 5), Conceptual Thinking (Chapter 9), Abstract Thinking (Chapter 12), and Intuitive Thinking (Chapter 17). Understanding how everything connects helps clarify why strategic thinking is so essential for success.

SEEING FROM A BROADER PERSPECTIVE

The benefits of highly developed Strategic Thinking are perhaps best summarized by Henry Mintzberg. His blog article titled "Strategic Thinking as 'Seeing,'" focuses on the complex nature of strategic thinking and how it comprises different forms of "seeing." Mintzberg states, "Most people would agree that strategic thinking means seeing ahead."[lxvii] However, Mintzberg views strategic thinking from a much broader perspective. In his article, he elegantly portrays many aspects of seeing, noting the role of each in optimized strategic thinking:

- *Seeing ahead* is when we identify and foresee what is to come next instead of simply extrapolating trends; thus, our frameworks are future-focused.
- *Seeing behind* means that to capture the future fully, we must leverage the lessons from the past and avoid unnecessarily reinventing the wheel.
- *Seeing above* is to see the big picture, as if you were in a helicopter hovering over a large forest.
- *Seeing below* is to see the value in the details. It's like getting out of the helicopter and walking through the forest to experience what is going on at the coalface.
- *Seeing beside* is to be dissatisfied with conventional wisdom, to seek different perspectives, and to leverage lateral thinking to pursue organizational success.
- *Seeing beyond* is where the creative meets the pragmatic; it is using innovative thinking to generate new and fresh ideas that are contextually relevant.
- *Seeing it through* means recognizing that great strategies are useless if they are never executed, which is why strategic thinkers see things through.

In the context of Fluid Thinking, executives with well-developed Strategic Thinking engage naturally with these styles of seeing. This capability makes them highly competent at the Specification and Strategy Formulation stages of the 4S Strategy Methodology.

AM I COMING THROUGH LOUD AND CLEAR?

Interestingly, we have found through our testing that individuals with lower Strategic Thinking also struggle to communicate clearly and succinctly. They typically speak in a stream of thought bubbles, delivering a lot of information, but in a less structured way. This delivery style is linked to the way their brain thinks and processes information. For example, although leaders with lower Strategic Thinking might understand the individual modules of a concept, they often struggle to communicate them in the correct sequence. While they will cover all the modules, they frequently introduce them in random order—thus A, B, C, and D might become C, A, D, and B. Arguably, all the key data is there, but the sequencing of it derails the team, making it difficult to understand what their leader is trying to explain. At the same time, the leader can feel as though no one is listening to them.

In my experience, good communication is a three-stage process:

1. **Get clarity first**. Get your ideas clear in your own mind before you start communicating them.
2. **Find your flow**. Mentally work out the sequence of what you want to communicate and how to communicate it effectively before you speak or write.
3. **Communicate clearly**. Deliver the communication clearly and succinctly.

Good communication relies on higher levels of Strategic Thinking capability; without it, working out the optimal sequence of communication can be a stumbling block. Regrettably, those who struggle with this issue often communicate important topics on the fly, which leads to misunderstandings and can make it impossible for their teams to execute their manager's strategy effectively.

OPHELIA: STRATEGIC THINKING GONE AWRY

Ophelia is Services Director at a major medical institution. She is responsible for all operational matters, along with compliance, governance, and management of medical staff. Disciplined, hardworking, and highly organized, Ophelia has a reputation for running her organization like a Swiss watch. She is known as Ms. Fix It, as there seems to be no problem she cannot solve. Often, Ophelia is called upon to drive unpopular, albeit necessary, changes. Indeed, since joining the organization, she has implemented significant changes, which have resulted in reduced costs and superior resource allocation.

Ophelia's direct and somewhat abrasive approach is sometimes off-putting to her colleagues. Her brusque communication style creates friction, as she leads with strength to ensure compliance, often alienating others in the process.

Despite these challenges, Ophelia has an impressive reputation for delivering results within budget. Besides being a qualified medical doctor, she has an MBA from an Ivy League university. Ophelia always meets her key performance indicators and believes her many strengths position her well for a promotion.

When the role of Senior Director opens up within her organization, she sets up an appointment with Mark, her CEO, hoping to get his input and endorsement for the role. However, the conversation does not go as expected. During the meeting, Mark explains that while the organization values Ophelia greatly and views her as a crucial operational asset, he has concerns about her strategic thinking capacity. Mark highlights that applicants require proven ability in this area, as strategic thinking is a critical skill for the Senior Director role.

Ophelia is stunned by Mark's words. She continues to listen as Mark explains that while her strong problem-solving skills and hands-on approach are assets in her current role, they alone are not enough to get her promoted. The Senior Director position requires a visionary thinker who can help guide the organization's three-to-five year strategy. Further, to deliver outcomes effectively as Senior Director, Ophelia would need to take a more collaborative and consultative leadership approach when communicating with internal and external stakeholders.

Agitated, Ophelia contemplates the feedback she just received. Mark's comments about her lacking the strategic thinking skills needed for the more senior role really stung. How could her strategic thinking be deficient when she had received top marks in the corporate strategy course she completed for her MBA? Why, on so many occasions, had she been given positive feedback? Wasn't she their go-to person to drive operational change? Sure, she sometimes took a harsh approach, but how else could she get results and achieve her deliverables? She had to be firm because many of the senior personnel were very resistant to change.

Feeling indignant and deflated, Ophelia lets the confusion wash over her. Nothing Mark told her makes any sense. Only one thing seems clear: the promotion she's been seeking feels farther away than ever. For someone whose nickname was Ms. Fix It, there appears to be no quick fix in sight.

IMPACT OF LOWER STRATEGIC THINKING

Too frequently, people with lower Strategic Thinking find themselves consigned to operational roles because they lack the leadership capabilities needed for more strategic positions. Even when they know exactly what to do, they have difficulty defining how to do it. Because they have difficulty formulating a strategy, they tend to leap into action and then struggle to communicate their strategy to their teams. Consequently, they often end up doing a lot of the work themselves.

In the following sections, I use Ophelia's story to illustrate how underdeveloped Strategic Thinking impacts strategic performance and limits career progression.

STUCK IN AN OPERATIONAL MINDSET AND POOR LEADERSHIP

Ophelia had a bulldozing predisposition and planned on the fly. She preferred to tackle each challenge as it came. Amidst all the action, she failed to step back and think. She did not specify and document the desired outcomes to ensure a successful strategic initiative, nor did she provide clear direction to her team. In her mind, it was clear enough, so why waste valuable time? This lack of clarity meant that her team frequently struggled to execute deliverables. This dominant operational mindset hindered Ophelia's Strategic Thinking capability and leadership communication style, creating a career ceiling.

LACK OF VISION

Regrettably, Ophelia's vision was far more linear, meaning that she focused on the task that was immediately in front of her and took one step at a time until she reached her goal. While this approach served her well in her current position, Ophelia's limited perspectives would cause her to stumble in a more senior strategic role.

CONFLATING CORPORATE STRATEGY AND STRATEGIC THINKING

Despite earning top marks in the corporate strategy courses for her MBA, Ophelia's academic understanding had not transitioned into her workplace. This frustration is common, as many individuals can talk about corporate strategy and have a breadth of knowledge on best practices. However, because of their lower Strategic Thinking capability, they can still struggle to apply their Crystallized Knowledge of corporate strategy, particularly in situations they haven't faced before and in times of rapid change.

UNCLEAR COMMUNICATION

We also saw Ophelia battling the problem of poor communication. That's why she usually just rolled up her sleeves and did the work herself. Her team and colleagues were frequently frustrated by this approach, which created a cycle of negative feedback about her leadership style and communication, inevitably limiting her career options.

BENEFITS OF HIGHLY DEVELOPED
STRATEGIC THINKING

Strategic Thinking underpins a person's ability to articulate clearly and specify their future vision and desired outcomes, as well as the ability to formulate a strategy to achieve the desired outcome. In addition, it provides the capability to step back and first think about how to approach a project, rather than planning on the fly and jumping straight into action.

Finally, it supports a person to communicate their vision and strategy succinctly and effectively because they have taken the time to create a clear mental picture in their own mind, rather than just sharing a stream of thought bubbles about the future as they pop into their head.

OPHELIA: CAREER PROGRESSION AFTER
BRAIN COACHING

Ophelia's story shows us how paramount Strategic Thinking is, as her lack of it blindsided her and halted her career growth. Indeed, if she had been given the more senior role she wanted, her lower Strategic Thinking might have stalled the growth of her entire organization. A sad story.

Thankfully, her career did not stall. Developing better Strategic Thinking ability created a new ending for Ophelia. She is still very much in the game because brain coaching repositioned her on the career progression track. Ironically, with her enhanced Strategic Thinking, Ophelia was later promoted above her CEO. However, I'm not sure that she actually thanked him for pointing out the limitations of her previously lower Strategic Thinking.

KEY TAKEAWAYS

- The ability to think strategically is a non-negotiable skill in the corporate world, particularly for senior executives and C-suite roles. Having knowledge about corporate strategy and best practices will never be enough unless you can apply your knowledge using highly developed personal Strategic Thinking.

- Strategic Thinking underpins the first two stages of the 4S Strategy Methodology—that is, Specification and Strategy Formulation. In Stage One, you define the desired outcomes and identify any risks. In Stage Two, you formulate the strategy to achieve your desired outcomes and convey that strategy to your team.

- Leaders with lower Strategic Thinking frequently fail to pause and think before jumping into action. Not taking time to define a project thoroughly and determine the appropriate approach leads to confusion and poor execution.

- Individuals with lower Strategic Thinking have an operational mindset that limits their ability to get promoted to more senior roles that require strategic vision and the ability to communicate clearly and leverage teams.

- When your Strategic Thinking is highly developed, you find it easy to define the desired outcomes, assess and mitigate risks, formulate a strategy, and articulate the strategy to your team.

Chapter 12
ABSTRACT THINKING

"If you fail to plan, you plan to fail."
—Benjamin Franklin

Pillar
Three

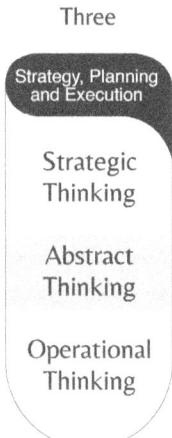

Strategy, Planning
and Execution

Strategic
Thinking

Abstract
Thinking

Operational
Thinking

Well-developed Abstract Thinking is fundamental to effective strategic planning. *Strategic planning* requires the analytical capacity to break down a complex strategy into smaller implementable pieces. The *strategic plan* defines who does what task, when they do it, and how they need to interact and collaborate with others to execute the plan effectively.

Abstract Thinking facilitates the ability to manipulate information to plan out a project, as well as the ability to delegate a task to someone competently. This is a vital Subconscious Thinking Habit, as it directly impacts a leader's performance and their team's productivity. The more thorough the strategic plan is, the better the team will be able to execute it effectively and efficiently.

It is easy to underestimate the role of strategic planning, but it is fundamental to success. Let's use writing the music for a song as an example. The composer first comes up with a tune. Then they break the tune down into notes and chords. And, finally, they transcribe it onto sheet music. It is only after all this that another musician can come along and easily play the song.

Strategic planning is a lot like breaking down music, except you are breaking down a process in a way that allows someone else to understand it and then execute it, much like musicians would play a song according to the score. Without sheet music, musicians would need to rely on their ability to hear the music accurately, develop their own mental musical score sheet, and then reproduce the original music perfectly. All of this would mean that there would be a high risk of the musicians not being on the same page musically, with detrimental consequences. The same happens in business if a strategic plan is poorly developed, which also inhibits the ability to communicate it clearly, resulting in team members not being on the same page.

Now, let's apply our songwriting analogy to the business environment. You can think of the song as the strategy, the sheet music as the strategic plan, and the musicians as the team that executes the strategy and strategic plan. So often, leaders are not charting the sheet music, and then they wonder why their team is failing to play the song as the songwriter intended. Likewise, team members get frustrated when managers expect them to play a song, but without the guidance of sheet music. The bottom line is this: whether you want to attain a goal in music, in business, or in life, you need all three modules to achieve a successful outcome.

THE ROLE OF ABSTRACT THINKING IN 4S STRATEGY METHODOLOGY

The Subconscious Thinking Habit of Abstract Thinking underpins the third stage in the 4S Strategy Methodology. As you learned in

Chapter 10, Stage Three involves planning how you will execute a strategy and mitigate any risks along the way. To explore the Strategic Planning component in a tangible way, we will return to our home-building metaphor and jump back into role-playing mode.

4S STRATEGY METHODOLOGY: STAGE THREE— STRATEGIC PLANNING (BUILDER ROLE)

In Chapter 11, you wore the hats of the Project Owner and the Architect. Now, it's time to put on your Builder hat as we unpack Stage Three of our 4S Strategy Methodology: Strategic Planning (see Figure 23).

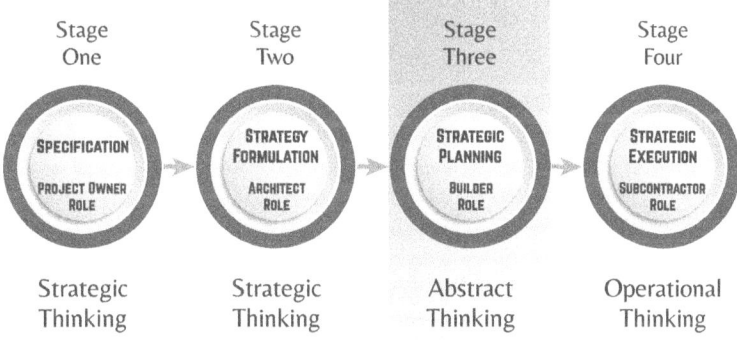

Figure 23. 4S Strategy Methodology: Stage Three—
Strategic Planning (Builder Role)

As the Builder, you will leverage the strategic thinking undertaken by the Architect to develop the strategic formulation and design. Then you will generate your own high-level strategic plan for executing the design. This plan will cover the sequence of steps your team and your Subcontractors will need to undertake to turn the Architect's design of a home into a physical home.

This strategic planning process involves breaking down all the elements required to build the home into modules comprising related tasks, which you will then delegate to your team leaders and the associated tradespeople and subcontractors (e.g., the electrical module covers all the tasks a qualified electrician would need to carry out.) The purpose of this is to create a timeline that optimizes building the home in an efficient and timely manner. To achieve this, some tasks will be undertaken in parallel to minimize elapsed time, while others will need to be staggered and undertaken serially. For instance, the foundation will need to be laid first, followed by building the home's framework. These steps will need to be implemented separately. In contrast, the roofing and external walls can be built in parallel. Then your teams can build the internal walls, connect the plumbing, install the electrical system, and so on.

Both the quality of the home and the schedule will depend on the quality of your strategic plan in your role as the Builder. The way you choose to streamline and delegate the tasks will impact the outcome, the speed of construction, and the total time from start to finish.

As you can see, the strategic plan is a big responsibility that requires high Abstract Thinking to guide the mental process of breaking down the building process. If the Builder's Abstract Thinking is underdeveloped, the strategic plan will lack clarity and completeness. As a result, the building process will be negatively impacted, and the consequences will be substantial, including unanticipated rework, timing delays, and cost overruns.

STRATEGIC PLANNING IN BUSINESS

Most of us are not Builders, but the same principles apply to business. Like the home Builder, executives require excellent Abstract Thinking skills to help them break a strategy down into chunks and create a strategic plan. The importance of thinking through a whole project and gaining the clarity needed for effective delegation should not be underestimated. Without a comprehensive strategic plan, delegation becomes messy and ineffective, with team leaders lacking the clarity required to deliver the desired outcomes.

Well-developed Abstract Thinking gives you greater confidence when monitoring a project's progress. When you have a strategic plan that outlines key modules and tasks and identifies potential risks and how to mitigate them, you can lead project meetings more effectively. Moreover, you can intervene early when necessary to ensure that the project's quality, cost, and timing are proactively managed.

SUBCONSCIOUS THINKING HABIT MODEL FOR ABSTRACT THINKING

Leaders with high Abstract Thinking have little difficulty developing strategic plans that their teams can execute efficiently. When you are competent at abstractly manipulating information in your mind, you can develop a well-thought-out strategic plan without a struggle. Regrettably, for those with lower Abstract Thinking capacity, strategic planning is often a chaotic process.

Here is an example of how lower Abstract Thinking ability might play out in business:

Cue: Your manager asks you to prepare a strategic plan that outlines the implementation of a new organizational strategy.

Routine: You subconsciously run your Abstract Thinking routine.

Output: You produce a strategic plan that is incomplete and poorly documented. Because you did not take enough time to think things through, the project tasks are poorly defined, and your plan is missing vital timelines. In addition, as virtually no risk assessment was undertaken, the plan fails to consider dependencies and contingency factors.

THE SCIENCE BEHIND ABSTRACT THINKING

After clients have improved their Abstract Thinking, they report that they are much better at developing a strategic plan, delegating tasks more effectively, and keeping projects on track. In addition, they find that they are more effective at anticipating and mitigating risks associated with the execution process.

With all this in mind, let's return to Mintzberg's influential article on strategic planning.[lxviii] He makes an important distinction when he says, "By redefining the planner's job, companies will acknowledge the difference between planning and strategic thinking." Mintzberg's view aligns with our definition of strategic planning, and he highlights that analysis drives the process. It is easy to understand why many strategic plans fail to deliver, as they have not been appropriately analyzed and the implementation process has not been adequately documented. Without a strategic plan, implementation will be challenging and impacted by unanticipated risks; and effective delegation will be virtually impossible.

Citing Arie de Geus, who was Corporate Planning Director of Royal Dutch Shell and in charge of business and scenario planning, Mintzberg amplifies the point that the actual purpose of strategic planning is not simply to make a plan. Instead, it is to *change the mental models* that executives have in their minds. This subtle distinction is helpful, as it accentuates that executives need to provide next-level thinking to lead the thinking of others. They achieve this by creating new mental models of the business and then clearly communicating them to their teams as part of the delegation process.

IF YOU'RE A LEADER, YOU'RE A PROJECT MANAGER

From a Fluid Thinking perspective, using Abstract Thinking to optimize the strategic planning process is similar to successful project management. Interestingly, most executives inevitably act as unofficial project managers from time to time. In her *Forbes* article titled "Project Management Isn't Just for Project Managers: 4 Skills You Need to Know," Dana Brownlee highlights that most requests for project management training come from individuals who are not project managers.[lxix] Brownlee asserts that organizations greatly value and understand the need for this skill in all leaders, not just project managers.

Executives unquestionably benefit from having a solid understanding of the fundamental principles of project management. These principles are part of your Crystallized Knowledge, just as your Abstract Thinking capacity is in the domain of your Fluid Thinking. High Abstract Thinking strongly supports you in applying your planning knowledge effectively and helps you delegate optimally.

Understanding the complementary nature of Crystallized Knowledge and Fluid Thinking helps you lead in a way that optimally leverages both you and your team. Before you can lead the thinking of others effectively, you must first create a clear strategic plan in your own mind.

STRATEGIC PLANNING IS RISKY BUSINESS

As you learned in Chapter 11, risk analysis is a vital component of Strategy Formulation. This is also true for Strategic Planning. Indeed, at every point in our 4S Strategy Methodology, we emphasize the importance of undertaking a risk analysis, as it forces your brain to look at things from different perspectives. Performing risk analysis from a broad perspective is inherently strategic and prevents us from being blindsided later by issues we failed to identify in advance. This is essential because if you don't perceive a risk, you can't mitigate it.

In the Strategy Formulation stage, your ability to analyze risks relies on your Strategic Thinking; however, in the Strategic Planning stage, you rely on your Abstract Thinking to identify potential risks from a multidimensional viewpoint. Abstract Thinking assists us in undertaking thought experiments and helps us imagine the future. The ability to anticipate future problems is extremely powerful because it can help prevent large amounts of rework. In addition, being aware of any risks helps you keep a project on track and ensure that tasks are executed successfully.

Risk analysis also aligns with Edward De Bono's hat concept—specifically his black hat, representing risk-driven thinking. Although some consider the black hat to be negative, it is more appropriate to consider it as a devil's advocate hat because it forces us out of our comfort zone. De Bono sheds light on the fact that we need to consider risks, dangers, obstacles, potential problems, and downsides when thinking critically and strategically.[lxx]

DRIVING DELEGATION

Delegating successfully relies on a clear strategic plan, advance delegation preparation, and effective communication. In order to lead the thinking of others and after documenting your strategic plan for a project, it is imperative to think through how you will delegate modules and tasks optimally. We suggest the following approach:

1. **Planning delegation**—Consider what modules and tasks you want to delegate, and to whom. You will need to provide appropriate context for the overall strategic plan, including a summary of the key steps, potential risks, and any other relevant background information.
2. **Preparing to delegate**—Think through in advance how you want to communicate each task to be delegated, including the experience level of the delegatee, the amount of detail you want to cover, and the type of language that will be most effective with each delegatee.
3. **Communicating the task to the delegatee**—This needs to be done clearly and succinctly. Communicate with

the delegatee only *after* you have completed the first two steps. Otherwise, if you just shoot from the hip, you will leave the delegatee confused, and you will probably be disappointed with what they deliver.

This trifecta creates the support structures needed to scaffold successful implementation and execution from the top down. As with all things in life, there is no holy grail that ensures perfect results; but this is a great way to mitigate potential problems and drive the timely execution of high-quality outcomes. Regrettably, many leaders struggle to delegate effectively due to their lower Abstract Thinking. As a result, they end up navigating sub-par deliverables and undertaking heavy loads of rework to address the situation.

Eli Broad was a successful businessperson who built two Fortune 500 companies: KB Home and Sun America. In his book, *The Art of Being Unreasonable: Lessons in Unconventional Thinking*, he sheds light on the importance of delegation. A key takeaway is that good leaders identify their top priorities and delegate everything else, as an inability to delegate causes significant roadblocks for managers.[lxxi] I couldn't agree more wholeheartedly with Eli Broad.

TO DELEGATE WELL, YOU NEED TO COMMUNICATE WELL

Regardless of whether the news is good, bad, or neutral, people need clear and straightforward briefings to ensure high-quality output. Unfortunately, many leaders struggle to delegate and communicate with their teams effectively, which leads to everybody being on a different page. Corporate Trainer Dana Brownlee refers to the lack of alignment between leaders and their teams as "the disease of 'the right hand not knowing what the left hand is doing.'"[lxxii] This is a common problem for many organizations and one they are consistently trying to navigate and overcome.

From my experience, this inconsistency in communication is not intentional, nor are executives deliberately trying to obscure information. The problem is that they are time poor. And so, they do not pause to think through a strategy, create a plan, and outline the associated processes in advance.

This lack of mental clarity creates top-down confusion about what needs to be done and how to do it. However, when leaders take time to reflect and develop a strategic plan, that document can become the vehicle that drives the execution of the strategy.

Now, the clarity can travel down the food chain, so everyone is on the same page and heading in the same direction. The contextualization of the strategic plan is often the missing link in effective delegation and communication.

EVEN BATMAN HAD ROBIN

Even superheroes have sidekicks, and that's why executives and leaders have teams to support them. John C. Maxwell in his book titled *Developing the Leaders around You* sums it up nicely, "If you want to do a few small things right, then do them yourself. If you want to do great things and make a big impact, learn to delegate."[lxxiii]

It can be a significant challenge to take a hands-off approach as a leader, but it frees you up to drive strategic innovation that results in the growth of your organization. Deborah Grayson Riegel, in her *Harvard Business Review* article titled "8 Ways Leaders Delegate Successfully," cited a 2015 Gallup study that queried 143 CEOs on the Inc. 500 list and found that those who delegated authority effectively led companies that grew faster, generated more revenue, and created more jobs.[lxxiv] So, there is enormous benefit to be gained by improving your Abstract Thinking, and thus, your ability to delegate, rather than just dispensing orders.

Additionally, in Jesse Sostrin's article, "To Be a Great Leader, You Have to Learn How to Delegate Well," we find more evidence regarding the value of strategic delegation. Sostrin states that to raise the ceiling on your leadership potential, you need to extend your presence through the actions of others. [lxxv] This suggests a clear correlation between effective delegation and increasing your leadership potential.

JOSHUA: A STRUGGLING SUPERHERO WITHOUT A STRATEGIC PLAN

Joshua is a young, up-and-coming executive who manages a team of ten individuals in the administration department of a multinational finance company. He is a bright, encouraging, and supportive manager who can easily motivate his team. Joshua's management style is very collaborative and inclusive, and while that often works in his favor, he is a bit too close to his team. Although the blurred boundaries between friendship and management have advantages, they make it challenging for Joshua to navigate situations that require him to be the boss.

Joshua is a hands-on manager who takes time to understand the details of what his team is doing. When a team member needs help, he is always ready to lend a hand. Because of his helpful nature, Joshua has earned a reputation for delivering quality outcomes on time. This affords him a lot of respect from his colleagues and managers; however, upper management would be surprised to learn these outcomes are not fully a team effort. The truth is that the team relies on Joshua's hard work and long hours to achieve their deliverables.

Now it's Monday morning and Diane, who is the head of administration and Joshua's immediate manager, has called him into a meeting. Diane greets him with a warm smile. After they take their seats, she explains that his performance and reliability have caught management's attention. In recognition of this, Joshua is being promoted to a more senior position. Now, instead of managing only ten people, he will have eight direct reports, each of whom manages a team of approximately ten people. Upon hearing this news, Joshua's head begins to spin. While he is excited, the idea of managing eighty people is daunting.

The next morning, he wonders how he can continue to take a hands-on approach with a much larger team. Joshua knows his collaborative process has been the reason for his success. This approach allows him to be immersed in the details, to control issues in real-time, and to stay one step ahead. What will happen when he keeps his sleeves rolled down and his deliverables depend on his direct reports?

Joshua realizes he will need to transform his leadership style. Instead of leading from within the trenches, he will need to take a broader, more strategic approach. This concerns Joshua. While he appreciates the need for strategic planning, it has never been his strong suit. It seems like a lot of mental work with little productive output. He much prefers figuring things out as he goes along and winging it when needed, and this approach hasn't failed him so far.

When Joshua arrives at the office, he goes to the follow-up meeting Diane had scheduled. A smile spreads across Diane's face as she tells him that she has developed a new strategy for the administration department. Not only that, but she has decided to appoint Joshua to roll it out with his new team.

Don't panic, Joshua thinks to himself, as he smiles and nods.

Continuing, Diane explains that she wants him to undertake the strategic planning for the new approach she plans to implement. This means he will need to develop a detailed project plan so his new, expanded team can operationalize the strategy effectively. Diane describes what the plan needs to cover—the key tasks, people, resources required, etc. Joshua will need to provide realistic budgets and timelines, along with an insightful assessment of associated risks and their relevant mitigation strategies. Their meeting ends on a high note with Diane saying she knows he is the right person for the job.

After hearing all that is required, he is concerned. His mind was never good at planning out the steps needed to achieve a goal, much less strategically sequencing them. And because he always focuses on the task immediately in front of him, he rarely thinks ahead to consider potential risks.

Joshua knows this new responsibility will require a lot of delegating, a skill he has never fully developed. In fact, he doesn't even like the idea of giving people orders because, to him, it feels inauthentic. Besides, whenever he delegated work in the past, it never came back precisely the way he had expected. He is never quite sure how much detail and direction to provide, so his instructions are usually vague. Half the time, he skips delegation and just does the work himself because his team cannot produce the same high quality output he does.

IMPACT OF LOWER ABSTRACT THINKING

Too often, leaders with lower Abstract Thinking rush into a complex project without taking time to break it down into smaller chunks and think through how best to achieve the desired outcome while simultaneously minimizing risks. Without a formal strategic plan, execution can become haphazard, leading to unforeseen problems, delivery delays, cost overruns, heavy rework, and major confusion about who is supposed to be doing what and when.

Below, I use Joshua's story to illustrate how underdeveloped Abstract Thinking impacts strategic performance and challenges career success.

LACK OF PLANNING

Joshua compensated for his lack of Strategic Planning ability by managing every detail himself. This approach left little room for him to step back and consider the optimal way to tackle a project so he could leverage his team. Because Joshua did not take time to think through every aspect of a project in advance and evaluate the risks, he needed to make frequent adjustments along the way. This improvisational approach had a negative effect on his team's productivity, and his people were irritated by the constant changes in project tasks and timelines.

Joshua's lower Abstract Thinking capability would have detrimentally impacted his ability to develop a comprehensive strategic plan to implement Diane's new strategy. It was like being asked to run a race with his feet tied together.

INEFFECTIVE AT DELEGATION

Joshua was well aware of the importance of delegation, but he was still no closer to overcoming his hands-on predisposition. Metaphorically, Diane gave Joshua a Batman-sized mission. He needed his whole team to collaborate in order to succeed. It would be a group effort that required at the very least Robin, the Batmobile, and his trusted butler Alfred Pennyworth—all of whom would need a clear briefing before taking action. Joshua understood this, and it was why his thoughts of inadequacy began creeping in. Once he realized he was the project manager of Diane's latest strategic initiative, the challenge of his new role became more apparent. Joshua now understood that you cannot micromanage every detail when you have a team of eighty people.

INEFFECTIVE AT COMMUNICATION

The idea of delegating gave Joshua so much distress that he avoided it as much as possible. Part of the problem was that he saw himself more as a peer than as the leader of his team, and that made him uncomfortable giving orders. He also had difficulty gauging how much detail to provide, so his instructions were often vague. Besides, explaining things seemed to take too much time. Rather than deal with all these challenges, he usually opted to do the job himself.

Although Joshua's team liked him, his people were frustrated by his ineffective communication. His superficial explanations of tasks often led to misunderstandings and work that did not meet his expectations.

LONE WOLF MANAGEMENT STYLE

Although Joshua looked like part of the pack, he was very much a lone wolf, doing a lot of the legwork by himself behind closed doors. This management style is dangerous, as it leads to burnout and capped career progression. Joshua wasn't isolating himself intentionally, but his choice to be overly hands-on had consequential effects. As a lone wolf, he would have had serious difficulty in quickly transitioning to the pack lead role.

So, why do individuals like Joshua unwittingly lead as a lone wolf? Below are some common reasons.

- **Anxiety**—Many individuals have anxiety about delegating tasks, as they don't want to feel as though they are giving orders and leading harshly.
- **Time Poor**—It takes time to plan proper delegation, and most people prefer to use that time to do the work themselves. However, as leaders progress and tasks become more complex, the DIY method is unsustainable.
- **Perfectionism**—Many individuals who struggle with delegation are perfectionists. They feel others can't produce the quality of work needed, so why bother delegating in the first place?

- **Uncertainty**—Their benchmarks are uncertain. How much detail is too much? How much is too little? Their lack of clarity causes them to avoid delegation.

- **Miscommunication**—Many managers think they have delegated appropriately to their staff, only to be disappointed with the work that's delivered. This disappointment is usually because of a miscommunication between the two parties. This happens when the instructions lack appropriate framework, context, and detail.

BENEFITS OF HIGHLY DEVELOPED ABSTRACT THINKING

As mentioned, Abstract Thinking underpins strategic planning by using the brain's subconscious capacity to predict the actions required to achieve a goal. The forward-looking orientation of Abstract Thinking is highly nuanced, and it is an essential capability for all executives. This thinking ability is not grounded in a physical environment. It requires a high level of mental agility to manipulate strategies, concepts, and tasks pragmatically in the mind, as a precursor to executing them in the physical world. When leaders can resist the urge to leap into action, they engage with creating mental models that others can easily understand during this communication and delegation process. Strategic planning ensures proactive and productive activity, instead of reactive responses. This is why it is so essential for strategic success.

JOSHUA: A STRATEGIC PLANNING SUPERHERO AFTER BRAIN COACHING

Joshua was not alone in his lower Abstract Thinking capacity. Indeed, our testing has shown that it is fairly common for executives to have low-to-moderate Abstract Thinking. As such, many leaders can routinely struggle with Strategic Planning and also delegating in a way that maximizes their own and their team's performance and productivity. However, through Abstract Thinking brain exercises and guidance, this struggle can be overcome.

As a result of having enhanced his Abstract Thinking, Joshua found it much easier and quicker to develop appropriate strategic plans. Brain coaching also vastly improved his ability to plan, prepare and communicate delegated tasks to his team members. Diane noticed his much improved leadership capability and confidence when undertaking the large assignment she had given him. So, she was very comfortable to recommend him for a promotion to another division which he was duly offered, and which he accepted with relish.

KEY TAKEAWAYS

- Abstract Thinking is fundamental to Strategic Planning. This habit facilitates the ability to manipulate information and develop mental models. It also provides the clarity necessary to sequence tasks appropriately and to delegate effectively.
- Abstract Thinking underpins the third stage of the 4S Strategy Methodology. In the Builder role, you plan out how to execute a strategy while also assessing and mitigating risks.
- Leaders with lower Abstract Thinking generally don't take the time to formulate a comprehensive strategic plan before beginning a project. Failure to think things through thoroughly in advance leads to miscommunication, confusion about work assignments, frequent changes to tasks and schedules, unnecessary delays, budget overruns, morale issues, and unsatisfactory deliverables.
- Leaders with lower Abstract Thinking often have a lone wolf management style that leads to be burnout. Those who struggle to delegate find themselves burdened by a disproportionate amount of work because they prefer to do everything themselves. This overly hands-on approach

limits the ability to get promoted to more senior roles that require the ability to leverage teams.

- When your Abstract Thinking is highly developed, you take a proactive approach to strategic planning instead of operating in reaction mode. Because your brain can manipulate information and create mental models with ease, you have no difficulty breaking projects down into modules and sequencing tasks. The strategic plans you develop provide clarity, helping you track projects, anticipate and mitigate risks, delegate tasks, and keep your teams well-informed.

Chapter 13
OPERATIONAL THINKING

"One way of looking at it is to see operational thinking as being about keeping the wheels of an organization turning, while strategic thinking is concerned with making sure they are being steered in the right direction."[lxxvi]
—*Dr. Neil Thompson*

Pillar
Three

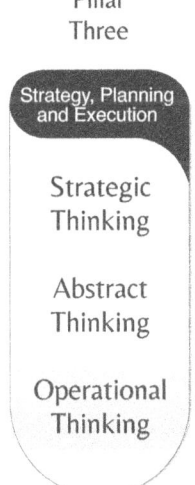

Strategy, Planning and Execution

Strategic
Thinking

Abstract
Thinking

Operational
Thinking

From a Fluid Thinking perspective, underdevelopment in any area often leads to subconscious behaviors that can thwart your career progression or even impede your ability to succeed in life, in general. While all Subconscious Thinking Habits cause difficulties when they are underdeveloped, a few can also create problems when they are overdeveloped. As you learned in previous chapters, overdevelopment is associated with an entirely different, but equally challenging, set of derailers. Just like Innovative Thinking (see Chapter 8), the Operational Thinking habit can be overdeveloped or underdeveloped. Both imbalances have their drawbacks. Here again, we are striving for Baby Bear's *just right* level.

When our Operational Thinking is ideally balanced, we can work through a process, task, issue, or problem practically and pragmatically while also managing others to deliver the solution. Individuals with optimum Operational Thinking delegate clearly and precisely. For example, when assigning a task, they give an explicit deadline such as "This needs to be done by 3 p.m. on Friday" rather than saying, "I need this ASAP."

Because we find overdeveloped Operational Thinking in almost ninety percent of the people we test, I will concentrate on this aspect. We hypothesize that overdevelopment occurs largely because individuals are typically recognized for being hands-on and for their ability to get things done through their own personal efforts, rather than for stepping back and managing others to deliver the desired outcome. As such, they get promoted early in their career as the go-to person who always gets things done. Unfortunately, what was as asset on the way up in middle management becomes a liability in more senior roles.

As you'll see a bit later in this chapter, Operational Thinking is related to Strategic Execution, which is the final stage in the 4S Strategy Methodology. In business, Strategic Execution is critical. However, it is even more crucial to know which hat you should be wearing when.

THE ROLE OF OPERATIONAL THINKING IN THE 4S STRATEGY METHODOLOGY

The Subconscious Thinking Habit of Operational Thinking underpins the final stage in the 4S Strategy Methodology. As you learned in Chapter 10, Stage Four corresponds to the implementation process, which involves building each module in the strategic plan and a mitigating any risks along the way. To illustrate this process in a practical way, we will return once again to our home-building analogy.

4S STRATEGY METHODOLOGY: STAGE FOUR— STRATEGIC EXECUTION (SUBCONTRACTOR ROLE)

In previous chapters, you wore the hats of the Project Owner, the Architect, and the Builder. Now, it's time to put on your Subcontractor hat as we explore Stage Four of our 4S Strategy Methodology: Strategic Execution (see Figure 24). As you will soon see, the nature of the Subcontractor role is narrower and more self-contained than the Builder role.

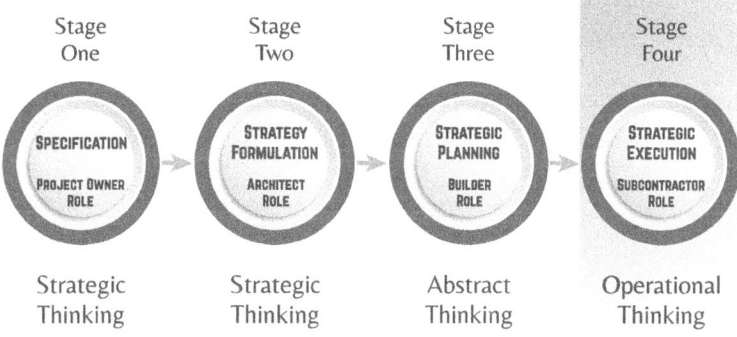

Figure 24. 4S Strategy Methodology: Stage Four—
Strategic Execution (Subcontractor Role)

The Subcontractor is more focused on the execution of the specific modules and tasks that have been delegated to them. In contrast, the Builder is more focused on the bigger picture, which includes developing a strategic plan that integrates the various modules and determining how to assign the individual modules and tasks.

Imagine yourself as the electrical Subcontractor. You are responsible for planning and executing the installation of the required electrical system, which is the module that the Builder has delegated to you.

Because you have done many electrical installations before, you can leverage your past experience to optimize how you execute your assigned module. However, you will need to collaborate with the other Subcontractors to ensure an integrated execution of the Builder's overarching plan. For example, you need to be aware of what is happening with the plumbing and plastering, so you can install each electrical component at the appropriate time while accommodating the plumbing and plastering needs and still meeting the Builder's deadline.

The aim is for each Subcontractor to think through strategically how they will collaboratively execute their respective modules while simultaneously assessing and mitigating any potential risks. When all this is achieved under the planning and guidance of the Builder, Strategic Execution is optimized.

STRATEGIC EXECUTION IN BUSINESS

Now that you understand Strategic Execution from a concrete, practical perspective, let's examine what it means to wear the Subcontractor hat in the context of a business environment where the boundaries between roles are less tangible.

When you're building a home, the Builder assigns modules and tasks to the Subcontractors who are responsible for executing them. Analogously, business leaders delegate modules and tasks to other people who do the work. When you're a business leader, you need to think of your teams as Subcontractors. It is their job to build each module of the organization's overall strategy, step by step. That's why leaders need to delegate clearly and give their teams agency to carry out their assigned tasks while still proactively monitoring their progress.

Executives are meant to develop strategies (Architect) and do high-level planning (Builder); however, when their Operational Thinking is overdeveloped, they over-focus on the process of execution (Subcontractor). Instead of wearing the Architect's hat or the Builder's hat, they put on the Subcontractor's hat and try to do the work of their team members. This habit inevitably becomes a subconscious roadblock to their success and career progression.

The reality is that Strategic Execution is frequently derailed by well-intentioned and hard-working leaders who have overdeveloped Operational Thinking. These individuals take a lone wolf approach. Because they prefer to work alone, other people tend to leave them alone and vice versa. Regrettably, working in silos carries a significant cost and results in poor collaboration.

SUBCONSCIOUS THINKING HABIT MODEL FOR OPERATIONAL THINKING

Because Operational Thinking is typically overdeveloped, many executives take a do-it-yourself approach to executing strategic initiatives rather than leveraging the full capability of their team members.

Here's an example of how overdeveloped Operational Thinking can play out in the workplace:

Cue: Your manager asks you to execute a module of their organizational strategic plan.

Routine: You subconsciously run your overdeveloped Operational Thinking routine.

Output: You jump straight into operational mode, taking on the heavy workload yourself and handing out only menial tasks to your team members to execute.

THE SCIENCE BEHIND OPERATIONAL THINKING

Significantly, Operational Thinking is closely related to the cognitive skill of *concrete logic*, which is based on our physical senses—in essence, what we can see, hear, touch, etc. It is a cognitive skill that operates in the here and now. Thus, Operational Thinking focuses on physical objects, immediate experience, and precise and literal interpretations of information to achieve the best results.

As you learned from Piaget's theory of cognitive development in Chapter 1, the concrete operational stage of development occurs between the ages of 7 and 11. From my perspective, this stage is underpinned by Operational Thinking. It's worth remembering that cognitive development in children comprises more than the acquisition of Crystallized Knowledge. In the context of my framework, it is during this stage that the child continues to enhance their Fluid Thinking by starting to develop their Subconscious Thinking Habit of Operational Thinking.

It is incredible to realize that many of our current Subconscious Thinking Habits were formed when we were so young. Most adults have overdeveloped Operational Thinking. Consequently, they are too "hands on." Being too operationally driven can inhibit the optimization of Strategic Thinking (see Chapter 11) and Abstract Thinking (see Chapter 12). This negatively impacts the formation of strategies, the development of strategic plans, and delegation.

The giveaway sign of a leader with overdeveloped Operational Thinking is that you often hear them say, "By the time I explained it to someone, I could've done it myself." When you meet Lydia, you will see how these imbalances can interfere with leadership capacity.

LYDIA: GO-GETTER WITH NOWHERE TO GO

Lydia is a young go-getter who has built a reputation as the right hand of the head of production at a national manufacturing company. She is known as "The Fixer" because she is the go-to person whenever a problem arises. She has extensive subject-matter expertise and can sort out issues at lightning speed.

Her boss, Jacinta, finds her practical, down to earth, and reliable, and greatly appreciates that Lydia always volunteers to help.

220

Jovially, Jacinta delegates many tasks to Lydia. Jacinta's motto is: "If you want something done, give it to a busy person." Lydia is always very busy, but she takes everything in her stride and is always up for a good challenge.

Lydia enjoys her work, as it allows her to get in deep and get things done. She finds rolling up her sleeves and taking a hands-on approach personally rewarding. Lydia knows she can be relied upon to leverage her vast experience and work out how to solve any production problems that come up. Because of her vast knowledge and can-do attitude, she is often sent across the country to fix issues. Lydia especially enjoys and values this element of her role.

Although she is always comfortable learning new things, Lydia is not the type to read the instructions before starting an unfamiliar task. Instead, she prefers to jump in and take a trial-and-error approach. She works speedily and diligently, executing on the fly. On the odd occasion when a new task stumps her, she takes things one step at a time until she remedies the situation. Although this approach often leaves her needing to correct unforeseen issues later, Lydia is never put off by long hours or rework. She would rather launch into a task and figure it out along the way than waste precious time strategizing.

Lydia admits she doesn't have much patience for people who prefer to analyze problems, especially when they are slow to implement solutions. She is confident that she is the best person for the job and rarely feels the need to delegate. Besides, whenever she entrusted work to someone else in the past, they took twice as long to do the task and delivered half the quality. So why even bother?

Lydia is happy with her salary and the perks of her current job, and she enjoys the travel her position requires. At the same time, she feels somewhat frustrated. At her last performance review, Jacinta had called her a "specialist contributor." Lydia didn't even know what that title meant. Although the title sounded impressive on the surface, deep down Lydia thought it was rather obscure and maybe even a bit snobbish. She prefers things to be more down to earth. In addition to giving Lydia this ambiguous title, Jacinta had been rather evasive about Lydia's prospects for career progression. Despite being happy for now, Lydia doesn't want to be stuck as a specialist contributor forever and wonders what is holding her back from being considered for other opportunities.

Although the organization values her niche skill set and pays her well, Lydia's inability to work strategically and delegate effectively creates a ceiling for her career progression. Failure to plan ahead results in poor delegation and compromised execution for her peers and team members.

Regrettably, due to Lydia's overdeveloped Operational Thinking and lower Abstract Thinking, she finds herself pigeonholed into a niche that will be difficult to overcome. She needs to rewire her brain by undertaking scientifically designed deliberate practice exercises in order to enhance her Strategic Thinking and Abstract Thinking, and thereby balance out her overdeveloped Operational Thinking.

IMPACT OF UNBALANCED OPERATIONAL THINKING

When a person has overdeveloped Operational Thinking, they exhibit the following behaviors:

- Overly action-oriented, preferring to get started on a project rather than thinking things through
- Prefers to plan on the fly
- Does too much of the heavy lifting themselves, rather than managing their team members to achieve an outcome
- Reluctant to delegate because they don't plan out in advance how to delegate effectively, and so they are often disappointed with the work they receive from the delegatee
- Frustrated that others often take more time than they do to achieve an outcome

When a person has underdeveloped Operational Thinking, they exhibit the following behaviors:

- Overly theoretical in their thinking
- Perceived by others as being impractical because their ideas are often not very pragmatic
- Open to managing team members to deliver outcomes, but often too hands-off, providing insufficient guidance
- Often unclear when delegating tasks because of their lower practicality

BENEFITS OF BALANCED OPERATIONAL THINKING

When your Operational Thinking is optimally balanced, instead of diving in and doing most of the heavy lifting yourself, you are comfortable stepping back and managing your team members to deliver an outcome. In addition, you have the ability to collaborate effectively with other team leaders when taking on broader and more complex projects. You delegate clearly, giving precise instructions and specific target completion dates. Instead of rolling up your sleeves and diving into the details of a project, you lead your team from a vantage point that gives you a wider perspective, providing guidance when needed.

LYDIA: OPTIMUM EXECUTION AFTER BRAIN COACHING

Predictably, after completing our brain coaching program, Lydia's Operational Thinking fit nicely into that *just right* category, neither overdeveloped nor underdeveloped—and it was now nicely complemented by her improved Strategic Thinking and Abstract Thinking. This Baby Bear level of Operational Thinking supports her in pulling back, so she is no longer too hands-on or overly action-oriented. It builds on her strong pragmatism and also empowers her, so she feels more comfortable delegating and leveraging her team to achieve the required outcomes: a win-win for everyone involved.

At a subsequent performance review, Jacinta complemented Lydia on her much-improved leadership style and more hands-off approach. They agreed that Lydia would substantially increase the size of her team, now that she had demonstrated her ability to guide her team members to achieve outcomes and mentor them to improve their overall skill levels. Lydia was excited by the new challenge, and Jacinta was relieved because, previously, Lydia had been a high-risk, single point of failure if she were to fall ill or leave the company.

Lydia was happy to kiss the title of "Specialist Contributor" goodbye.

KEY TAKEAWAYS

- Operational Thinking corresponds to Stage Four of the 4S Strategy Methodology for Strategy, Planning, and Execution. It facilitates the ability to work through a process, task, issue, or problem pragmatically while also managing others to deliver the solution.
- Ideally, Operational Thinking needs to be balanced—that is, neither overdeveloped nor underdeveloped.
- Most people have overdeveloped Operational Thinking, which results in an overly hands-on approach that lacks sufficient advance planning because they prefer to be action oriented.
- Operationally driven individuals prefer to work alone and do most of the work themselves. Their inability to delegate tasks effectively often limits their opportunities for personal growth and career advancement. They don't realize that while being hands on and action oriented on the way up can be an asset, it quickly turns into a liability in more senior roles.
- Although relatively rare, people with underdeveloped Operational Thinking tend to be overly theoretical. Because they lack practical orientation, these individuals take a very long time to figure the next step in a process.

PART V

PILLAR FOUR

SOCIAL LEADERSHIP

Pillar
Four

Social
Leadership

Nonverbal
Thinking

Perspective
Thinking

Intuitive
Thinking

Chapter 14
INTRODUCTION TO SOCIAL LEADERSHIP

"The key to successful leadership today is influence, not authority."
—*Kenneth Blanchard*

Social Leadership is an art. I define Social Leadership as an individual's capacity to leverage their social, interpersonal, and emotional skills to lead and motivate people to deliver a desired outcome. A great metaphor for this is an orchestra conductor, who is responsible for the quality of music even though they do not play a single note.

Pillar Four: Social Leadership comprises the three Subconscious Thinking Habits shown in Figure 25.

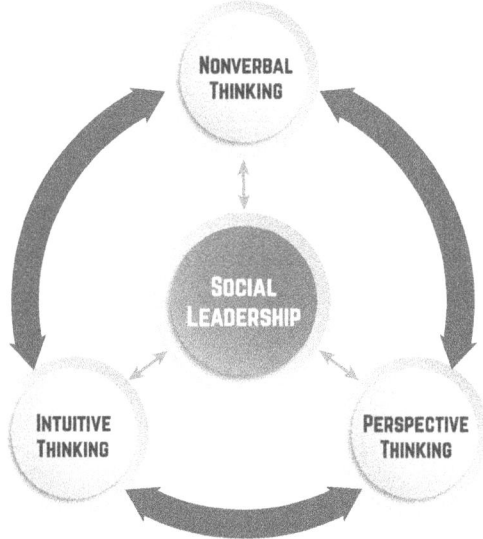

Figure 25. Social Leadership Pillar

227

When these are in balance, you can achieve the connectedness you desire and re-energize yourself, your team, and how you lead.

- **Nonverbal Thinking** enables you to sense subconsciously when something is "not quite right" with another person. This skill relies primarily on observing subtle changes in people's body language. Nonverbal Thinking pertains mainly to one-on-one interactions with individuals.[10]
- **Perspective Thinking** is the ability to sense subconsciously and understand another person's perspective (even when you don't agree with it). This skill also plays a critical role in empathizing with others.
- **Intuitive Thinking** is the ability to observe subtle changes in your wider working environment subconsciously, including the aptitude to read a room full of people. It also underpins your gut feelings and street smarts. Intuitive Thinking pertains mainly to group interactions (i.e., one-to-many or many-to-many).

In business, optimum Social Leadership is a non-negotiable and an increasingly critical factor in long-term career progression, which is why it merits having its own Pillar in the Subconscious Thinking Habits framework. The habits in this Pillar are more sensory than logical. Unlike habits based on rational thinking skills—such as Analytical Thinking (Chapter 7) and Abstract Thinking (Chapter 12)—Social Leadership habits use our perceptual skills when we are interacting with others.

SOCIAL GLUE

Leaders need to build an atmosphere of everybody sticking together to deliver an outcome. They need to create *social glue* to motivate

---

[10] I say "mainly" because Nonverbal Thinking usually pertains to one-to-one interactions. While you also rely on this habit when interacting with groups, you can concentrate on only one group member at a time.

their people to perform at their best. While subject-matter expertise is essential to be a great leader; it is no longer the differentiator for advancement. Instead, career growth is increasingly determined by an individual's capacity to connect authentically with their team and peers while also optimizing collaboration and performance growth.

Interestingly, people can be highly skilled at controlling their attention, solving complex problems, and strategizing and planning, yet still struggle with Social Leadership. When Social Leadership skills are less than ideal, a leader has difficulty bringing their people along on the journey with them. Without this social glue, their people become demotivated and less willing to use their complete skill set to implement a leader's strategy collaboratively and competently. This lack of buy-in and enthusiasm hinders the quality of work produced and compromises the overall success of a project or department.

SOCIAL LEADERSHIP AND EMOTIONAL INTELLIGENCE

Emotional intelligence is the cognitive ability that underpins interpersonal relationships and behavior. Daniel Goleman popularized this term in his book titled *Emotional Intelligence*, which was published in 1995.[lxxvii] In his 1998 book, *Working with Emotional Intelligence*, Goleman defines emotional intelligence as "the capacity for recognizing our own feelings and those of others, motivating ourselves, and for managing emotions well in ourselves and in our relationships."[lxxviii] This definition underscores why having emotional intelligence is paramount to being successful as a leader. As Goleman says, "CEOs are hired for their intellect and business experience—and fired for lack of emotional intelligence."[lxxix]

According to Goldman, "Empathy and social skills are *social intelligence*, the interpersonal part of emotional intelligence. That's why they look alike."[lxxx] From my viewpoint, Nonverbal Thinking, Perspective Thinking, and Intuitive Thinking are key drivers of what

Goleman refers to as emotional intelligence and social skills. Collectively, I refer to these Subconscious Thinking Habits as Social Leadership.

Although I have not touched on this topic previously, it is worth noting that *all* the Subconscious Thinking Habits I discussed earlier in this book also impact emotional intelligence and social skills. When they haven't been optimized, they can derail overall leadership style and performance. Below is a snapshot of how the Subconscious Thinking Habits I covered in the first three Pillars can also affect emotional intelligence.

Focused Thinking: Individuals with lower Focused Thinking are easily distracted during conversations because their minds naturally wander. When this happens, others perceive them as being absent from the discussion. This gives others the impression that the person with lower Focused Thinking considers the conversation unimportant and damages rapport.

Analytical Thinking: During a conflict, people with lower Analytical Thinking often initially react at a feeling or emotional level, instead of stepping back and analyzing why the conflict is occurring. They can display anger and frustration quickly. Obviously, this is an ineffective way to engage with conflict from a Social Leadership perspective. Alternatively, the individual may shut down and then spend a significant amount of time churning the situation over internally before taking corrective action. Both reactions negatively impact performance and productivity.

Innovative Thinking: When an individual has overly high Innovative Thinking, they struggle to discern unwritten social and corporate boundaries. This problem can compromise working relationships in various ways. For example, one of my clients had a habit of asking colleagues and external experts for favors, but never offered to return a favor. Not surprisingly, others began to recognize this pattern of requests and eventually became less willing to grant my client favors.

Conceptual Thinking: People with exceptionally high Conceptual Thinking can come across as arrogant because their thinking speed is very fast. Because they are easily irritated by those who think more slowly, they don't suffer fools gladly. They can also lack the social graces required to filter their opinions. These bristling interactions put their peers and teams into a negative emotional state, compromising the quality of work others produce.[lxxxi] When you consider all the undesirable effects these types of behaviors could have on others, it is easy to understand why leaders with extremely high Conceptual Thinking often create an underlying cycle of resentment within their teams. This derails the quality of their Social Leadership ability.

Strategic Thinking: Individuals who have lower Strategic Thinking tend to be overly wordy and they often communicate in an unstructured manner, leaving their colleagues and peers confused about what is expected of them. Low Strategic Thinking capability can damage professional relationships, as others become increasingly frustrated by the lack of clarity over the long term.

Abstract Thinking: When a person's Abstract Thinking is lower, they struggle to plan and delegate effectively. Lack of clarity and precision in a leader's thinking compromises their ability to communicate and delegate tasks effectively. Consequently, their team members will repeatedly ask for further clarification, causing frequent interruptions. Over time, people avoid working with these types of leaders.

Operational Thinking: When Operational Thinking is overdeveloped, individuals tend to plan on the fly and take a fire-aim-ready approach. This overly action-driven leadership style always results in large amounts of rework and causes team members to become frustrated—usually because the goalposts are constantly moving.

As a result, people aren't drawn to working with these types of leaders, either.

As you can see, all ten Subconscious Thinking Habits must be intricately balanced to optimize emotional intelligence and Social Leadership capability—thereby synergistically delivering harmony and performance.

KEY TAKEAWAYS

- Social Leadership is an art that relies heavily upon the optimized sensing capabilities related to the Subconscious Thinking Habits of Nonverbal Thinking, Perspective Thinking, and Intuitive Thinking.
- When your Nonverbal Thinking is optimized, you can quickly and easily pick up subtle changes in nonverbal cues such as body language and facial expressions, which then helps you determine when something is off with the individual with whom you are communicating.
- Metaphorically, you use Perspective Thinking to walk a mile in another person's shoes so you can genuinely understand where they're coming from and be empathetic, even if you don't agree with their position on a topic.
- You rely on Intuitive Thinking to scan your environment subconsciously, grasp group dynamics, and read the room at a meeting or when delivering a presentation. It underpins our gut feel and street smarts.
- Nonverbal Thinking, Perspective Thinking, and Intuitive Thinking play an important role in optimizing emotional intelligence and Social Leadership capability. However, the other seven Subconscious Thinking Habits impact emotional intelligence and Social Leadership, too.

Chapter 15
NONVERBAL THINKING

"The most important thing in communication is to hear what isn't being said." —Peter Drucker

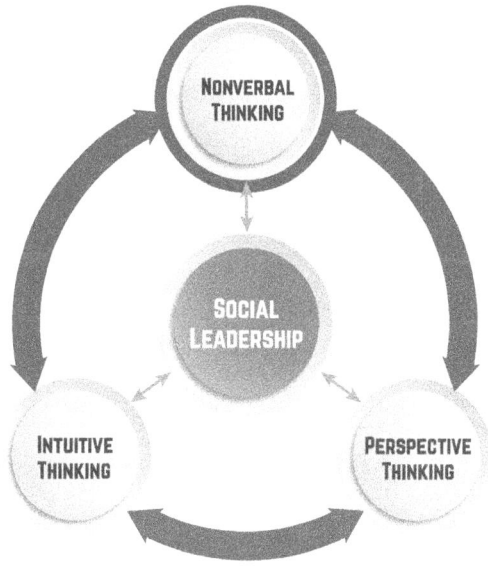

I define Nonverbal Thinking as a subconscious sensing cognitive ability that allows us to read and calibrate interpersonal feedback by noticing subtle changes in an individual's body language. It assists us in picking up on small and nuanced changes in body language, facial expressions, tone of voice, and so on—all of which are important when building rapport with an individual. While Nonverbal Thinking predominantly comes into play during one-to-one interactions, we also use it during group interactions; however, the latter requires continually shifting our focus from one individual to the next.

People with underdeveloped Nonverbal Thinking are usually unaware of their colleagues' subtle nonverbal cues. This can cause disgruntled professional relationships. However, we have found it is uncommon for successful senior executives to test low in this area, primarily because it is becoming increasingly difficult to progress into senior leadership roles with significantly compromised Social Leadership skills.

Others often perceive leaders with lower Nonverbal Thinking capability to be deliberately bulldozing their way through meetings. However, it is more likely that this approach is unintentional, as these leaders are simply unable to notice nonverbal cues; so, they unwittingly push their own agenda. Unfortunately, this approach does not pave the way for others to follow willingly.

Taking a traditional Crystallized Knowledge approach to training and coaching might help bridge communication gaps temporarily; however, the executive will invariably default to their original behavior under stress because lower Nonverbal Thinking is a *subconscious* derailer. Although leaders who use traditional Crystallized Knowledge approaches might experience temporary periods of adjustment, their Social Leadership will continue to be compromised, damaging relationships and ultimately capping their career progression. To address this issue fully, leaders would need to enhance their Nonverbal Thinking using a deliberate practice approach to reprogram this Subconscious Thinking Habit.

In Pillar Two: Complex Problem-Solving, I touched on Robert Katz's seminal article, "Skills of an Effective Administrator." He asserted that leaders need technical skills (i.e., subject-matter expertise), conceptual skills,[11] and human skills to be effective. Katz understood how human skills help create well-rounded leaders who engender confidence in their people.

---

[11] Closely related to my concept of Conceptual Thinking, which is discussed in Chapter 9.

Katz's view on the role of human skills in leadership is similar to my concept of Social Leadership. From my perspective, Nonverbal Thinking is a key component of what Katz refers to as "human skills" because this habit supports a person both when they are working as a member of a group and when they are leading a team. In leadership, we use Nonverbal Thinking to build collaboration and drive momentum. Thus, Katz's work provides a solid framework we can leverage to unpack the Subconscious Thinking Habit of Nonverbal Thinking.

"Non-verbal communication is an elaborate secret code that is written nowhere, known by none, and understood by all." —Edward Sapir

As American anthropologist and linguist Edward Sapir astutely articulated, "Non-verbal communication is an elaborate secret code that is written nowhere, known by none, and understood by all."[lxxxii] His statement aptly sums up Nonverbal Thinking, coining the exquisite phrase "an elaborate secret code."

Let's examine why I find Sapir's comment to be an apt observation about Nonverbal Thinking. First, it's a "secret code." So, while some people may understand that it exists, the code itself remains a mystery. Most people tap into this code subconsciously, as they are not consciously aware of it.

Second, because the code is "written nowhere, known by none," it is practically impossible to articulate and document. Therefore, we cannot categorize it as Crystallized Knowledge. Rather, it falls into the category of Fluid Thinking.

Third, it's "understood by all." I would say the secret code is understood by most, but not all. To those with lower Nonverbal Thinking, this code usually remains a complete mystery, as their brain did not encode their Nonverbal Thinking habit effectively when they were growing up.

SUBCONSCIOUS THINKING HABIT MODEL FOR NONVERBAL THINKING

Remember the habit model? It is hard to forget by now. But we have to frame the picture, and context is essential. Those who struggle with Nonverbal Thinking, rarely, if ever, recognize the cue.

If you have underdeveloped Nonverbal Thinking, it plays out as follows:

Cue: A colleague's facial expression or body language changes subtly while you are conversing with them.

Routine: You subconsciously run your underdeveloped Nonverbal Thinking routine.

Output: Unfortunately, you are oblivious to their nonverbal cue changes; so, you continue unabated without recognizing the need to check in with the other person.

Individuals with lower Nonverbal Thinking have great difficulty observing the subtle cues that show shifts in body language, tone of voice, facial expressions, and so on. Consequently, they have trouble dancing the nonverbal rapport dance with others.

THE SCIENCE BEHIND NONVERBAL THINKING

Goleman and Boyatzis's *Harvard Business Review* article titled "Social Intelligence and the Biology of Leadership" is a valuable resource to us as we explore the more scientific aspects of Social Leadership and Nonverbal Thinking.[lxxxiii] This article touches on the evolving research in behavioral neuroscience, which is the study of how

236

our brains react when we interact with others. The authors' work reveals interesting insights into what makes a good leader. I will explain how their insights support our approach to delivering brain coaching to clients who need help navigating Social Leadership in demanding situations.

Goleman and Boyatzis also referred to work undertaken by their colleague Fernandez-Araoz, who found that many new C-suite executives hired for "...their self-discipline, drive, and intellect were sometimes later fired for lacking basic social skills."[lxxxiv] This observation sheds light on why executives who have excellent technical and intellectual skills can be professionally limited by their inadequate Social Leadership skills.

Goleman and Boyatzis also examined research in the field of behavioral neuroscience that identified *mirror neurons*. Widely distributed throughout the brain, mirror neurons monitor and mimic what another person's brain is doing and instantaneously activate the very same areas in our own brain. These brain cells are largely responsible for our subconscious ability to mirror and reproduce another person's emotions, body language, movements, and intentions. When we engage in social interactions, our brain is constantly changing as we both consciously and subconsciously react and respond to the other person. Thus, our own emotions, body language, movements, and intentions are constantly changing, too.

Most of us have experienced the feeling of being completely in sync with another person. If this ever happened to you, you might have said, "We were on the same wavelength." Until recently, this attunement phenomenon was not well understood. But the latest research in neuroscience explains that we are able to empathize and tune into others because our brains become "fused into a single system."[lxxxv] Metaphorically speaking, mirror neurons operate as a kind of *neural Wi-Fi network*, creating brain interconnectedness between people and subconsciously helping us connect and navigate our social interactions. Essentially, when we connect into this neural Wi-Fi network, each of us can feel the shared experience instantly.[lxxxvi]

Let me explain how this plays out in real life. Have you ever noticed that when someone smiles at you, you usually smile back? This reflexive behavior is an example of mirror neurons and neural Wi-Fi network in action. Similarly, people find yawning contagious. Here's another example. When someone shares a particularly emotional experience with you, do you feel their emotions? If so, that is mirror neurons and the neural Wi-Fi network in action.[12]

It's not only __what__ you say that matters, but also __how__ you say it.

The neural Wi-Fi network is especially important in organizations because people will automatically and subconsciously mirror the feelings and actions of their leaders. Goleman and Boyatzis cite a study by Marie Dasborough, who found that receiving positive feedback accompanied by negative emotional signals (e.g., frowns) made people feel worse than receiving negative feedback accompanied by positive emotional signals (e.g., smiles). So, effectively, the delivery had a greater impact on the test subjects than the actual message did. For leaders, the key takeaway is: it's not only *what* you say that matters, but also *how* you say it.

Goleman and Boyatzis's examination of the research on mirror neurons underscores why it's so vital to have an optimal level of Nonverbal Thinking ability. You need to be able to connect into the neural Wi-Fi network reliably in order to pick up on other people's nonverbal cues, including their body language, facial expressions, tone of voice, and so much more. Having the ability to perceive those cues subconsciously is critical to cracking what Sapir

---

[12] If you remain detached and in a rational state of mind, one or more of your Social Leadership habits may be underdeveloped.

referred to as the "secret code." Individuals with lower Nonverbal Thinking struggle to detect the nonverbal cues, and this reduced capability undermines their Social Leadership skills.

A leader will have difficulty navigating social situations when their capacity to connect and build rapport with others is compromised. When an individual has difficulty receiving the neural Wi-Fi signal, there will inevitably be some technical difficulties.

THE COST OF COMPROMISED CONNECTION

Leadership style can be a blessing or a curse. When it is a curse, Social Leadership skills can be significantly enhanced by developing the related Subconscious Thinking Habits, particularly Nonverbal Thinking.

In their *Harvard Business Review* article titled "How to Develop Your Leadership Style," Peterson, Abramson, and Stutman state, "Few things are more frustrating for talented professionals than hitting the ceiling in their career because they lack appropriate leadership style."[lxxxvii] These authors view leadership style and personality as separate. They see *leadership style* as mutable and define it as what you do, how you do it, and how often you do it. In contrast, they see *personality* as a more fixed and immutable aspect of a person.

Based on their own work and decades of proprietary research, which included engagements with over 12,000 executives, Peterson et al. identified the markers most commonly used by executives to express status in the workplace. Together, these markers define an executive's leadership style. The authors undertook an extensive review to identify the hallmark of a balanced leadership approach and identified two categories of leadership markers:

- **Powerful Markers** are aligned with status and power. They are associated with confidence, competence, charisma, and influence; however, they are also associated with arrogance, abrasiveness, and intimidation.

- **Attractive Markers** are aligned to warmth and attractiveness. These are related to agreeableness, approachability, likability; however, they are also associated with diffidence, lack of confidence, and submissiveness.

While the authors note that Powerful Markers and Attractive Markers are neither inherently good nor bad, they observe that executives who display Powerful Markers frequently view individuals who display Attractive Markers as being weak. Conversely, those who display Attractive Markers often view their colleagues with Powerful Markers as rude.

They further note that people's leadership styles fell into five categories based on their balance of Powerful and Attractive Markers, spanning a spectrum that includes the following:[13]

- Powerful
- Lean Powerful
- Blended
- Lean Attractive
- Attractive

Peterson et al. note that a blended style is rare, and it involves balanced use of Powerful Markers and Attractive Markers. People who have a blended leadership style are seen as having "presence," according to the authors.

The authors also examined the difference in nonverbal styles between those with Powerful Markers and those with Attractive Markers. For context, see Table 5, which outlines the nonverbal styles and behaviors associated with each type of marker.[lxxxviii]

---

[13] Within the authors' framework, the term "Lean" means "leaning toward." For example, "Lean Powerful" describes leaders who display a mix of both Powerful Markers and Attractive Markers, but still lean toward the "Powerful" style.

Table 5. A Guide to Leadership Markers within the Context of Nonverbal Style

Powerful Markers	Attractive Markers
Backward leans	Forward leans
Physical distance	Physical closeness
Eye contact when speaking	Eye contact when listening
Averted gaze when listening	Averted gaze when speaking
Tendency to stare	Tendency to break eye contact
Serious expressions	Happy expressions
Controlled movements	Natural movements
Talking while moving away	Body square while talking

From the research of Peterson et al., it is easy to see how costly lower Nonverbal Thinking ability can be. A lack of balance between Powerful Markers and Attractive Markers leads to a lack of connection. The authors recommend that executives take a blended approach, but also tweak their style as appropriate, depending on the context.

We have found this to be true in our brain coaching experiences across many companies in a multitude of countries. Executives who display predominately Powerful Markers tend to come across as intimidating, have lower social skills, and be less collaborative. Plus, they are often unaware of their impact on people. In such situations, we enhance the executive's Social Leadership Subconscious Thinking Habits as appropriate. This increases their ability to read the social signals, better equips them to soften their leadership style when needed, and it helps them be more adaptable in their approach when dealing with people.

In contrast, executives who display predominately Attractive Markers come across as very likable, but they often lack the gravitas, power, and visibility to inspire confidence in their leadership. They are also quite surprised to discover how much improving their Nonverbal Thinking and changing their nonverbal communication and physiology can enhance their status in the eyes of their peers and team members.

ANTONIO: VERY SMART, BUT SOCIALLY CLUELESS

Antonio is the vice president of finance at a prestigious global insurance organization. Smart as a whip, he is quick at analyzing numbers, generating deep insights, and developing innovative solutions to intricate problems. He is also highly competent at developing strategies to optimize potential opportunities and mitigate financial risks. These traits make Antonio a valued executive, and he wants to pursue continual promotion within his organization.

Despite Antonio's many positive attributes, his manager regularly speaks to him about a significant derailer: Antonio's people skills need major improvement. Team members and colleagues have voiced that he regularly misses nonverbal cues, often bulldozing through meetings. Antonio's overpowering leadership style inadvertently leads others to feel intimidated, unrecognized, or unheard. His colleagues don't understand why body language and nonverbal cues seem to fly right over Antonio's head.

During his last performance review, his manager pointed out that Antonio had rushed through a recent meeting. Instead of encouraging the attendees' input, Antonio pressed on, and his colleagues had felt excluded as a result. His manager asked if Antonio had seen the clear nonverbal signals the attendees had given him throughout the meeting. Unfortunately, Antonio never noticed his colleagues' discomfort as he hurried to wrap up the meeting.

Genuinely surprised by his manager's feedback, Antonio exclaimed, "Really? I had no idea!" He thought the meeting had gone reasonably well. Antonio was discouraged and admitted that body language had always seemed like a foreign language to him. Despite trying, he couldn't seem to crack it or learn it. Sapir's idea of nonverbal communication being a "secret code" certainly would have resonated with him.

To help Antonio learn nonverbal cues, his manager hired a personal mentor. While Antonio gained a solid understanding of nonverbal communication concepts quickly, he struggled to apply them in day-to-day work situations. Although he tried hard to leverage this mentoring, it only produced minor changes. Antonio continued to bulldoze through work, often blissfully unaware of nonverbal cues. As a result, his manager had to accept that, although Antonio's technical skills were a tremendous asset, his inability to improve his Social Leadership skills meant he could not rise higher within the organization.

This was a costly consequence that Antonio would eventually over-come. In the meantime, he continued to be blindsided by issues and conflicts that had been building up around him, culminating in harsh words from colleagues who often told him, "You just don't get it!" For Antonio, these admonishments were random and con-fusing. Despite his best efforts, he found it difficult to build rap-port with his team, colleagues, and professional network. It made him feel out of sync with others, as if he were a step or two behind the beat and couldn't find the pocket of his rhythm. He knew deep down this was because he struggled with the nonverbal rapport dance—the one he had learned all the steps to but could never perform.

Unfortunately for Antonio, no amount of conscious learning will correct this subconscious imbalance. Until the root cause associat-ed with his lower Nonverbal Thinking is addressed, the code will remain secret, regardless of how hard he works to treat the symp-toms using methods that engage only his conscious mind.

IMPACT OF LOWER NONVERBAL THINKING

Reviewing Antonio's situation supports us in understanding what it's like to operate with lower Nonverbal Thinking capability. Un-fortunately for Antonio, he didn't even realize that Sapir's nonverbal secret code even existed, let alone understand it. The concept of a neural Wi-Fi network to which everyone was connected would have been a mystery to him, and his mirror neurons just didn't seem to fire as other people's did. As I summarize the tangible impacts of Antonio's lower Nonverbal Thinking, see if any of the symptoms resonate with you or someone you know.

WHAT BODY LANGUAGE CUES?

Because lower Nonverbal Thinking inhibits the ability to notice subtle changes in body language, facial expressions, tone of voice, and so on, these cues never came up on Antonio's radar. His manager and mentor tried to explain some aspects of the nonverbal secret code to no avail. Although Antonio somewhat understood the concept intellectually, he couldn't relate to it because it simply wasn't part of his personal experience.

As a consequence, he continued to take a bulldozer approach at meetings and unwittingly overused his Powerful Markers. Because of his lower Nonverbal Thinking, Antonio was unable to identify and calibrate others' nonverbal cues; as a result, he couldn't tell when people weren't on board with him.

OUT OF STEP WITH THE NONVERBAL RAPPORT DANCE

Antonio seemed to be dancing to a different rhythm than everyone else. While others heard the music on the neural Wi-Fi network clearly, Antonio heard it only faintly. Because of his low Nonverbal Thinking, he received a weak signal that dropped frequently. When you can barely hear the music, it's very hard to dance to the rhythm.

It's interesting to observe when two people are in strong rapport. They seem to be doing what I call a subconscious nonverbal rapport dance. Without conscious awareness, they start to mirror each other's physical gestures, smiles, verbal rhythm, and tone of voice. Their mirror neurons seem to be firing in harmony, and they both have strong neural Wi-Fi network signals.

For Antonio, it was more important to deliver results than to engage with his people. He was focused on delivering his message and not particularly aware of the manner in which he delivered it. With his lower Nonverbal Thinking, he was unattuned to how he engaged with his people and unable to read nonverbal feedback, which is why he could never get in sync with the rapport dance. Sadly, it was easier for him just to stand alone in the corner of the dance floor.

WHY DIDN'T I SEE THAT CONFLICT COMING?

It is very important for a leader to be able to anticipate when conflicts are starting to arise so they can be managed early in the piece. Not everybody is comfortable or confident enough to verbalize conflict issues, especially in the early stages.

Typically, people will subconsciously provide nonverbal cues indicating they are unhappy with a situation. These signals open up an opportunity for a manager to inquire about what's happening. Individuals often express nonverbal cues over a period of time during various interpersonal interactions such as meetings. When these cues are not acknowledged and addressed, a large conflict can explode. For those who are unable to detect these signals, the conflict can seemingly come out of nowhere.

With his lower ability to pick up on nonverbal cues, Antonio fell victim to being blindsided to emerging conflicts, even though they had been bubbling just below the surface for some time.

SOCIAL LEADERSHIP IS A MYSTERY

To Antonio, it was a mystery how some of his peers could engage so easily with their team members, build rapport, and get their people to deliver above and beyond the call of duty. In contrast, Antonio felt he had to ride his team continuously to get the most out of them. Even after both his manager and his mentor had tried to educate him about nonverbal communication, social leadership skills still remained a mystery to Antonio.

Like many people, Antonio didn't realize there is a world of difference between being able to understand a concept intellectually (i.e., Crystallized Knowledge) and being able to apply newly acquired knowledge (i.e., Fluid Thinking). Consequently, the mentoring program did little to help him improve his social leadership ability.

BENEFITS OF OPTIMALLY DEVELOPED NONVERBAL THINKING

When Nonverbal Thinking is optimized, the brain can effortlessly, quickly, and subconsciously sense nonverbal cues. This then supports a person to make a conscious decision about a possible intervention or conversation that may be appropriate based on the nonverbal cue they picked up on.

We need to become aware of nonverbal cues before we can decide what to do with that information. When an individual's Nonverbal Thinking is suboptimal, their brain cannot pick up on the nonverbal signals and cues. Thus, there is no trigger upon which to base a decision. And so, the person continues on, oblivious to the situation at hand. It is important to note that people with lower Nonverbal Thinking do not deliberately ignore these signals. The problem is that their brain doesn't even perceive the nonverbal cue, let alone register that something needs to be addressed.

With optimal Nonverbal Thinking, our brain can easily tap into the wider neural Wi-Fi network and more readily connect with another person on a subconscious level.

ANTONIO: ENHANCED NONVERBAL THINKING AFTER BRAIN COACHING

Antonio's lower Nonverbal Thinking had been his blind spot, simply because he didn't know what he didn't know. However, after taking a deliberate practice approach to improve his Nonverbal

Thinking, Antonio was very surprised by how his improved neural Wi-Fi made it much easier for him to notice nonverbal cues quickly and effectively. It was as if someone had suddenly shared with him Sapir's "elaborate secret code" to nonverbal communication, and he could see and hear the world with new eyes and ears.

In addition, brain coaching gave him the ability to choose his leadership style. Whereas previously his default style was dominated by Powerful Markers, he now understands the importance of balancing his approach with Attractive Markers and is more adept at applying a blended approach. Antonio's enhanced Nonverbal Thinking enables him to detect nonverbal cues and, having detected them, he can choose how to address the issue—a choice he had never had before.

Antonio was surprised and delighted to see that his ability to manage the human dynamics of his team had improved considerably, and his colleagues and team members were amazed by the changes in his behavior. What surprised Antonio the most was that his team now seemed to be more engaged, productive, and proactive.

KEY TAKEAWAYS

- Nonverbal Thinking underpins the ability to detect subtle changes in nonverbal communication such as body language, facial expression, tone of voice, etc.
- When Nonverbal Thinking is lower, people literally cannot detect subtle nonverbal communication cues, and so they cannot react to those signals. This is very frustrating for their team members and colleagues who feel that they are being deliberately ignored or brushed aside.
- For those with lower Nonverbal Thinking, nonverbal communication seems like a secret code that, unfortunately, remains hidden. It is a mystery to them.
- The brain's mirror neurons underpin a metaphorical neural Wi-Fi network that enables people to track, subcon-

sciously, each other's emotions, physical movements, subtle changes in body language, and intentions. This enables people to get on the same wavelength easily, instantaneously, automatically, and without conscious awareness.

- When Nonverbal Thinking is optimal, a leader can quickly and effectively build rapport by tapping into others' nonverbal communication cues and ensuring that their own neural Wi-Fi is operating effectively.

Chapter 16

PERSPECTIVE THINKING

"Everyone is right from their own perspective so don't judge anyone prior to knowing why they had that perception." —Giridhar Alwar, My Quest for a Happy Life [lxxxix]

Perspective-taking is part of the social glue that helps an organization stick together and run smoothly. In business, a leader's willingness to hear and consider different points of view is crucial to building relationships, collaborating with others, creating better cooperation, and cultivating authentic connections—all of which are skills that can be appropriately applied when Social Leadership capability is optimized.

The Subconscious Thinking Habit of Perspective Thinking underpins our ability to look at a situation from multiple orientations. This habit gives you a more expansive view and helps you avoid getting blindsided because you failed to take other people's perspectives into account. Having well-developed Perspective Thinking is like having eyes in the back of your head. With the ongoing chaos and rapid change in today's world, we all need a high level of Perspective Thinking.

Perspective Thinking also supports our ability to have empathy for others by leveraging sympathy and compassion. Having the capacity to understand what someone else might be thinking and feeling not only supports you in being more empathetic, but also gives you an edge in leadership and negotiation.

There is a high cost associated with lower Perspective Thinking. Repeatedly ignoring others' perspectives and ideas has detrimental effects on personal and professional relationships. People who lack the ability to show empathy appropriately can appear cold and indifferent. This makes social bonding and collaboration difficult, as others will feel unheard and discounted.

SUBCONSCIOUS THINKING HABIT MODEL FOR PERSPECTIVE THINKING

When you have well-developed Perspective Thinking, you are open to entertaining ideas, approaches, and opinions other than your own. You are able to look at a situation from different angles and are receptive to hearing alternative different points of view. However, if your level of Perspective Thinking is suboptimal, here's how this habit might play out:

Cue: A team member tries to offer a different position on an issue.

Routine: You subconsciously run your underdeveloped Perspective Thinking routine.

Output: Instead of acknowledging that person's alternative viewpoint, you reiterate your own position, rapidly shutting down any discussion.

THE SCIENCE BEHIND PERSPECTIVE THINKING

In this section, I highlight three important academic research studies that underscore key aspects of my framework for Perspective Thinking.

THE CAPACITY TO IMAGINE WHAT OTHERS ARE THINKING AND FEELING

Put simply, perspective-taking is the ability to imagine what the other person might be thinking. By contrast, the authors define empathy as the ability to imagine what the other person might be feeling.

In their 2008 paper titled "Why It Pays to Get Inside the Head of Your Opponent," Galinsky et al. explore the importance of having perspective when involved in negotiations.[xc] The authors define *perspective-taking* as the ability to consider the world from another person's point of view. They explain that this involves understanding and anticipating the other person's interests, thoughts, and potential behaviors. Put simply, perspective-taking is the ability to imagine what the other person might be *thinking*. By contrast, the authors define empathy as the ability to imagine what the other person might be *feeling*.

Galinsky et al. opine that, when negotiating, it is valuable to understand not only what the other party is thinking but also what motivates their thinking. Having perspective allows you to tailor a deal that can work for both parties. However, the authors caution that over-empathizing during negotiations can come at a personal cost if you try too hard to make the other party happy.

ALL POWER + NO PERSPECTIVE = INEFFECTIVE LEADERSHIP

In their 2014 paper titled "Acceleration With Steering: The Synergistic Benefits of Combining Power and Perspective-Taking,"

Galinsky et al. state, "Effective leadership is like a successful car ride. To go places, you need gas and acceleration—power is a psychological accelerator. But you also need a good steering wheel, so you don't crash as you speed down the highway—perspective-taking is that psychological steering wheel. When you anchor too heavily on to your own perspective, and don't take into account the viewpoints of others, you are bound to crash." [xci]

The authors paint a vivid and accurate picture; heavy reliance on your personal perspective alone will almost always end in needing to call roadside assistance. They emphasize that influential leaders such as CEOs, politicians, and military commanders who fail to understand their people's perspectives are more prone to miscommunicating and mishandling contentious issues and conversations. However, leaders who look at the world from multiple perspectives handle these situations with greater ease.

The authors conclude that effective leaders need both power and perspective. All power and no perspective often results in ineffective leadership styles that stall and cap both personal and professional progression.

It is easy to see how underdeveloped Perspective Thinking can derail a career. Without well-developed Social Leadership skills, even the best minds will struggle to take the driver's seat. People want to be led, not owned.

SPATIAL IQ

In her 2012 *Harvard Business Review* article titled "Improving Your Spatial IQ Can Lift Your Social IQ," Professor Amy Shelton observes that spatial IQ and social IQ are intrinsically linked in the brain. According to Shelton, "People with strong social skills are better at seeing other people's perspectives—literally." [xcii] She notes, "…[S]omething about your social nature affects the way you engage in the task when you're taking another person's point of view." [xciii]

Shelton also found a possible link between social skills and the ability to read a map. In the same article, she posits that the ability to see the physical world from others' perspectives appears to predict our spatial learning style, suggesting a correlation between the way we navigate our physical and interpersonal worlds.[xciv]

Shelton's opinions are consistent with my experience in working with individuals who have underdeveloped Perspective Thinking. I, too, have found that people with lower Perspective Thinking usually have lower directional and orientation skills. This might explain why they are often prone to invading people's personal space.

IMPACT OF RESONANT LEADERSHIP VERSUS DISSONANT LEADERSHIP

In 2012, Boyatzis wrote a fascinating journal article titled "Neuro-science and the Link between Inspirational Leadership and Resonant Relationships" that pulls together a wide range of research and touches on why many bright, innovative, and intellectual leaders unintentionally act in ways that compromise their level of personal effectiveness.[xcv] While we will explore this in more depth later, the overarching takeaway is Boyatzis's concept of neurological *coherence*.

The *Default Mode Network*[14] is a very important in Boyatzis's work because it underpins his concept of a resonant leader. Boyatzis defines a *resonant leader* as one who coaches with compassion.[xcvi] Resonant leaders are seen as charismatic. They take a vision-driven approach that motivates and creates an exciting view of the future of a business, product, service, or program.[xcvii] Importantly, this type of leader subconsciously seeks to connect positively, engaging with a coachee's Default Mode Network. This compassionate

---

[14] This network is activated when we are engaging with or being engaged by others. It is also known as the *social network* and the *Empathic Network*.

approach enables the coachee to be open to new ideas, feel new emotions, think outside the box, and put their spectrum of talents to full use. Thus, a resonant leader encourages their people to be more innovative and more open to adapting to changes in technology and their organizational environment.

Conversely, according to Boyatzis, a *dissonant leader* coaches for compliance, telling people what they should do instead of motivating them to do it.[xcviii] Dissonant leaders significantly deactivate or suppress their coachees' Default Mode Network.[xcix] People avoid interacting with dissonant leaders, and those who work for them typically produce the minimum amount of work needed to get by.[c] It makes sense when you consider that the behaviors of dissonant leaders are often perceived as threatening and demanding. Instead of acknowledging successes, these leaders are predisposed to focusing on what needs fixing and call attention to the weaknesses of the team and individual team members. This subconscious management style can be demotivating and demoralizing and can trigger a maddening negative behavioral cycle for the leader and team members alike. In addition, dissonant leaders tend to be more task-focused and less visionary, which inhibits both openness to change and innovativeness in their people.

Everything comes back to what is going on inside a leader's head—specifically, in their brain. A resonant leader's brain is more connected than a dissonant leader's, as the former's neural circuits are more coherent. Citing the research of David Waldman at Arizona State University, Boyatzis explains, "…'[C]oherence' occurs when the left and right parts of the brain are in greater coordination (i.e., activated at the same time)…"[ci] Drawing again from Waldman and others, he further asserts that coherence is the differentiator that makes a leader well-rounded, authentic, and charismatic.

Boyatzis's concept of neurological coherence is what I call *brain balance*. It's a key reason why we encourage people to develop their Subconscious Thinking Habits, which are vital to success and help support having a coherent Social Leadership style. Boyatzis's research validates our findings, which are based on extensive experience with leaders who have lower Social Leadership skills. From Boyatzis's work, it is clear why the behavioral derailers we identify in our testing often stem from a lack of neurological coherence.

ARE YOU A PEA OR AN NEA?

Let's continue to delve into Boyatzis's insights into social leadership capability. In the same article that discusses resonant and dissonant leaders, he reviewed the results of a study that examined two very different coaching styles.[cii] One focused on the Positive Emotional Attractor (PEA) and the other focused on Negative Emotional Attractor (NEA). Figure 26 describes the attributes associated with each coaching style.

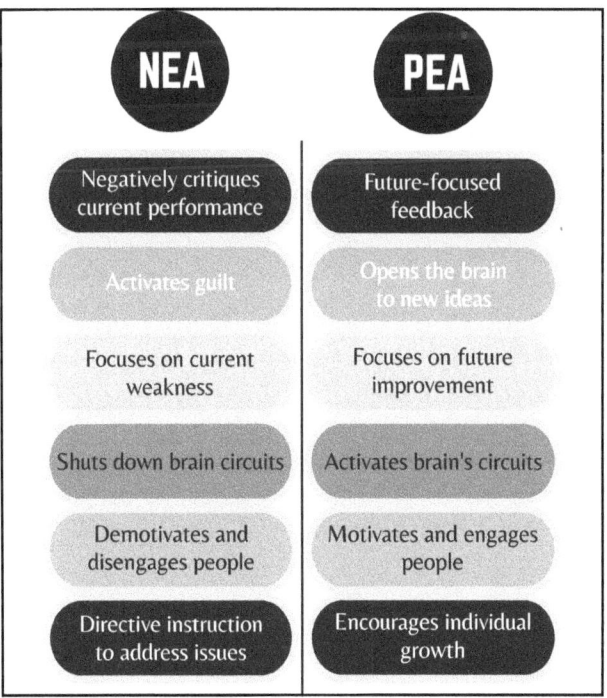

Figure 26. Characteristics of NEA and PEA Coaching Styles

The study participants much preferred the PEA approach, which incorporates future-focused feedback. This style of coaching stimulates the brain's visual cortex, which is involved in imagination. Thus, PEA coaching positively activates components of the Default Mode Network.

In contrast, NEA coaching provides feedback on how a person is doing in their current assignments and focuses on overcoming their weaknesses. Boyatzis found that NEA coaching activates the parts of the brain that are connected to self-consciousness and guilt, so it's no surprise that NEA coaching was less well-received.

The key takeaway is that PEA coaching enables people's brains to be more open to new ideas and more creative, adaptable, and motivated. Conversely, NEA coaching shuts the brain down and reduces people's openness to changing and adapting.

It is interesting that so many leaders unwittingly use a NEA approach when mentoring and developing their people. They focus on telling people what to do without attending to how to motivate them, and this often results in their team members going into a NEA state of mind and then shutting down.

PEA coaching requires more than some hyped-up jargon and a smile. It is a subconscious capacity within the brain. Just knowing its features does not support a leader in applying them because lower Perspective Thinking can inhibit its application.

THE BENEFITS OF A PEA COACHING STYLE

A client I'll call Jim had a habit of jumping into fix-it mode whenever his direct reports delivered work. (A habit that had resulted from his overly developed Operational Thinking.) Jim genuinely thought this was the best way to help his people grow and develop, but he missed the crucial step of acknowledging the parts of the work that had been done well.

During our brain coaching sessions, we addressed Jim's annoyance with his direct reports. He thought they made slow and incremental improvements in their rework even when he had clearly laid out the path for them. This was an excellent opportunity to integrate Boyatzis's work into our coaching. Like many of my clients, Jim had an epiphany when he realized he had been sending his direct reports into an NEA state of mind, inadvertently shutting down their brains and openness to ideas, as well as unintentionally demotivating them.

"It is amazing how much more intelligent my people have become since I've been doing your Fluid Thinking Program." — *"Jim" (a client)*

We combined our deliberate practice brain exercises with targeted coaching to help Jim enhance his Perspective Thinking. This equipped him to apply a PEA coaching approach. Much to his surprise, the quality of his team's work and turnaround times dramatically improved. This leads me to recall one of my absolute favorite brain coaching moments. Jim joked, "It is amazing how much more intelligent my people have become since I've been doing your Fluid Thinking Program."

NIA: "MY WAY OR THE HIGHWAY"

Nia is the managing director of a business unit that was part of a large conglomerate. She has been with the organization for ten years, steadily working her way up the corporate ladder. Nia has an excellent understanding of how her company works, including its processes, politics, strengths, and weakness.

Nia is a proud Type A personality, feisty, and chasing C-suite roles—specifically, the title of CEO. It is no secret that she feels equipped to match and outperform the current CEO. Nia believes her leadership style is just right, and that she is well-positioned to become the current CEO's successor.

Everyone knows where Nia stands on most topics. Though she can be friendly and approachable, her tendency to be overzealous and overconfident is not warmly received by some of the board members, her senior colleagues, and her team. Additionally, Nia is very protective of her business unit and her team, which results in unnecessary confrontations with a cross-section of people from other departments. Like everyone else, she has positive and negative traits; however, Nia sees only her positives, and this tendency complicates her professional relationships.

Nia particularly enjoys giving presentations to the board. She finds it exciting to get up and share her work and credentials, and she delivers her presentations with passion and enthusiasm. However, some board members feel Nia can be too enthusiastic, bordering on aggressive. This behavior is challenging, as people find it hard to connect with her.

Despite all her passion and enthusiasm, Nia's colleagues and team members are put off by her tendency to see things only from her own narrow perspective. Rather than having two-way conversations, Nia prefers to deliver monologues, as she intends her passionate opinions to be received but never challenged or debated. Understandably, her colleagues and team members never feel heard or included. This problem is amplified by her willingness to listen only to those who reinforce her opinions.

Nia's colleagues feel she lacks empathy, which makes her appear cold and indifferent to others' feelings and opinions. Additionally, she has a habit of unwittingly invading people's personal space, which makes everyone uncomfortable.

In a recent meeting, Mateo, a new hire who reports to Nia, wanted to impress her. So, he took the initiative to analyze a problem the business unit was trying to solve. He explored the issue deeply, desiring to understand it from multiple angles. Mateo came to the meeting excited, hoping Nia would value the insights he had generated and that his analysis would prove valuable to the business unit. However, as soon as he began his presentation, he felt the tension mounting in the room. Experienced members of the team knew Nia would not be receptive to Mateo's work because she is notoriously critical of new ideas, especially when they don't align with her own views.

Mateo's peers were on the money because Nia cut him off almost immediately. Speaking to him dismissively in front of his peers, Nia said, "When you have obtained my level of experience and expertise, then you can put forward your opinions. Until then, it is best to listen and learn." Unsurprisingly, Mateo shut down. Taking a cue from his peers, he was never tempted to share any original thinking with Nia or the team. He had gotten the message: the glass is only as full as Nia says it is.

Clearly, Nia has several derailers to overcome. Her Nia-tinted glasses compromise her Social Leadership capability. While she sees herself as well positioned for the CEO role, her lower empathy and difficulty in recognizing others' perspectives are blind spots that will cost her promotional prospects unless she improves her Perspective Thinking. As we all know, results alone are no longer the only metric used to determine who is chosen for coveted C-suite positions.

IMPACT OF LOWER PERSPECTIVE THINKING

Lower Perspective Thinking has business consequences associated with lower Social Leadership capability and reduced ability to engage and motivate team members, as Nia found.

DIFFICULTY WITH NEGOTIATION

It is almost impossible to negotiate with people who have lower Perspective Thinking. Just like Nia, they lack social awareness. Because they struggle to appreciate others' perspectives and empathize appropriately, they often take a "my way or the highway" approach that leaves no room for negotiation.

In business, this leadership style pushes away team members and colleagues. It creates negative perceptions throughout the organization and, consequently, can limit a person's career advancement opportunities.

UNWITTING NEA COACHING APPROACH

Leaders with lower Perspective Thinking generally take an NEA approach to coaching, just as Nia did. This leadership style lowers motivation and ultimately comprises the quality of the team's output. Many of us can relate to how demoralizing it can be to work for someone who doesn't seem to care about how we think or feel. However, it's not that people with lower Perspective Thinking are uncaring; it's usually that they are unaware of how their behavior comes across because they have difficulty seeing or feeling things from other points of view.

ISSUES WITH PERSONAL SPACE

Because people with lower Perspective Thinking commonly lack spatial awareness and struggle with directional orientation, they often invade others' personal space inadvertently. When our personal space is violated, it can make us very uncomfortable.

For those who are navigating this issue, a lot can be gained once this Subconscious Thinking Habit is fully developed. It creates a whole new way to navigate professionally and personally, eliminating those subconscious behaviors that can derail career opportunities.

BENEFITS OF HIGHLY DEVELOPED PERSPECTIVE THINKING

Highly developed Perspective Thinking enables you to orient yourself quickly in new environments and understand other people's perspectives. This then supports you in successfully navigating a tricky negotiation or a complex conflict. In addition, it is paramount to possess empathy skills, as having them gives you the ability to understand and share feelings with team members, colleagues, and social contacts.

Another key benefit of optimized Perspective Thinking is that an executive will be more open to using a Positive Emotional Attractor (PEA) coaching approach, which is important for motivating people. This approach helps open others' brain circuits to new ideas and encourages individual growth.

NIA: ENHANCED PERSPECTIVE THINKING AFTER BRAIN COACHING

With her enhanced Perspective Thinking, Nia is noticeably more willing to entertain different perspectives and encourages her team members to present original ideas. Now that she has replaced her disapproving leadership style with a PEA coaching approach, she is amazed at how much better her people perform. She guides them in a positive manner to stretch their thinking, rather than immediately criticizing their work and ideas.

She has also replaced her Nia-tinted glasses with significantly more valuable and useful empathy-tinted glasses, which enable her to see and take the time to understand other people's viewpoints.

Finally, Nia has positively enhanced her personal brand and improved her relationships with everyone in the organization, including the CEO and board. The company is now more open to promoting her to a more senior role that requires well-developed Perspective Thinking and strong Social Leadership skills overall.

KEY TAKEAWAYS

- Perspective Thinking is integral to our subconscious ability to sense what other people are thinking and feeling.
- Empathy is underpinned by Perspective Thinking. Higher levels of Perspective Thinking correlate with higher levels of empathy.
- People with higher Perspective Thinking are generally more competent negotiators. They are better positioned to achieve win-win outcomes because they have a sharpened sense of what's important to the person with whom they are negotiating.
- Higher Perspective Thinking supports using a Positive Emotional Attractor (PEA) coaching approach, which results in much better performance than a Negative Emotional Attractor (NEA) approach. Unfortunately, dissonant leaders who use an NEA approach are usually unaware that they are doing so, nor are they aware of the damaging impact a continuous stream of negative critique has on people.
- Resonant leaders who use a PEA coaching approach are seen as more charismatic. They take a vision-driven approach and create a more engaging view of the future. Resonant leaders are very adept at subconsciously tapping into the neural Wi-Fi network. Having this ability, they can help their team members be more creative, adaptable, and motivated.
- People with lower Perspective Thinking often have a "my way or the highway" attitude because they find it difficult and time-consuming to understand other people's perspectives fully.

Chapter 17
INTUITIVE THINKING

"Intuition involves a sense of knowing, without knowing how one knows based on the unconscious processing of information." —Seymour Epstein

Have you ever gotten a strong sense about someone or something that later turned out to be true? Whether you call it a premonition, intuition, or just a hunch, this instinctual response arises from your subconscious brain. When we get this gut sense, we can have an idea about something even though we have no proof. Intuitive Thinking doesn't require evidence because it doesn't engage with rational processes or necessarily rely on explicit data and facts.

Intuitive Thinking is more elusive than the other Subconscious Thinking Habits, and its softer, less-precise nature makes it challenging to define. Robin Hogarth's definition resonates best with my view of Intuitive Thinking:

"The essence of intuition or intuitive response is that they are reached with little apparent effort, and typically without conscious awareness. They involve little or no conscious deliberation."[ciii]

Almost everyone is familiar with the term Spidey-Sense, which was made famous by the *Spider-Man* movies. *Spidey-Sense* is the superhero's precognitive ability to perceive danger before it happens. Well-developed Intuitive Thinking is similar to Spidey-Sense in that it gives us the capacity to sense subconsciously information in our environment. We might feel uneasy or confident in a situation, depending on our intuitive impressions. But no matter how well attuned our Spidey-Sense is, we should never base important decisions solely on intuition.

In some ways, Intuitive Thinking resembles Nonverbal Thinking (see Chapter 15); however it's important to note a key difference between these two habits. Whereas Nonverbal Thinking applies to one-on-one interactions, Intuitive Thinking applies more to group dynamics and enables a person's broader environmental awareness. For example, Intuitive Thinking gives you the ability to sense whether or not people are on board with you when you're addressing a group (e.g., during a meeting or presentation). In common parlance, we call this *reading the room*. People with high Intuitive Thinking also have the ability to *see the writing on the wall*—that is, they can correctly predict future events by interpreting the subtle environmental signs that indicate something is about to happen.

SUBCONSCIOUS THINKING HABIT MODEL FOR INTUITIVE THINKING

Individuals with lower Intuitive Thinking are less tuned in to their environment and less aware of group dynamics. They commonly miss indicators that people with higher Intuitive Thinking get a gut feeling about.

Because Intuitive Thinking is subtle and highly nuanced, I will provide two examples of how this habit might play out when it is underdeveloped. Here is the first one:

Cue: It is obvious to others that the people in the room appear to be unengaged during your presentation.

Routine: You subconsciously run your underdeveloped Intuitive Thinking routine.

Output: Because you don't recognize when the group is exhibiting subtle signs of disengagement, you're unaware that you've lost your audience; so you just keep on talking without adjusting your approach.

Could you relate to that scenario? If not, here's another example:

Cue: You have a weak gut feeling that something isn't quite right about the project you're working on.

Routine: You subconsciously run your underdeveloped Intuitive Thinking routine.

Output: Because your gut is giving you a weak signal, you choose to ignore it. Later, the issue you suspected (but dismissed) becomes a major problem.

Unfortunately, lower Intuitive Thinking impacts personal efficacy, deliverables, and professional relationships, particularly in group situations, such as during meetings, training sessions, and presentations.

THE SCIENCE BEHIND INTUITIVE THINKING

Rhythm is music's pattern in time, and like music, our thinking has different rhythms, depending on what we are trying to achieve. Understanding and mastering these rhythms allows us to leverage our thinking to conduct our metaphorical orchestra made up of team members and colleagues.

Taking the lead from Daniel Kahneman, who won a Nobel Prize in behavioral economics for his work concerning human judgment and decision-making, I will expand on the concept of the rhythm associated with thinking.[civ] In his book *Thinking, Fast and Slow* Kahneman theorizes that humans have two diverse thinking systems: System 1 (fast) and System 2 (slow).[cv]

System 1, fast thinking, remains below the conscious threshold and requires little effort, as information is processed subconsciously and automatically. System 1 assists us in anticipating threats and recognizing opportunities. Fast thinking is more prone to bias and error. From my perspective, System 1 resembles the Subconscious Thinking Habit of Intuitive Thinking. The gut feelings associated with intuition arise because our brains subconsciously process environmental data quickly—much faster than our conscious brain can process information.

System 2, slow thinking, is much slower than System 1 and requires deliberate, conscious effort. System 2 is used for analysis and critical thinking, both of which require controlled and conscious mental processes. Slow thinking is less prone to bias and error, as decisions are more considered. From my perspective, System 2 aligns with the Subconscious Thinking Habits that rely on rational thinking, such as Analytical Thinking (see Chapter 7), Conceptual Thinking (Chapter 9), and Abstract Thinking (Chapter 12).

During his 2018 speech at the World Business Forum in New York, Daniel Kahneman said, "Intuition is thinking that you know, without knowing why you do."[cvi] He also explained that intuition can be right or wrong. Critically, Intuitive Thinking can be right or wrong as well. That is why we separate Intuitive Thinking, which is based on subconscious sensing, from the conscious decision-making process.

TUNED IN

In Chapter 15, I touched on an influential *Harvard Business Review* article by Goleman and Boyatzis titled "Social Intelligence and the Biology of Leadership." According to the authors, a *finely tuned leader* can operate in a wide range of contexts, leveraging gut feelings and good instincts while still gathering reliable data input for decision making.[cvii]

In this article, Goleman and Boyatzis explain that intuition is partly driven by the spindle cells present in the brain. *Spindle cells* are about four times larger than other brain cells and have an extra-long branch that attaches them to other brain cells, allowing feelings and thoughts to be transmitted faster than other types of brain cells can transmit information. According to the authors, spindle cells help us gauge an individual's trustworthiness quickly and give us the ability to read if they are an appropriate candidate for a job.[cviii]

The authors also contend that the extra-long spindle cells facilitate ultra-rapid transmission and connection of people's emotions, beliefs, and judgments. Behavioral scientists call this our *social guidance system*. From my perspective, spindle cells enable our sense or gut feel when we use our subconscious Intuitive Thinking because the information processing occurs rapidly and below the conscious threshold.

DANGER ZONE: INTUITIVE THINKING ISN'T INFALLIBLE

When making important decisions, we must use Analytical Thinking to complement our Intuitive Thinking. Complex problems need to be broken down so potential solutions can be evaluated before the ideal solution is chosen and implemented. The process cannot be rushed, nor should we try to solve complex problems by engaging at a purely intuitive level.

This is why it is so important to develop brain balance. Just as your car needs to be firing on all cylinders to deliver optimum performance, all ten Subconscious Thinking Habits must be functioning at optimal levels to achieve the best possible outcomes. You cannot rely solely on the habits you happen to be strong in. When you achieve brain balance, it's much like driving a car with a souped-up engine. You have more power at your disposal. Thus, brain balance has a synergetic effect, allowing us to take a broader $1 + 1 = 3$ approach.

POSSIBLE IMPACT OF COVID-19 ON INTUITIVE THINKING

I will touch on this only briefly, but it's worth mentioning that our new clients since the start of COVID-19 are showing an interesting pattern. Their Intuitive Thinking scores have dropped relative to Intuitive Thinking scores before COVID. While the reasons for the decline are not entirely clear, this trend does not surprise me, considering how difficult it has been to navigate the devastating complexities of COVID. As we adapted to the constraints of this pandemic, many of us found ourselves working from home. We became isolated from our families, friends, and colleagues. Instead of engaging with people in person, we started relying on technology to communicate virtually. Email and messaging platforms became more popular than ever, and videoconferencing replaced face-to-face meetings at the office.

In the Zoom era, we needed to learn to read a room when we are not physically in the room. Cues are different, contexts are different, and common ground is not so common anymore. We could all use more confidence and greater sensing capability in this unfamiliar environment. I believe this is why our clients' test scores are showing an increased need to enhance Intuitive Thinking skills. Now, more than ever, we could all use a heightened Spidey-Sense.

NATHAN: AM I MISSING SOMETHING?

Meet Nathan and Lara. They work at the same international travel corporation where Nathan is Head of Talent Development and Lara is Head of Talent Acquisition. Their personalities could not be more different. While Nathan is an extrovert, Lara is introverted, more measured, and always pragmatic. Because they both work in Human Resources, they attend many meetings together. Lara is always looking out for Nathan and happily lends him an extra pair of eyes and ears.

Nathan is fairly new to the company, having worked there only a year, and he is still struggling to get oriented with the corporate landscape. His friendly personality keeps him on good terms with most of his colleagues, and his role keeps him organically connected to heads of departments, as he helps them with succession planning and the professional development of their teams. Despite Nathan's access to the company's inner workings, he still lacks a sense of who the real power players are. He also doesn't know who he can trust, besides Lara, nor is he aware of who belongs to which clique.

Although Nathan is technically competent in his role, he lacks the capacity to read the work environment, as his gut instinct is almost non-existent. He is more book smart than street smart, which leaves him looking green in his role and somewhat naïve. Without Lara's help, Nathan would be lost.

Nathan and Lara recently took our assessment, and both were excited to receive their Fluid Thinking Reports. While we found Lara's Intuitive Thinking to be high, Nathan's scored on the lower end of the scale. I explained this meant Nathan would be unaware of subtle cues and messages in his environment. He would struggle to grasp the nuances of office politics and have difficulty understanding how his decisions impact others and their departments.

Nathan was displeased to receive my feedback. According to him, I had gotten it wrong. He didn't see himself this way at all. To my relief, Lara broke out into laughter at his response. Jovially, Lara explained how she regularly bailed Nathan out of sticky situations when he had unwittingly stepped on someone's toes. Keeping her tone constructive and light-hearted, she continued to share examples of other situations when Nathan had behaved the way I described. At a recent meeting, the senior managers became irritated when he continued to over-explain a point. Fortunately, Nathan had successfully picked up on her not-so-subtle signal and moved on to the next topic.

Nathan was understandably disappointed by our feedback. But after reflecting upon Lara's examples, he began to understand why some people never seemed to take a strong liking to him. Humbled, Nathan shared that in his previous role, he had been given similar feedback about his lack of awareness of people and the environment.

Nathan asked if his lower Intuitive Thinking impacted his ability to detect problems going on below the surface. Lifeguard Lara gently reminded him of all the times she had prompted him to chat with this person or that person. She also highlighted some of the many occasions when she had brought departmental issues to his attention. Nathan was surprised by the volume of evidence and thanked Lara for having his back. Then, he turned to me and asked, "I can fix this, right?" I reassured him that we certainly could.

As our meeting was wrapping up, Lara and I knew the penny had finally dropped for Nathan when we saw him break into a grin. We encouraged him to share his epiphany, and he told us he had gone on vacation last month. While he was away, his executive assistant had worked very hard to spruce up his office. Nathan had been back at work for two weeks before he noticed that something was different about his office. But even then, he still couldn't quite put his finger on it. Thankfully, his assistant had taken his obliviousness in stride. All three of us were chuckling over Nathan's story when Lara exclaimed, "By George, I think he's got it!" Her perfectly timed *My Fair Lady* segue left us all in a positive frame of mind.

IMPACT OF LOWER INTUITIVE THINKING

Like Nathan, people with lower Intuitive Thinking often feel as if their radar isn't picking up on important, but subtle, aspects of their working environment and group dynamics.

DIFFICULTY READING THE ROOM

With his lower Intuitive Thinking, Nathan had difficulty sensing group dynamics and, in particular, reading the room when he was giving a presentation. While he focused on the content he was delivering, his underdeveloped Spidey-Sense had difficulty reading the overall mood of the attendees. Because he could not pick up on the signals of restlessness from the attendees, he had to rely on Lara to prompt him to adapt his presentation style or speed.

LOWER GUT FEEL

Nathan had difficulty sensing when problems were bubbling just below the surface and understanding the subtle politics of the organization. Even when he did get a gut sense that something was not quite right, the signal was so low that he paid no attention to it. Then he would be blindsided when things blew up. In contrast, Lara's high Intuitive Thinking sent her flashing warning lights, which she was only too happy to share with Nathan.

NOT SO STREET SMART

You know that feeling you get when somebody is not being straight with you? It's often referred to as the BS meter. Unfortunately for Nathan, his BS meter virtually never went off; and so, less scrupulous executives would use him to further their political ambitions in the organization. Nathan was totally oblivious to this until Lara came to his rescue using her finely tuned street smarts.

BENEFITS OF HIGHLY DEVELOPED INTUITIVE THINKING

When your Intuitive Thinking is functioning optimally, your internal radar is highly sensitive, enabling you to detect subtle environmental cues. This internal radar supports you in having a finely tuned gut feel and sharply honed street smarts. In addition, it underpins the ability to read a room without consciously thinking about it.

Developing Intuitive Thinking is a pivotal step in optimizing Social Leadership capability because it rapidly brings things that just don't seem right to your conscious attention, allowing you to investigate the situation in more detail. Interestingly, based on anecdotal feedback from our clients, we have found that when people ignore a signal generated by their gut sense and higher Intuitive Thinking, the issue inevitably comes back to cause them grief down the road.

NATHAN: ENHANCED INTUITIVE THINKING AFTER BRAIN COACHING

After completing our brain coaching program, Nathan is no longer blindsided by people, nor is he oblivious to office politics. Now, he is adept at recognizing when an issue is brewing, so he can be proactive about addressing it in advance.

With his enhanced Intuitive Thinking, Nathan is also more competent at reading the room and no longer relies on Lara to be his environmental awareness guide when dealing with groups of people or sensitive political situations. Nathan finds his newfound astuteness very liberating.

In the past, Nathan was seen as somewhat naïve even though he was technically very good in his role. The senior executives respect him more now, and they are more comfortable taking him into their confidence regarding their talent needs. With his stronger BS meter, Nathan now has more direct conversations with his internal clients, so he can better understand their needs. In the past, Nathan often succumbed when executives coerced him into authorizing their requests to attend prestigious off-site programs. But now, he resists this pressure and helps executives come up with improved and more targeted talent development solutions.

KEY TAKEAWAYS

- Intuitive Thinking underpins your gut feel and is used to sense, subconsciously, when things are not quite right or when a problem might be brewing in the environment.
- Your Intuitive Thinking also impacts your street smarts and helps you detect when someone is trying to deceive you.
- Intuitive Thinking acts as a type of brain radar that you use to navigate nuanced social and political landscapes. It's like having an early warning system that gives you insights into group dynamics and alerts you when people-related problems might be developing.
- Daniel Kahneman, in his book *Thinking, Fast and Slow* refers to System 1 as fast thinking (which, from my perspective, is related to Intuitive Thinking) and System 2 as slow thinking (which I relate to Analytical Thinking). Kahneman warns that System 1 thinking is more prone to bias and error. I concur. While we can use Intuitive Thinking to identify potential issues, we need to complement it with Analytical Thinking when making important decisions.
- The average Intuitive Thinking test scores we observed before COVID-19 were higher than our newer clients' scores during the pandemic. My hypothesis is that the markedly reduced face-to-face contact time we experienced during the peak of COVID-19 decreased the effectiveness of individuals' internal Intuitive Thinking radar, leading to lower test results.

PART VI

UNLOCKING THE POWER OF YOUR BRAIN HABITS

Chapter 18
MENTAL CHI

"Strength is not born from strength. Strength can be born only from weakness. So be glad of your weaknesses now, they are the beginnings of your strength."
—Dr. Claire Weekes

After all the stories and science, we find ourselves back at the nexus of it all: the yin and yang of the bicameral brain. By weaving all the threads of understanding together, we can finally turn over the tapestry and see the bigger picture, as understanding brain balance and Subconscious Thinking Habits is the foundation for understanding Mental Chi.

Understanding the connective tissue, the yin and yang, the division and connection of the brain's hemispheres is crucial as we begin to pivot and negotiate collectively the pressure of growing workloads. When we take an intentional approach to enhancing the right hemisphere's Fluid Thinking capability, we begin the journey of upgrading our brain app. Balancing both hemispheres of the brain facilitates our ability to leverage and utilize the left hemisphere's Crystallized Knowledge more easily and effectively.

The critical takeaway is that this process of development and balance leverages the complementary capabilities of both hemispheres of the brain. It is a vital process to understand, as traditional teaching approaches are overly focused on developing the left hemisphere while having very little understanding of how important the right hemisphere is to the process of learning novel skills. As a result, in most people, the right hemisphere learns and develops in an *ad hoc* and unintentional manner.

Developing the right hemisphere to create better brain balance by optimizing the Subconscious Thinking Habits is not only good science, but also an invitation to enhance equanimity in your professional and personal life.

Addressing the gaps inherent in conventional approaches to teaching, training, and developing children and adults is the nexus of subconscious success. Developing the right hemisphere to create better brain balance by optimizing the Subconscious Thinking Habits is not only good science, but also an invitation to enhance equanimity in your professional and personal life.

Brain balance is the process of engaging with the Subconscious Thinking Habits that currently derail your output. Though many view these as weaknesses, I echo Dr. Weekes, suggesting that they are "…the beginnings of your strength." The process of developing each cognitive derailer into a strength is the beginning of brain balance and puts you on the road to achieving Mental Chi.

WHAT IS MENTAL CHI?

The American Heritage Dictionary defines *chi* as follows:

> The vital force believed, in Taoism and other Chinese thought, to be inherent in all things. The unimpeded circulation of chi and a balance of its negative and positive forms in the body are held to be essential to good health in traditional Chinese medicine.

While Taoism and Chinese philosophy are powerful and rich in wisdom, I confess I am no expert in philosophy. So, allow me to borrow from this definition, as it has influenced what I call Mental Chi.

Mental Chi is the state of optimal cognitive competency that is achieved by intentionally balancing the brain. It occurs when the left and right hemispheres of the brain are operating in harmony and balanced, as shown in Figure 27. Fluid Thinking and Crystallized Knowledge come together effortlessly to deliver high levels of cognitive performance consistently and easily.

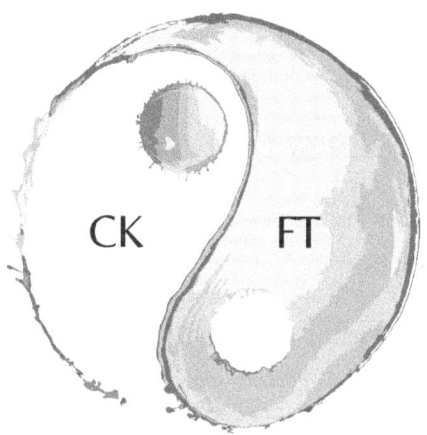

Crystallized Knowledge (Conscious Mind Habits)	Fluid Thinking (Subconscious Thinking Habits)
Traditional approach to education, training, development, coaching, and mentoring.	Thinking skills that operate below our conscious threshold and drive productivity and performance.
Focus on Content (what you learn)	**Focus on Process (how you learn)**
Subject-Matter Expertise:	Process - Cognitive Abilities
• Accounting • Marketing • Engineering	• Adaptability • Agility • Ability to pivot

Figure 27. Mental Chi Achieved through Brain Balance

Many individuals occasionally experience a state of mental performance that is noticeably higher and more effective, while also using less mental energy. Usually, it is difficult to access. This state, often referred to as being *in the zone*, is the infancy of Mental Chi. The *zone* is brain balance in action, whereas Mental Chi is the mastery of brain balance through deliberate practice, so that optimal output becomes second nature and successful performance becomes a subconscious routine.

WHY BRAIN BALANCE IS SO IMPORTANT

Taking inspiration from the harmony and balance represented in the yin and yang symbol, we can explore the importance of balancing both hemispheres of the brain through an analogy. If a person were to have severely impaired vision in one eye, it would significantly impact their capacity to drive. They would likely have monocular vision, which undermines the ability to perceive depth. Plus, they would have considerably reduced peripheral vision. When driving, this person would find it difficult to judge how far away a pedestrian or a cyclist might be. Depending on the severity of their vision impairment, their driver's license may be subject to restrictions, such as limited geographical area, speed constraints, daylight driving only, and so on.

A person with monocular vision views the road using only one hemisphere of the brain, which is quite dangerous. In contrast, an individual with stereoscopic vision can view the road using both hemispheres of the brain. The integration of the images from the left and right hemispheres supports optimal depth perception, so a person can judge distance more accurately and have wider peripheral vision. Leveraging the input from both hemispheres enhances the ability to estimate accurately the car's distance from a cyclist or a pedestrian, which is vital for safe driving.

The goal of this analogy is to highlight the complexities encountered when the left and right hemispheres of the brain do not work in harmony. Relying on your accidental brain app is like driving with monocular vision. While you might be able to get by, it impairs your ability to live your personal and professional life consummately.

Thus, Mental Chi is the metaphorical equivalent of stereoscopic vision. And the good news is that it is accessible to everyone.

YOUR BRAIN'S SWEET SPOT

Tennis, golf, baseball, cricket, softball, hockey, and other sports use the term *sweet spot*, which the Cambridge Dictionary defines as "the part of a surface that gives the most power for the least effort, for example, when hitting a ball." Curiously, the sweet spot is also salient to our discussion of brain balance, as the emphasis on *the most power for the least effort* is at the core of Mental Chi.

When your left and right hemispheres operate in a complementary way, you achieve the highest ROI on your mental effort and energy.

When your left and right hemispheres operate in a complementary way, you achieve the highest ROI on your mental effort and energy. This cognitive balance shifts everything, improving your performance and leadership, increasing your productivity and overall resilience, and supporting your ability to focus. All of this happens subconsciously and with ease.

Mental Chi is the *subconscious* sweet spot that changes your game.

COGNITIVE WAX ON, WAX OFF

Remember *Karate Kid?* This movie tells the story of a teenager named Daniel who wants to learn the art of karate. His sensei, Mr. Miyagi, teaches Daniel in a novel way, giving him arduous chores, such as sanding the floor, painting the fence, and, most notably, waxing Mr. Miyagi's collection of vintage cars. Making sweeping motions in the air to demonstrate the correct technique, Mr. Miyagi instructs Daniel: "Wax on, right hand. Wax off, left hand. Wax on, wax off."

It is easy to foresee the young man becoming increasingly frustrated by these seemingly menial tasks that appear to have nothing to do with karate. Predictably, Daniel's frustration boils over, and he wants to quit. Mr. Miyagi pauses to give him a lesson, fine-tuning his odd-job skills and aligning them with the art of karate. A frustrated Daniel keeps on until one day when, out of the blue, Mr. Miyagi launches a full-on attack. Much to Daniel's surprise, he is able to fend off the sensei easily.

This scene is powerful, but in the context of Mental Chi, it is a beautiful example of deliberate practice in action. Unbeknownst to Daniel, the chores Mr. Miyagi prescribes are specifically tailored for learning karate. By performing the repetitive motions these tasks entail, Daniel subconsciously develops the hand movements that underpin the most fundamental defensive blocks in karate.

From Daniel's perspective, Mr. Miyagi was just having him do random chores. But his sensei knew the repetitive motions were building the cognitive "muscle memory" that Daniel would need to execute karate moves in unexpected situations. Through deliberate practice, Daniel unwittingly developed the subconscious habits that prepared him to thrive when under attack.

Karate Kid provides an apt metaphor for the process of achieving Mental Chi. The first step is to develop the necessary Subconscious Thinking Habits by repeatedly performing tailored deliberate practice exercises. The second step is to increase the difficulty of those exercises, and then to apply the enhanced capability in business and real-life situations. The latter requires specific contexts for developing cognitive competency that can be used without conscious awareness. Thus, Mental Chi is a subconscious cognitive state characterized by a balance of mental readiness and mental calm.

Being in the zone cognitively is Mental Chi in effortless action. Most people have experienced the zone, but not effortlessly and only fleetingly—with no control over how to get into it. There was a difference between the way Daniel and his opponents received their training—don't worry, I won't give away the ending. Mr. Miyagi trained Daniel in a counterintuitive manner that didn't seem to make much sense in the conventional world. Many individuals would have given up, but Daniel's consistent practice and application made the difference.

The chores Daniel did were the means of subconsciously developing his capability to use his defensive karate blocks. Similarly, our clients undertake increasingly more difficult cognitive activities and exercises in order to develop their Fluid Thinking, which then equips them to operate in the zone of Mental Chi.

Brain balance is only as powerful as its degree of personalization; it is not a one-size-fits-all prescription. That is why it takes tailored deliberate practice to achieve a state of Mental Chi that enables you to stay in the zone effortlessly. While I am no karate sensei, I know the art of cognitive wax on, wax off—and I can show you a few other expert moves, too.

ENHANCING BRAIN HABITS TO ACHIEVE COGNITIVE MASTERY

It is time to bring everything together. Understanding the benefits of Mental Chi is an integral part of the conversation this book is starting. In the previous chapters, you saw how costly it can be to be derailed by inefficient Subconscious Thinking Habits. Now, please allow me to give you a preview your brain's full potential once your Subconscious Thinking Habits have been optimized to achieve brain balance.

Table 6 shows how all ten Subconscious Thinking Habits function collectively when they have been optimized and integrated to deliver cognitive mastery. As you read each description, take a moment to reflect upon your own brain app. Can you relate to some of these strengths more than others?

Table 6. Cognitive Mastery with All Subconscious Thinking Habits Optimized

Pillar One: Controlling Attention	
Focused Thinking	• You have control over how you leverage your focus to increase productivity, performance, and time management. • You are no longer sucked into the procrastination vortex. • You reclaim mental energy, avoid burnout, and often gain at least an hour of productivity each day—all of which significantly improve work-life balance.
Pillar Two: Complex Problem-Solving	
Analytical Thinking	• You can digest large amounts of information rapidly and find it easy to identify which details are most important, enabling you to generate relevant insights quickly. • You can quickly, easily, and accurately define complex problems.
Innovative Thinking	• You can generate multiple creative solutions to a well-defined problem speedily and with little conscious effort. • You are agile, having the capacity to pivot swiftly, strategically, and effectively as circumstances change.
Conceptual Thinking	• You evaluate potential solutions to complex problems quickly and easily against the agreed-upon criteria before selecting the most advantageous solution. • You are very confident in your decision-making ability. • You are adept at thinking on your feet and can respond competently in a variety of professional situations.

Pillar Three: Strategy, Planning, and Execution	
Strategic Thinking	• You are comfortable stepping back and creating clarity before undertaking a project, rather than just diving in. • You can define concisely what a successful project outcome should look like and develop a clear, strategic path forward to deliver that outcome. • You communicate the strategy to others plainly and succinctly.
Abstract Thinking	• You quickly and easily plan out the stages of a project, the associated timelines, and the necessary resources. • You are adept at identifying the risks associated with a project and can mitigate them in advance. • You delegate effectively and effortlessly.
Operational Thinking	• Like an orchestra conductor, you focus on managing your team to achieve outcomes, instead of becoming too involved in implementing the plan. • You lead strategically and pragmatically, avoiding the trap of being too hands on.
Pillar Four: Social Leadership	
Nonverbal Thinking	• You readily process nonverbal communication and react quickly and appropriately. • You understand the secret code of nonverbal communication, engendering trust, and building rapport easily.
Perspective Thinking	• You navigate complex social and relational situations smoothly. • You are empathetic and can readily see things from another person's perspective. • As a natural leader, you are collaboratively driven.
Intuitive Thinking	• You are highly adept at observing the signals in your environment (e.g., you have the ability to "read the room" when presenting). • Acutely attuned to your gut feelings, you investigate situations that make you feel uneasy, which prevents you from getting blindsided later. • You have a superb BS meter, which readily enables you to detect when someone is trying to mislead you.

COGNITIVE MASTERY BEYOND THE OFFICE

A personal highlight regarding achieving Mental Chi happened outside the corporate environment. A client had finished our program and asked a personal question. As a golf enthusiast with a respectable handicap of six, he wanted to achieve an even-par round—easier said than done. So, we stepped back to see how he might leverage the Subconscious Thinking Habits in the game of golf to achieve this goal.

After mentally walking through the steps, we discussed how he needed to engage strategically with each hole and occupy a state of Mental Chi, putting himself in the mental zone. Remarkably, he achieved the par round without changing a single thing about the way he physically hit the ball—it was all about his cognitive, mental, and strategic approach to the game.

The well-known saying "we need to work smarter, not harder" applies to all aspects of work and life. We can attain Mental Chi by enhancing our Subconscious Thinking Habits to develop brain balance. Mental Chi is the ultimate game changer and differentiator.

KEY TAKEAWAYS

- Mental Chi is the state of cognitive mastery brought about by brain balance.
- When the left and right hemispheres of the brain operate in harmony, Fluid Thinking delivers high levels of cognitive performance and enables you to apply the left hemisphere's Crystallized Knowledge skillfully.
- Brain balance and Mental Chi provide the most brain power with the least amount of effort, creating a sense of equanimity that improves both your professional and personal life.
- The first step in developing Mental Chi is to identify inefficient Subconscious Thinking Habits. The second step is to

undertake tailored deliberate practice exercises. The third step is to increase the difficulty of those exercises. The final step is to engage in the practical application of your enhanced Fluid Thinking in real-life situations.

- Rapid and ongoing change is inevitable. Achieving Mental Chi equips you to achieve brain balance and perform optimally. This, in turn, enables you to thrive in a world of change.

Chapter 19

REWIRING YOUR BRAIN FOR THE FUTURE

"Our brains renew themselves throughout life to an extent previously thought not possible." —Michael Gazzania

So, we have come to the end of the road, and hopefully, we are parting fellow travelers on the journey of understanding the power of optimized Fluid Thinking. That was my goal, to highlight what is possible and to show you what you are capable of becoming.

As I mentioned in the Introduction, we have all been subjected recently to a massive amount of external disruption which has also generated considerable internal, personal disruption. The days of living in a steady-state environment and having to deal solely with incremental change are well behind us. Ongoing disruption will only accelerate from here.

As I share with my clients, the greatest gift you can give yourself to handle this ongoing disruption is to enhance your Fluid Thinking significantly, so you can be optimally equipped to thrive in an ever-changing world. During my many years as a brain coach, I have seen clients radically redefine their careers by mastering Mental Chi.

I have seen brain balance push individuals through their professional ceiling and provide a steppingstone to elevate them to C-suite roles. I have been tasked to make a client CEO ready, who transitioned very effectively into a global CEO role. I have seen clients gain back an hour in each day and obtain much better work/life balance. I have seen clients double their revenue in just two years, while others have made their full year's profit in just one quarter. I feel privileged to watch leaders develop enhanced Fluid Thinking and achieve sustained leadership behavioral changes.

Balancing the hemispheres of the brain turns good thinking into great thinking and good personal performance into exceptional personal performance.

The Four Pillars of Subconscious Success provide the framework for developing brain balance, which is the foundation of Mental Chi. The ten Subconscious Thinking Habits equip the brain to elevate in every area. They enhance performance and productivity and even stretch professional potential and promotion opportunities. Balancing the hemispheres of the brain turns good thinking into great thinking and good personal performance into exceptional personal performance. And career trajectories change dramatically when the brain is balanced. Critically, brain balance also boosts mental energy to support higher levels of resilience, which is incredibly valuable and necessary in today's world.

THE DIFFERENCE BETWEEN SURVIVING AND THRIVING

The rapid progression of digital disruption has launched us into the early stages of the Fourth Industrial Revolution, according to the World Economic Forum. The impact of this is in its infancy, but the WEF predicts that we are facing a reskilling emergency. This emergency will require fifty percent of all employees to be reskilled by 2025, and a billion people will need reskilling by 2030.[cix] The impact of reskilling is starting to disturb the waters of global industries, with ripple effects that are far-reaching and pervade almost all facets of organizations and entrepreneurial offerings.

In his 1970 book, *Future Shock*, Alvin Toffler states: "Future shock is the shattering stress and disorientation that we induce in individuals by subjecting them to too much change in too short a time."[cx]

From my perspective, Toffler predicted the World Health Organization's burnout syndrome over fifty years ago.

"To survive, to avert what we have termed future shock, the individual must become infinitely more adaptable and capable than ever before," says Toffler. Again, a very prescient forecast made before the concepts of neuroplasticity and fluid reasoning were well understood.

This is why I am so passionate for everyone to look at optimizing their Fluid Thinking. This underpins Toffler's comment about being "more adaptable" and supports the learning agility required to make a person "more capable than ever," as Toffler suggested.

An enhanced agile learning capability will be the most valuable skill and asset a person can have to succeed during this massive reskilling program.

In this context, a brain upgrade becomes essential for anyone who desires to thrive in the future, and not just survive. This need is purely due to the increased load from continuous disruption and the enormous reskilling requirements that will be placed on the right hemisphere of everyone's brain—both because of the novelty learning required and because of the need to adapt continually to the rapidly changing digital environment. An enhanced agile learning capability will be the most valuable skill and asset a person can have to succeed during this massive reskilling program.

On top of the workload and the ever-increasing quantity and speed of information, the introduction of industry-wide reskilling will require organizations to develop their leaders' and employees' Fluid Thinking capability. Cognitive competence will play a significant role in an individual's and the organization's capacity to learn, apply, adapt, and pivot successfully.

YOUR PERSONAL BRAIN APP CHECKUP

We have covered a lot of ground in our quest to understand subconscious success. Along the road, we encountered many twists and turns, and we tried not to take things too seriously. It is likely that more than once you recognized the behaviors of a colleague in the stories, or maybe you even saw some of your own familiar traits.

Now, I invite you to take a moment to reflect on the quality of your current brain app. While our comprehensive Fluid Thinking test provides an objective and *quantitative* assessment of a person's Fluid Thinking, the short *qualitative* questionnaire below offers the opportunity to gain a glimpse into your own Subconscious Thinking Habits. Assign a score (from 1 to 10) to each item in the list to indicate how much the descriptions resonate with you. Use the following rating scale:

1 ...... 2 ...... 3 .... 4 ...... 5 ...... 6 ...... 7 ...... 8 ...... 9 10

Not like me   Somewhat like me   Very much like me

		Score
Pillar One: Controlling Attention		
Focused Thinking	I have difficulty staying focused on my top priorities. I am often distracted by things that interest me, rather than focusing on the task I need to be working on.	
Pillar Two: Complex Problem-Solving		

Analytical Thinking	I have difficulty breaking down a complex problem into its component parts quickly and efficiently. I have issues dealing with a lot of detailed information.	
Innovative Thinking	I have considerable difficulty generating creative solutions to a problem, especially if I have never encountered that type of problem before.	
Conceptual Thinking	I have trouble seeing the big picture because I don't readily grasp how the details connect to the broader plan. I often struggle to come up with a good answer quickly when I'm put on the spot.	
Pillar Three: Strategy, Planning, and Execution		
Strategic Thinking	I find it challenging to develop an original strategy and give my team a clear path forward when I'm dealing with a situation I haven't encountered before. I have difficulty communicating clearly and succinctly.	
Abstract Thinking	It takes me a lot of time and mental effort to construct a project plan that outlines the tasks and timelines required to execute a strategy. I have difficulty delegating effectively.	

Operational Thinking	I often find myself rolling up my sleeves and working alongside my team, even when I know I should be stepping back and leading them. When tackling a new project, I tend to dive right in instead of pausing to think through my approach.	
Pillar Four: Social Leadership		
Nonverbal Thinking	I have difficulty picking up on subtle shifts in another person's body language.	
Perspective Thinking	I often have trouble seeing another person's point of view. I find it difficult to empathize with others.	
Intuitive Thinking	Because I find it difficult to trust and rely on my gut feelings, I tend to ignore them, only to find problems come back to cause me grief. I lack confidence in my ability to discern when someone isn't being straight with me.	

Now, use the guidelines below to interpret your score *for each individual Subconscious Thinking Habit*. (Note that we do not tally the individual scores at the end because an aggregate score is not especially meaningful. Rather, it is the impact of each habit that is important.)

Score of 7-10: Strong cognitive derailer which would have a major negative impact on thinking, learning, adapting, and performance

Score of 4-6: Moderate cognitive derailer which would have a moderate-to-significant negative impact on thinking, learning, adapting, and performance, particularly during times of high stress or when under time pressure

Score of 1-3: Cognitive strength which would have a positive impact on thinking, learning, adapting, and performance

How did you do? Are you well-equipped for future success or could your brain app use an upgrade?

If you would like to learn even more about how to unlock your cognitive capital, adaptability, and learning ability—and leverage your brain's potential to increase your performance—we invite you to take a complimentary assessment of one of your ten Subconscious Thinking Habits called Focused Thinking. This test measures your distractibility and your ability to control your attention. To get your free assessment, visit:

https://www.enigmafit.com/focusedtest

ACKNOWLEDGMENTS

No person is an island. My interactions with people from all walks of life in a diverse range of business and personal contexts have been fundamental in building my curiosity about how the brain uses Subconscious Thinking Habits to process information, think, learn, and adapt—and, thereby, generate enhanced Fluid Thinking.

I would like to acknowledge the pivotal people who have encouraged and supported me on this journey for their input and inspiration, which has resulted in bringing this book to life.

To my wife, Susan, without whose robust encouragement, love, and support, this book would have never been started, let alone finished. Susan has been a pillar of strength both as a business partner and a life partner.

To my editor, Anna Paige, for her patience, guidance, expertise, and the numerous hours she spent refining the technical aspects of a complex topic into an easy-to-read manuscript. Her great sense of humor during the whole process was immensely valuable and supportive.

To Alyssa Dukich whose witty humor helped turn the dry subject of the brain into an easy-to-understand topic by contributing humorous input when I was writing up the real life client stories to which readers can easily relate.

Helga Rowe pioneered fundamental research into the nonverbal testing and development of fluid intelligence in children. I thank her for providing me with the historical background context for her work. Dr. Rowe was truly an inspiration, and she has become a dear friend to my wife, Susan, and me.

To Graeme Lee, our program director, for his professional operational and technical capability for the entirety of our Fluid Thinking journey. He has been extremely innovative and a tower of support during the whole process.

To Julie Thibault who was a great sounding board by sharing her insights from undertaking the Fluid Thinking Program. She was able to provide guidance on what would be most interesting from the reader's viewpoint.

To Kate Bradshaw for taking complex concepts and turning them into simple diagrams that aid in the understanding of Fluid Thinking and help readers navigate their way through the book.

To Jeff Sullivan who provided important suggestions and input to the structure and content of the book during the early stages.

To Alan Hamilton for his assistance in proofreading the book—a very valuable contribution.

Last but not least, I would like to thank all my clients with whom I've had the privilege of working throughout the years. They provide me with unique insights into how our brains work in real-world situations. It is extremely rewarding to see the transformations that occur in their lives. I'm deeply grateful to have the opportunity to guide them. I'm also very appreciative of the contributions and collaborative support I receive from my team and colleagues when working with our clients.

GLOSSARY

adaptability—The mental capability to change your thinking and behavior intentionally, competently, and effectively in order to adapt to changes in your environment.

agility—The speed and efficiency with which a person can change their thinking and behavior to adapt to changes in their environment.

bicameral brain—In neuroscience, *bicameral* refers to the two hemispheres of the brain and, specifically, the differential—and highly specialized—roles of the left and right hemispheres.

brain balance—The state of mental agility, competency, adaptability, and ease created by enhancing the brain's right hemisphere in order to balance the left hemisphere's *Crystallized Knowledge* and routinization.

cognitive derailer—A subconscious inefficiency in thinking or behavior that occurs below an individual's conscious awareness. Can be developed into a *cognitive strength* using targeted and specifically designed *Fluid Thinking* exercises.

cognitive routine—An encoded, subconscious brain program that is created by strengthening neural pathways through repetition. Performed automatically without the individual being aware of it.

cognitive strength—A subconscious efficiency in thinking or behavior that occurs below an individual's conscious awareness and supports the ability to work smarter, not harder.

Conscious Mind Habit—A habit of which an individual is consciously aware. Typically, related to a routine physical activity (e.g., brushing their teeth) or a physical craving (e.g., reaching for chocolate when stressed).

Crystallized Knowledge—The knowledge that an individual has accumulated throughout their lifetime, including subject-matter expertise, mastered skills, and past experience. Akin to book smarts.

deliberate practice—In the context of my framework, a method of strengthening the brain routines associated with targeted *Subconscious Thinking Habits* by repeatedly engaging in challenging and fun *Fluid Thinking* activities that become increasingly complex over time.

discovery learning—A proactive method of learning by doing practical activities whereby the individual discovers and takes ownership of their learning process and outcomes, rather than passively receiving information.

effectiveness vs. efficiency—Terms used to describe and measure thinking capability. *Effectiveness* refers to the quality of the thinking (i.e., high or low), whereas *efficiency* relates to the speed of the thinking (e.g., fast or slow).

Fluid Thinking—The raw cognitive capability that enables agile thinking, providing the ability to adapt quickly to new and *novel* problems, opportunities, and disruptions. Also supports effective, efficient learning and the ready application of newly acquired knowledge. Akin to street smarts.

Fluid Thinking Development Theory—My own hypothesis of how we think, learn, and adapt. Focuses on improving the right-hemisphere's Fluid Thinking capability in adulthood to create the *brain balance* needed for subconscious success.

Four Pillars of Subconscious Success—The core framework for developing *brain balance*. Establishes the categories for subconscious cognitive improvement through a sequential system of ten *Subconscious Thinking Habits*.

learning agility—The ability to acquire new knowledge quickly and to apply that knowledge in *novel* situations. A subconscious brain ability underpinned by *Fluid Thinking*, not an academic skill. Impacted by all ten *Subconscious Thinking Habits*.

Mental Chi—The state of cognitive competency achieved by ideally balancing both hemispheres of the brain in order to operate easily in the optimal performance zone. Leverages the right hemisphere's *Fluid Thinking* to adapt quickly and facilitates effective utilization of the left hemisphere's *Crystallized Knowledge* to deliver peak performance.

neuroplasticity—The brain's ability to rewire and physiologically change itself in response to environmental interactions such as repeated mental and physical activities.

novel(ty)—Not previously known or used by a person. Refers to cognitive challenges that require an innovative and adaptive approach to thinking because they cannot be resolved by relying on pre-existing *cognitive routines* or knowledge.

novelty-routinization theory—A view on brain function based on the research of Elkhonon Goldberg. Posits that the left hemisphere of the brain specializes in processes that are driven by well-established *cognitive routines* based on past strategies, experiences, and knowledge, whereas the right hemisphere specializes in *novel* cognitive challenges.

schemas—The mental models the brain uses to organize knowledge and guide cognitive processes and behaviors. Jean Piaget defined a *schema* as a cohesive, repeatable action sequence that is tightly interconnected and governed by a core meaning.

Subconscious Thinking Habits—The ten thinking functions that occur below an individual's conscious threshold. Can be quantitatively measured to determine the person's *cognitive strengths* and *cognitive derailers*. Must be optimized to achieve *brain balance* and *Mental Chi*.

ENDNOTES

[i] "The half-life of professional skills is 5 years." *EAB*, October 2, 2018. https://eab.com/insights/daily-briefing/workplace/the-half-life-of-professional-skills-is-5-years/.

[ii] Shook, Ellyn, and Mark Knickrehm. "Reworking the Revolution." Acrobat. *Accenture*, January 2018. https://www.accenture.com/_acnmedia/pdf-69/accenture-reworking-the-revolution-jan-2018-pov.pdf.

[iii] Ratey, John J. *A User's Guide to the Brain: Perception, Attention, and the Four Theaters of the Brain*. New York, NY: Vintage Books, 2002.

[iv] Piaget, Jean. *The Origin of Intelligence in the Child*. Translated by Margaret Cook. 3. 1st ed. Vol. 3. 8 vols. New York, NY: Routledge, 2011.

[v] Piaget, 1936.

[vi] Piaget, 1936.

[vii] Vygotsky, Lev S. *Mind in Society: The Development of Higher Psychological Processes*. Edited by Michael Cole, Vera John-Steiner, Sylvia Scribner, and Ellen Souberman. Revised ed. Cambridge, MA: Harvard University Press, 1978.

[viii] Piaget, 1936.

[ix] Piaget, 1936.

[x] Piaget, 1936.

[xi] Duhigg, Charles. *The Power of Habit*. London, England: Random House Books, 2013.

[xii] Duhigg, Charles. Habits: How They Form and How to Break Them. Interview by NPR Fresh Air. *NPR*, March 5, 2012. https://www.npr.org/2012/03/05/147192599/habits-how-they-form-and-how-to-break-them.

[xiii] Duhigg, Charles, 2012.

[xiv] Ramón y Cajal, Santiago. *Advice for a Young Investigator*. Translated by Neely Swanson and Larry W Swanson. Bradford, PA: Bradford Books, 1897; Cambridge, MA: The MIT Press, 2004.

[xv] Konorski, Jerzy. *Conditioned Reflexes and Neuron Organization.* Translated by Stephen Garry. 1st ed. Cambridge, England: Cambridge University Press, 1948.

[xvi] Doidge, Dr. Norman. *The Brain That Changes Itself: Stories of Personal Triumph from the Frontiers of Brain Science*. Reprinted. London, England: Penguin Books, 2007.

[xvii] Mintzberg, Henry. "Planning on the Left Side and Managing on the Right." *Harvard Business Review*, July–August 1976. https://hbr.org/1976/07/planning-on-the-left-side-and-managing-on-the-right.

[xviii] Mintzberg, 1976.

[xix] Mintzberg, 1976.

[xx] Goldberg, Elkhonon. "A New Look at the Old Riddle : Novelty, Routines and the Evolution of the Bicameral Brain." *Japanese Journal of Cognitive Neuroscience* 20, no. 3+4 (February 1, 2019): 129–38. https://doi.org/10.11253/ninchishinkeikagaku.20.129.

[xxi] Goldberg, 2018.

[xxii] Goldberg, 2018.

[xxiii] Goldberg, 2018.

[xxiv] Mintzberg, 1976.

[xxv] Mintzberg, 1976.

[xxvi] Duckworth, Eleanor. "Piaget Rediscovered." The Arithmetic Teacher 11, no. 7 (1964): 496–99. http://www.jstor.org/stable/41186862. (The original text contains the phrase "principle goal," which probably should be "principal goal.")

[xxvii] Mintzberg, 1976.

[xxviii] Horn, John L. "Intelligence—Why It Grows, Why It Declines." *Society*, Trans-action, 5, no. 1 (November 1967): 23–31. https://doi.org/10.1007/bf03180091.

[xxix] Rowe, Dr. Helga A. H. *Language-free Evaluation of Cognitive Development*. Hawthorn, Victoria, Australia: Australian Council for Educational Research, 1986.

[xxx] Rowe, 1986.

[xxxi] Rowc, 1986.

xxxii Cattell, 1963.

xxxiii Ericsson, K. Anders, Michael J. Prietula, and Edward T. Cokely. "The Making of an Expert." *Harvard Business Review*, July 1, 2007. https://hbr.org/2007/07/the-making-of-an-expert.

xxxiv Ericsson, K. Anders, and Robert Pool. *Peak: Secrets from the New Science of Expertise*. Boston, MA: Mariner Books/Houghton Mifflin Harcourt, 2017.

xxxv Adams, Linda. "Learning a New Skill Is Easier Said Than Done." *Gordon Training International*, August 2015. https://www.gordontraining. com/free-workplace-articles/learning-a-new-skill-is-easier-said-than-done/.

xxxvi Zahidi, Saadia, Vesselina Ratcheva, Guillaume Hingel, and Sophie Brown. "The Future of Jobs Report 2020." *World Economic Forum*, October 2020. https://www.weforum.org/reports/the-future-of-jobs-report-2020.

xxxvii Carroll, Lewis, John Tenniel, and Hugh Haughton. *Alice's Adventures in Wonderland ; and, Through the Looking-Glass and What Alice Found There ; Alice's Adventures Under Ground*. New York, NY: Penguin Classics, An Imprint of Penguin Books, 2012.

xxxviii "In Search of Lost Focus: The engine of distributed work." *The Economist Intelligence Unit Limited*, 2020. https://lostfocus.eiu.com/.

xxxix Snachner, Emma. "How Has the Human Brain Evolved?" *Scientific American Mind*, 24, 3, 76 (July 2013). doi:10.1038/scientificamericanmind0713-76b. https://www.scientificamerican. com/article/how-has-human-brain-evolved/.

xl Simon, Herbert A. "Designing Organizations for an Information-Rich World," in *Computers, Communications, and the Public Interest*, ed. M. Greenberger. The Johns Hopkins Press (1971): 40–41.

xli "Burn-out an 'occupational phenomenon': International Classification of Diseases." *World Health Organization*, May 28, 2019. https://www.who.int/news/item/28-05-2019-burn-out-an-occupational-phenomenon-international-classification-of-diseases.

xlii Killingsworth, Matthew A., and Daniel T. Gilbert. "A Wandering Mind Is an Unhappy Mind." *Science* 330, No. 6006 (2010): 932–32. https://doi.org/10.1126/science.1192439.

xliii Rubinstein, Joshua S., David E. Meyer, and Jeffrey E. Evans. "Executive Control of Cognitive Processes in Task Switching." *Journal of Experimental Psychology: Human Perception and Performance* 27, no. 4 (2001): 763–97. https://doi.org/10.1037/0096-1523.27.4.763.

xliv Yerkes, Robert M., and John D. Dodson. "The Relation of Strength of Stimulus to Rapidity of Habit-Formation." *Journal of Comparative Neurology and Psychology* 18, no. 5 (November 1908): 459–82. https://doi.org/10.1002/cne.920180503.

xlv Gino, Francesca. "Are You Too Stressed to Be Productive? Or Not Stressed Enough?" *Harvard Business Review*, October 5, 2017. https://hbr.org/2016/04/are-you-too-stressed-to-be-productive-or-not-stressed-enough.

xlvi *World Health Organization*, 2019.

xlvii Killingsworth and Gilbert, 2010.

xlviii *The World Economic Forum*, 2020.

xlix Dörner, Dietrich, and Joachim Funke. "Complex Problem Solving: What It Is and What It Is Not." *Frontiers in Psychology* 8, no. 1153 (July 11, 2017). https://doi.org/10.3389/fpsyg.2017.01153.

l Dörner, Dietrich. "On the Difficulties People Have in Dealing with Complexity." *Simulation & Games* 11, no. 1 (March 1, 1980): 87–106. https://doi.org/10.1177/104687818001100108.

li Dörner and Funke, 2017.

lii Engelhart, Michael, Joachim Funke, and Sebastian Sager. "A Web-Based Feedback Study on Optimization-Based Training and Analysis of Human Decision Making." *Journal of Dynamic Decision Making* 3 (May 17, 2017): 1–23. https://doi.org/10.11588/jddm.2017.1.34608.

liii Smith, Melvin, Ellen Van Oosten, and Richard E. Boyatzis. "The Best Managers Balance Analytical and Emotional Intelligence." *Harvard Business Review*, June 12, 2020. https://hbr.org/2020/06/the-best-managers-balance-analytical-and-emotional-intelligence.

liv Indeed Editorial Team. "Definition and Examples of Analytical Skills." *Indeed Career Guide*, August 25, 2020. https://au.indeed.com/career-advice/career-development/analytical-skills.

[lv] Acar, Oguz A., Murat Tarakci, and Daan van Knippenberg. "Why Constraints Are Good for Innovation." *Harvard Business Review*, November 22, 2019. https://hbr.org/2019/11/why-constraints-are-good-for-innovation.

[lvi] Burgoyne, Alexander P., and David Z. Hambrick. "Sometimes Mindlessness Is Better than Mindfulness." *Scientific American*, August 31, 2021. https://www.scientificamerican.com/article/sometimes-mindlessness-is-better-than-mindfulness/.

[lvii] White, Holly. "The Creativity of ADHD: More insights on a positive side of a 'disorder.'" *Scientific American Mind*, March 5, 2019. https://www.scientificamerican.com/article/the-creativity-of-adhd/.

[lviii] Beard, Allison. "Defend Your Research: Drunk People Are Better at Creative Problem Solving." *Harvard Business Review*, May 1, 2018. https://hbr.org/2018/05/drunk-people-are-better-at-creative-problem-solving.

[lix] Acar et al, 2019.

[lx] Katz, Robert L. "Skills of an Effective Administrator." *Harvard Business Review*, September 1974. https://hbr.org/1974/09/skills-of-an-effective-administrator.

[lxi] Katz, 1974.

[lxii] Yerkes and Dodson, 1908.

[lxiii] Sullivan, John. "6 Ways to Screen Job Candidates for Strategic Thinking." *Harvard Business Review*, December 13, 2016. https://hbr.org/2016/12/6-ways-to-screen-job-candidates-for-strategic-thinking.

[lxiv] Watkins, Michael D. "How to Think Strategically." *Harvard Business Review*, April 20, 2007. https://hbr.org/2007/04/how-to-think-strategically-1.

[lxv] Mintzberg, Henry. "The Fall and Rise of Strategic Planning." *Harvard Business Review*, January–February 1994. https://hbr.org/1994/01/the-fall-and-rise-of-strategic-planning.

[lxvi] Sullivan, 2016.

[lxvii] Mintzberg, Henry. "Strategic Thinking as 'Seeing.'" mintzberg.org, September 14, 2018. https://mintzberg.org/blog/strategic-thinking-as-seeing.

[lxviii] Mintzberg, 1994.

[lxix] Brownlee, Dana. "Project Management Isn't Just for Project Managers: 4 Skills You Need to Know." *Forbes*, July 14, 2019. https://www.forbes.com/sites/danabrownlee/2019/07/14/project-management-isnt-just-for-project-managers-4-skills-you-need-to-know/?sh=4ac39b811a8e.

[lxx] De Bono, Edward. *Six Thinking Hats*. Boston, MA: Little Brown and Company, 1985.

[lxxi] Broad, Eli, Swati Pandey, and Michael Bloomberg. *The Art of Being Unreasonable: Lessons in Unconventional Thinking*. 1st ed. Hoboken, NJ: John Wiley & Sons, 2012.

[lxxii] Brownlee, 2019.

[lxxiii] Maxwell, John C. *Developing the Leaders around You*. 1st ed. Nashville, TN: Nelson Business, 2005.

[lxxiv] Riegel, Deborah Grayson. "8 Ways Leaders Delegate Successfully." *Harvard Business Review*, August 15, 2019. https://hbr.org/2019/08/8-ways-leaders-delegate-successfully.

[lxxv] Sostrin, Jesse. "To Be a Great Leader, You Have to Learn How to Delegate Well." *Harvard Business Review*, October 10, 2017. https://hbr.org/2017/10/to-be-a-great-leader-you-have-to-learn-how-to-delegate-well.

[lxxvi] Thompson, Dr. Neil. "Linking Strategic and Operational Thinking." *Medium*, December 30, 2019. https://drneilthompson.medium.com/linking-strategic-and-operational-thinking-e0de043dbc99.

[lxxvii] Goleman, Daniel. *Emotional Intelligence: Why It Can Matter More than IQ*. New York, NY: Bantam Books, 1995.

[lxxviii] Goleman, Daniel. *Working with Emotional Intelligence*. New York, NY: Bantam Books, 1998: 317.

[lxxix] Goleman, 1995: 16.

[lxxx] Goleman, Daniel. Sociability: It's all in your mind. Interview by Sharon Jayson. *USA Today*, September 24, 2006. https://usatoday30.usatoday.com/news/health/2006-09-24-social-intelligence_x.htm.

lxxxi Goleman, Daniel, and Richard E. Boyatzis, "Social Intelligence and the Biology of Leadership." *Harvard Business Review*, September 2008. https://hbr.org/2008/09/social-intelligence-and-the-biology-of-leadership.

lxxxii Sapir, Edward. *Selected Writings of Edward Sapir in Language, Culture and Personality*. Edited by David G. Mandelbaum. Berkeley, CA: University of California Press, 1949. Reprint, Leicester, UK: Forgotten Books, 2016: 556.

lxxxiii Goleman and Boyatzis, 2008.

lxxxiv Goleman and Boyatzis, 2008.

lxxxv Boyatzis, Richard. "Neuroscience and the Link between Inspirational Leadership and Resonant Relationships." *Ivey Business Journal*, February 7, 2012. https://iveybusinessjournal.com/publication/neuroscience-and-the-link-between-inspirational-leadership-and-resonant-relationships-2/.

lxxxvi Goleman and Boyatzis, 2008.

lxxxvii Peterson, Suzanne J., Robin Abramson, and R. K. Stutman. "How to Develop Your Leadership Style: Concrete Advice for a Squishy Challenge." *Harvard Business Review*, November 1, 2020. https://hbr.org/2020/11/how-to-develop-your-leadership-style.

lxxxviii Peterson et al, 2020.

lxxxix Alwar, Giridhar. *My Quest for Happy Life*. 1st ed. Chennai, India: Notion Press, 2015.

xc Galinsky, Adam D., William W. Maddux, Debra Gilin, and Judith B. White. "Why It Pays to Get inside the Head of Your Opponent: The Differential Effects of Perspective Taking and Empathy in Negotiations." *Psychological Science* 19, no. 4 (April 19, 2008): 378–84. https://doi.org/10.1111/j.1467-9280.2008.02096.x.

xci Galinsky, Adam D., Joe C. Magee, Diana Rus, Naomi B. Rothman, and Andrew R. Todd. "Acceleration with Steering: The Synergistic Benefits of Combining Power and Perspective-Taking." *Social Psychological and Personality Science* 5, no. 6 (February 11, 2014): 627–35. https://doi.org/10.1177/1948550613519685.

[xcii] Shelton, Amy. "Improving Your Spatial IQ Can Lift Your Social IQ." *Harvard Business Review*, January 1, 2012. https://hbr.org/2012/01/improving-your-spatial-iq-can-lift-your-social-iq.

[xciii] Shelton, 2012.

[xciv] Shelton, 2012.

[xcv] Boyatzis, 2012.

[xcvi] Beugre, Constant D., James Dulebohn, Richard E. Boyatzis, Sebastiano Massaro, David V. Smith, and Dongyuan Wu. "The Neuroscience of Decision Making in Organizations." *Academy of Management Proceedings* 2020, no. 1 (July 29, 2020). https://doi.org/10.5465/ambpp.2020.13893symposium.

[xcvii] Boyatzis, 2012.

[xcviii] Boyatzis, 2020.

[xcix] Boyatzis, 2012.

[c] Boyatzis, 2012.

[ci] Boyatzis, 2012.

[cii] Boyatzis, 2012.

[ciii] Hogarth, Robin M. *Educating Intuition*. 1st ed. Chicago, IL: University of Chicago Press, 2001.

[civ] Kahneman, Daniel. *Thinking, Fast and Slow*. 1st ed. New York, NY: Farrar, Straus and Giroux, 2011.

[cv] Kahneman, 2011.

[cvi] Kahneman, Daniel. "Your Intuition Is Wrong, Unless These 3 Conditions Are Met." Presented at the World Business Forum, New York City, NY, November 16, 2016. https://www.thinkadvisor.com/2018/11/16/daniel-kahneman-do-not-trust-your-intuition-even-for-stock-picking/.

[cvii] Goleman and Boyatzis, 2008.

[cviii] Goleman and Boyatzis, 2008.

[cix] *World Economic Forum*, 2020.

[cx] Toffler, Alvin. *Future Shock*. New York, NY: Random House, 1970.

INDEX

ABOUT PHILLIP JOHN CAMPBELL

Phillip John Campbell is a cognitive scientist, an executive brain coach, and Founder and CEO of enigmaFIT, a global brain coaching and leadership development organization. He has dedicated his career to understanding and leveraging the science behind how the brain processes information and how it rewires itself to enhance our ability to think, learn, and adapt. Campbell has developed a breakthrough approach for measuring and enhancing an individual's subconscious Fluid Thinking, which drives adaptability, agility, performance, and leadership capability—all essential elements for success in today's world of disruption. For the past 25 years, he has been coaching Fortune 500 executives and entrepreneurs in the USA, Europe, UK, Asia, and Australia.

Phillip John Campbell is a coauthor of *Habits of Success: What Top Entrepreneurs Routinely Do in Business and in Life* (Leaders Press, 2021), a Wall Street Journal and USA Today bestseller. He served as Governor of the American Chamber of Commerce in Australia and was a long-time member of the Chamber's diversity and inclusion committee. Phillip John Campbell holds a Master of Cognitive Science from University of New South Wales in Sydney. It was at the university where he learned how to "connect the dots" optimally by engaging with the departments of Humanities and Information Technology–two very different, yet complementary disciplines.

Find out more about Phillip John Campbell's work at
www.enigmafit.com.

IF YOUR BRAIN WAS AN APP, WOULD IT NEED AN UPGRADE?

Apps are constantly being updated so their software is compatible with our latest phones, tablets, and computers.

Our brains have the same issue. We are trying to run at peak performance with brain software that was programmed when we were growing up.

The solution is to upgrade the brain's subconscious software so that it runs on autopilot in our fast paced world of disruption.

We invite you to take our complimentary assessment of one of our ten Subconscious Thinking Habits called Focused Thinking. Put your focus to the test.

Are you:
- Easily distracted by external interruptions
- Prone to procrastinating — busy, but not very productive
- Have difficulty staying focused on your top priorities
- Starting important projects later than ideal
- Side-tracked by your mind wandering and noisy environments

TO TAKE YOUR FREE ASSESSMENT, VISIT:

https://www.enigmafit.com/focusedtest

and jumpstart your Brain APP journey today!

www.ingramcontent.com/pod-product-compliance
Lightning Source LLC
Chambersburg PA
CBHW051132120626
46547CB00012B/769